Praise for
A TIME FOR (

"It is rare that an author and teacher as accomplished and influential as Caroline Myss would, with each book, discover whole new vistas, and then report back to us with her legendary clarity and passion. With *A Time for Grace* she has done it again. Anyone in need of healing—healing from illness, anxiety, fear, or heartbreak—will find enormous help in this book. It is a tonic made of light and wisdom."

— **Elizabeth Lesser,** co-founder, Omega Institute and author of *Broken Open: How Difficult Times Can Help Us Grow*

"In *A Time for Grace,* Caroline Myss offers a new model of transformation and healing that will shift how we perceive crisis and illness. A must-read."

— **Deepak Chopra,** author of *The Seven Spiritual Laws of Success*

"Caroline has been one of my most important spiritual teachers. In her new book, she continues to pierce both hearts and minds with arrows of truth."

— **Marianne Williamson,** author of *The Age of Miracles* and *A Return to Love*

"*A Time for Grace* is a powerful look at the mystical aspects of the process of deep healing. The extraordinary Caroline Myss provides profound insights into the nature of illness and the healing miracles that can occur. What I love about Caroline is that she isn't afraid to make waves and go way beyond convention to create new paradigms of health."

— **Judith Orloff, M.D.,** author of *Emotional Freedom*

"In this time of extraordinary evolutionary upheaval, Caroline Myss offers a powerful and wise prescription for self-healing that transforms and empowers the reader to gain sovereignty over their physical, emotional, and spiritual well-being."

— **Bruce H. Lipton, Ph.D.,** author of *The Biology of Belief* and *Spontaneous Evolution*

"In *A Time for Grace* Caroline Myss goes far beyond conventional thinking to describe with precision those areas of experience, those mystical and mysterious events that ultimately account for illness. I found this book to be extraordinarily intelligent and perceptive in charting ways to go deep into the soul to glimpse those faint issues that grow into large problems."

— **Thomas Moore**, author of *Care of the Soul* and *Writing in the Sand*

"Like no other author, Myss invariably manages to help us reach yet an even higher level of understanding of how to heal. Run, don't walk, and buy this book."

— **Mona Lisa Schulz, M.D., Ph.D.**, author of *The Intuitive Advisor* and *Heal Your Mind*

"In this book, Caroline Myss reminds us that, while we should be grateful for the gift of reason, we should also be aware that the mystery and holiness of life cannot be found in the dim light of reason alone. As *A Time for Grace* makes clear, the mystics teach that there is in each of us the capacity for mystical experience that transcends reason. Each chapter of this book echoes with the expansive energy of mystical awakening and offers ways we can cultivate this awakening in our lives."

—**James Finley, Ph.D.**, author of *Christian Meditation* and *The Contemplative Heart*

"Caroline Myss is the most outstanding voice in the field of spirituality and healing alive on the planet today. In *A Time for Grace* she challenges some of our culture's most cherished myths about healing, inviting the reader to exit the prison of reason and enter the 'field of grace' from which miracles spontaneously arise. Translating universal spiritual wisdom into modern language, Caroline illuminates the journey to empowering both psyche and soul."

— **Joan Borysenko, Ph.D.**, author of *Minding the Body, Mending the Mind* and *Your Soul's Compass*

A
TIME
FOR
GRACE

ALSO BY CAROLINE MYSS

Anatomy of the Spirit

Archetypes

Entering the Castle

Invisible Acts of Power

Sacred Contracts

Why People Don't Heal and How They Can

A
TIME
FOR
GRACE

SACRED GUIDANCE
for EVERYDAY LIFE

CAROLINE MYSS

HAY HOUSE, INC.
Carlsbad, California • New York City
London • Sydney • New Delhi

Copyright © 2009, 2023 by Caroline Myss

Published in the United States by: Hay House, Inc.: www.hayhouse.com •
Published in Australia by: Hay House Australia Pty. Ltd.: www.hayhouse.com.
au • *Published in the United Kingdom by:* Hay House UK, Ltd.: www.hayhouse
.co.uk • *Published in India by:* Hay House Publishers India: www.hayhouse.co.in

Design: Tricia Breidenthal
Indexer: J S Editorial LLC

All rights reserved. No part of this book may be reproduced by any mechanical, photographic, or electronic process, or in the form of a phonographic record-
ing; nor may it be stored in a retrieval system, transmitted, or otherwise be copied
for public or private use—other than for "fair use" as brief quotations embodied in
articles and reviews—without prior written permission of the publisher.

The author of this book does not dispense medical advice or prescribe the
use of any technique as a form of treatment for physical, emotional, or medical problems without the advice of a physician, either directly or indirectly. The
intent of the author is only to offer information of a general nature to help you
in your quest for emotional and spiritual well-being. In the event you use any of
the information in this book for yourself, the author and the publisher assume no
responsibility for your actions.

The Library of Congress has cataloged the earlier edition as follows:

Myss, Caroline M.
  Defy Gravity : healing beyond the bounds of reason / Caroline Myss. -- 1st ed.
        p. cm.
  Includes index.
  ISBN 978-1-4019-2290-0 (hardcover : alk. paper) 1. Healing--Religious aspects.
2. Spiritual healing. 3. Medicine--Religious aspects. 4. Teresa, of Avila, Saint,
1515-1582. Moradas. I. Title.
  BL65.M4M97 2009
  203'.1--dc22

                                        2009020697

Tradepaper ISBN: 978-1-4019-7645-3
E-book ISBN: 978-1-4019-7646-0
Audiobook ISBN: 978-1-4019-7730-6

This book was previously published with the title *Defy Gravity*
and the ISBN: 978-1-4019-2290-0

10 9 8 7 6 5 4 3 2 1
1st edition, October 2009
2nd edition, January 2011
3rd edition, November 2023

Printed in the United States of America

For my godchildren
Angela, Rachel, Eddie, Jimmy,
Basile, Lacey, Eben, and Sam

Contents

Preface

to the 2023 Edition

When I read my original introduction to this book (originally titled *Defy Gravity*) as preparation to write this preface to the new edition, I was truly pleased, as I realized I did not want to change a word of what I'd written 15 years ago. I did, however, feel inspired to elaborate on what I wrote then, as my belief in the power of grace—as well as our need for grace—has only deepened in the years since. I have also come to a very different understanding about the nature of the Divine that only enhances my belief in the intimate way the sacred moves within our lives and how deeply we need to rely upon faith and grace now more than ever. Writing a new preface gives me the opportunity to share what I have observed about the wonders of grace and how, why, and when grace flows into your life.

I am always asked questions about grace, such as, "What is grace?" and "How does grace work?" and "How do I know if I've ever had an experience of grace in my life?" Grace is one of those topics that fascinates people, and for good reason. Who does not want to believe that somehow, in some extraordinary way, grace is poured into your life just when you need it?

One way to understand grace is that it is a mystical force, not an intellectual or physical power. As a rule, an experience of grace does not explode into your life in ways that are obvious. Usually it is not until time passes—maybe a day, a week, or even longer—that you realize something slightly out of the ordinary has occurred. And that something out of the ordinary can be subtle, such as the way in which you spontaneously step out of your comfort zone to assist a stranger—emphasis on the word *spontaneously*.

Another download of spontaneous grace that occurs rather frequently in our lives happens during heated exchanges with our loved ones. When we find ourselves in the midst of a conflict, we are often tempted to say something—or do something—that is especially cruel, so much so that it carries the potency to destroy the relationship. It is not unusual to hear a voice asking you, "Are you sure you want to say that?" So many people have told me that it was that question, coming out of nowhere in the heat of the conflict, that caused them to storm out of the room instead of shouting that last remark—and how grateful they were that they'd left the room. I have also been told by people that they are living with the regret that they did not listen to that voice— preferring, out of pride, to deliver that final blow in the argument. As it turned out for so many, it was the final blow that destroyed the relationship. In fact, one man told me that while his divorce did not happen until eight years after that fatal argument, he could sense that something had shifted immediately in the quality of his marriage. And that shift gradually grew into the reason for the breakup.

A point of interest is that, regardless of how much grace assistance you receive, the choice to listen is still yours. Heaven's angels do not make our choices for us when we are at critical turning points in our lives. And yet, in keeping with the mystical, mysterious nature of the Divine, we are given direct guidance to act when we are unaware that we are in a dangerous or risky situation. Being unaware seems to *allow* for direct guidance and grace in a way that our conscious awareness blocks, as conscious awareness means we are in charge of the quality of choices that we make.

At the same time, a truth that is a "mystical operating principle" in your life is this: that guidance and grace support your well-being at all times. (Consider guidance and grace as two sides of the same coin.) You are never directed to do anything that will harm you or others. Rather, grace and guidance are infusions of a higher power or holy light that assists you in making a transition to a higher or more light-filled inner state of consciousness. And from that higher inner position, you are then capable of an empowered decision.

Another example of how softly grace directs a higher thought into your mind is to imagine that you are seated in a smoke-filled, crowded bar. You've been in that smoky room for so long that you have adapted to the increased pollution in the atmosphere. You are now in a health-threatening environment, though you are unaware that the room has become so toxic. Suddenly, you get a breath of fresh air from an open window. All your senses instantly respond to clean air coming into your lungs. You feel a jolt of energy run through your system, as if awakening you from a sleep state. The next thought you have is "I have to get out of here. I need some fresh air." And with that, you exit the bar into the clean evening breeze.

Grace operates exactly like fresh air coming into the smoke-filled, crowded thoughts in your mind. It is a single, clean message that has the power to engage all your senses and direct you to a more empowered, healthy choice. Grace is a holy power message that comes into your life during those times when you are (consciously or unconsciously) vulnerable, frightened, confused, lonely, or in need of immediate direction. The purpose of these transmissions of grace is to facilitate the most empowered choice you can make for yourself in that moment. Heaven cannot make our challenges or obstacles disappear in an instant, even though we often wish such things were possible. But in an instant it can assist us to shift our inner view, our attitudes, our fears. Grace empowers our capacity to make choices that we might prefer to avoid in our ordinary moments. But grace especially pours into us when we require assistance to better the lives of other people, or even one person.

Consider the grace of courage. Most of our everyday decisions do not require exceptional courage. But, inevitably, each of us will find ourselves in some type of situation that fills us with fear or makes us uncomfortable. Or we may find ourselves positioned to come to the aid of someone in need, as I witnessed one person doing so bravely a while ago. I heard yelling as I drove into a parking lot by my local grocery store. I approached the growing crowd to see that an extraordinary young woman had come to the aid of a homeless woman. Apparently, the woman was being targeted by a small group of people who did not want her in the neighborhood. As they yelled abusive comments at the homeless woman, this young girl stepped in, stood in front of her, and told them to leave her alone. She radiated courage and it was obvious that her strength, in turn, attracted the support of others. The aggressors quickly left and the group that had gathered pulled out their wallets to provide that homeless woman with much-needed financial assistance.

Grace does not require a crisis or dire situation to flow into your life. Grace also comes into your life during times of reflection and contemplation. Often, in times of creativity, the grace of inspiration pours into our souls. Many times, when we gaze into the calmness of nature, the grace of tranquility descends upon us. With or without our asking for these acts of mystical intervention, the graces of the Divine flow freely and abundantly into our lives.

And prayer is like turning a tributary of grace into a river that flows into you without obstacles. Grace, in all its many expressions, has the power to enhance a quality in you because you need that quality. Patience, for example, expands within you into the grace of endurance, giving you the strength to sustain yourself through what you would ordinarily consider an unendurable situation. Ordinary thinking expands into the grace of discernment, providing you with a capacity to maneuver more carefully through a decision.

Heaven cannot give us a second or different life path because the one we are on has a difficult passage, or even years of hardship. And we are really never given the type of guidance that explains why things are so difficult. Unfortunately for us, there is no such thing as the "grace of an explanation" or the "grace of personal justice." But prayer, grace, and guidance contain the holy authority to help us in ways that we are incapable of imagining. Though invisible and quiet holy resources, grace and guidance flow continually into our lives.

If you are like most people who listen to me speak about prayer, grace, and guidance, you would like to ask me about how to pray for grace. So let me close by answering that important question.

I learned as a medical intuitive that every thought, every emotion, every attitude, every judgment, every possible spark of life that we generate converts into an act of creation. We are always participating in acts of creation, directing the energy of our life force into actions in the physical and energetic domains of life. We are micro-engines of creation, co-creating with all other human beings.

Because every action we generate is an act of creation, every spark of life—from what you consider the most insignificant thought to those you are most conscious of creating—should rightfully be considered a prayer. Every thought generates an action and therefore a reaction. Every emotion you have engages the mystical laws of creation, such as magnetic attraction and cause and effect. When are you not participating in the holy act of creation? If you only realized how powerful you are, you would hold on to prayer as your lifeline, knowing that every thought you generate really does impact the whole of creation. And you would never again think of yourself as helpless or view any of your challenges as hopeless.

With that awesome view of your universe in mind, a simple prayer you might find useful is: "Hover over me, God. Fill in the grace-gaps for me when I am incapable of compassion and kindness. Help me live in harmony with nature, to do no harm to my fellow creatures. And give me the grace of courage to do more for others each day and to worry less about what tomorrow might bring."

Please read this book with an open and welcoming soul. Let the graces pour into you with every page. I assure you that the more you open yourself to the ways of the sacred, the more you will experience the wonders of grace, guidance, and miracles in your life. May the power of each grace transform your life in endless and blessed ways.

Caroline Myss

Foreword

Brilliance, passion, wit, forensic clarity, and a realistic unshrinking compassion—these are all qualities we have come to expect from the extraordinary work of Caroline Myss, and they are in abundant, vivid, and provocative display in *A Time for Grace*. What is also remarkable and inspiring about Caroline as a writer, teacher, and person, is that she is continually reinventing herself, constantly pressing forward to a more and more all-encompassing integration of mind, heart, body, and soul. For her, this search for the unified force field of truth is never a purely individual one; it takes place in the context of an urgent and radical confrontation with our world crisis that is now threatening the survival of the human race and much of nature, and it is born out of a passionate desire for planetary as well as personal healing.

It is this menacing crisis that is at the heart of *A Time for Grace*. Caroline Myss knows exactly where we are in a vast disaster of our own making, a growing catastrophe engendered by our addiction to and adoration of reason and the powers of control it opens up to us, and by our abandonment of the Sacred and the rigorous and exacting mystic laws that govern its application to life. Our survival is threatened on every side—by the demons our passion for domination of each other and of nature have unleashed, by our flawed and tribal understandings of religion that fuel instead of resolve conflict, and by our continuing refusal to face the personal and collective shadows of our greed, fear, cruelty, and unacknowledged despair at our untransformed human nature.

Caroline Myss offers us a way out of this nightmare—a way out that she has clearly forged in the core of her own life and from a lifetime's wrestling with the problems and possibilities of healing. This way out demands of us that we face two things—that the Age of Enlightenment—the age of the primacy of reason and of purely materialistic and scientific explanations of reality—has now revealed its bankruptcy and cannot offer us any real guidance, and that our greatest resource lies not in our technological wizardry or rational political "solutions" but in the truth of our inner divine nature and its astounding transparence to the divine's power of transforming grace. It is this power that Caroline has experienced in the heart of her own life and it is to this ultimate universal divine power that she returns us again and again in different increasingly revelatory ways throughout her new book, challenging all of us to learn the difficult lessons of humility, surrender, unconditional forgiveness, understanding of necessary ordeal and of mystical law that ensure its most potent operation.

One of the holiest joys of my life is my deep friendship with Caroline. What characterizes Caroline as a friend and as a sacred friend now to all of you in the pages of this book is her startling nakedness of soul, her unwillingness to let herself or anyone else off the hook of examining our darkest passions and the robust kindness and strong generosity of encouraging compassion that radiate from her hard-won knowledge both of human frailty and of the possibilities to transmute and transform that frailty. One of the things I admire most about this wonderful book is that in it I hear constantly the intimate voice of the soul-sister I know and love, speaking here from the full range of herself, and in a way that is at once humble and exalted, fierce, and consoling. A voice as varied, clear, and radical as Caroline's is rare in any culture: in our culture of denial, confusion, muddy and sophomoric spiritual and political correctness, it is of unique value. What it offers—even as it exposes our fantasies, addictions, and perversities—is a faith and witness we can believe in because they have been forged both from heartbreak at the state of the world and from radical experience of the potentially all-transforming power of Divine Love and Wisdom.

What Caroline also gives us—and this is, I believe, its greatest grace to us—is an extremely clear archetypal template for both inner and outer healing, one that distills for a vast audience and in contemporary language the difficult truths of universal mysticism. Caroline has found an utterly modern and timely way of describing for us the essential healing journey enshrined at the heart of the world's major mystical traditions. This journey at once demands us to transcend our "unreasonable" rational claims of personal security, safety, and control and to travel through sometimes extremely painful zones of surrender, unconditional forgiveness, and unillusioned confrontation with our own dark passions so as to discover the great gifts of soul, passion, power, and knowledge that are born in us when we enter into our own deepest divine identity. There is nothing easy or consoling to the mind or ego about such a journey; but what it offers, as Caroline makes marvelously and methodically clear, is a wholly new evolutionary level of empowerment.

It is this wholly new evolutionary level of empowerment—and so of both inner and outer healing—that our shattering and contemporary crisis is now calling us to. No one has a fiercer sense of "divine paradox" than Caroline—and she makes it clear that she knows that our modern dark night is potentially the crucible of a birth on an unprecedented scale of healed human beings aligned consciously with cosmic grace and mystical law and so imbued with their essential soul power and destiny.

In the journey from our contemporary confusion to the humbled surrendered clarity that can open us to such an evolutionary birth, Caroline Myss's *A Time for Grace* will play an indispensable role as guide and radiant torch of hope and possibility.

This is a book to read and savor again and again, to learn from and live by. I'm personally grateful to Caroline for continuing to risk the searing journey that makes such healing visions accessible to her and through her to us. In *Entering the Castle*, Caroline Myss guided us through the timeless path of wisdom opened up by Teresa of Ávila; in *A Time for Grace* Caroline claims her own authority as guide and radical mystic pioneer with the humility, intensity, and clarity that potentially ennobles us all.

Andrew Harvey

A Mystic's
Introduction to Healing

This is not an ordinary book on healing. It does not offer guidance on how to heal any particular illness, for example, nor does it proceed on the assumption that all illness is rooted in the mystery of wounds. Instead, this book challenges that approach to healing, and more—it invites the reader to examine the very real limitations of the holistic model of health and to explore a path that breaks with the conventional wisdom that the resources and skill of the mind is sufficient to ignite a transformation in a diseased body. Or, for that matter, that the mind alone can transport a person into the vast domain of the soul.

After working in the field of health and healing for more than two decades, I have come to believe that we as a society have not fully animated the body-mind-spirit trinity that is the foundation of this approach to health, for a simple reason: we are still enamored of the more familiar power of the mind and intimidated by the less familiar, the mystical and transformational regions of the soul. And, so, although we may use the language of the spirit, we frequently retreat into the methods of the mind, which primarily indulge our need to find reasons why events happen as they do in our lives. We seek to learn why we were hurt during our childhoods, for example, or what lessons lie hidden in the illnesses that we have developed. The underlying premise is that if we can excavate these reasons, then our lives will return to normal. We will recover our health, just as vibrant as it was before the illness struck. But that rarely happens, because this system of reasoning our way through illness and crisis is undermined by a fundamental flaw: We cannot reason our way back to health. Our intellect is an inadequate vehicle to carry us through the arduous journey of healing.

Healing requires far more of us than just the participation of our intellectual and even our emotional resources. And it certainly demands that we do more than look backward into the dead-end archives of our past. Healing is, by definition, taking a process of disintegration of life and transforming it into a process of return to life. The mind cannot accomplish such a task. Only the soul has the power to bring the body back to life. If it weren't for the fact that I have now witnessed this phenomenon several times, I would not venture into the territory of healing with enough confidence to share my findings with others. But I have been a witness to healings, and some might even say I have facilitated these healings because of what I now teach, namely, mystical wisdom blended with all that I have learned about human consciousness and this journey we share called life.

We all need to know the essential truths of healing, because at some point in our lives, each of us will have to call on them. No matter how healthy we may feel at any given moment, there will inevitably come a time when we will need to heal. I came to that conclusion after years of teaching in the field of health-related subjects, and that truth alone was enough to make me rethink my long-held reluctance to work directly with people in need of healing—people who were confronting painful, overwhelming diseases, such as cancer, rheumatoid arthritis, ALS (Lou Gehrig's disease), or multiple sclerosis. Although I had been a medical intuitive for many years, diagnosing people's ailments in collaboration with Dr. Norm Shealy, I had long since stopped giving individual readings on a professional basis. And even when I was giving readings, I had been able to keep my distance from the person I was helping, because the assistance I had to offer was mainly intuitive insight. Personal contact made me uncomfortable, but I did not have to meet the person in order to do an intuitive reading; phone communication worked just fine. That suited my need to keep any association with "healing" at arm's length. In the early days of my work as a medical intuitive, I did not understand myself well enough to pinpoint why I avoided any association with healing and clung to the professions of "writer" and "teacher" as if they were designer labels. Now, as I look back at that attitude, I have no doubt that my comfort with those labels was based on the fact that I never had to explain the occupation of writer or teacher, whereas describing myself as a medical intuitive always required a lengthy and exhausting description. As a matter of fact, it still does.

I realized that I was overwhelmed by the vulnerability that arises in each of us when we are in need of healing. It's that feeling of waiting on the edge of hope or hopelessness that few other conditions in life can activate within us. This vulnerability comes from an eruption in the life force itself, as if the force were red-hot lava threatening to break through your energy field and flood you with the vastness of eternity. You can tell when your life force is beginning to heat up toward that eruption point; it sends out distress signals like warning flares through your intuitive system. You begin to sense your body's stamina declining, and then the fear peculiar to the onset of an illness begins to filter through each one of your cells like the oncoming of a rare yet indescribable force of destruction. I've known that vulnerability, because I've suffered through my own eruptions and most likely will have more of them in the years to come. That's life, after all.

But this rice-paper-thin wall between health and illness, life and death, those who heal and those who can't, is exactly the wall I had successfully avoided until people began to experience healings during a number of workshops I was teaching. Interestingly, the healings occurred in only those workshops that were based on a new book, *Entering the Castle*, which I was introducing on a lecture tour. This book marked a turning point for me in that I dealt with a contemporary view of the classical mystical experience, encouraging the reader to discover his or her "inner castle"—a metaphor for the soul inspired by the magnificent teachings of the 16th-century mystical theologian Saint Teresa of Ávila. In her seminal work, *The Interior Castle*, which became the template for my work, Teresa clearly outlines the seven stages of mystical illumination based on a path of prayer and the pursuit of the knowledge of the soul. During the process of writing this book, including the formative five years before the writing began, I went through my own mystical awakening, which was precipitated by a serious health crisis.

As is always the case, we understand much more about a turning point in our lives only later, after we've reached that crisis—and survived it. When I look back at that time, I now marvel at how my health crisis, a year during which I had three seizures, seemed so carefully engineered to suit my next book project: updating the teachings of a renowned mystic who was also known to have had seizures. Like all great mystics, Teresa has risen to cosmic status, and her writings are studied, respected, and loved around the world, although her roots remain deeply planted in her religious origins. Her life as a Roman Catholic nun was the necessary setting to incubate the genius of her mystical insights, which are universal in their magnitude, depth, and capacity to lead an individual into a profound experience of mystical transformation. Suffice it to say that before my engagement with Teresa, prayer had been a mental act of repetition for me, and grace was something that I continually struggled to define for other people; after Teresa, prayer became the purest form of power for me, and grace became the conduit through which I understood that people heal.

As I studied Teresa's writings, I realized that the emptiness that people continually express today, their search for "something more" in their lives, is not a search for yet another job or yet another partner. People are missing a sense of awe in their lives, a connection to the sacred—a connection they can't make through their intellects. They don't want to talk about God; they want to feel the power of God. They want to be overwhelmed by awe in the way that only a mystical experience can provide. They want to silence that reasoning, demanding, inquisitive intellect and fall into the breathless experience of inner trust.

I have listened to so many people talk about their "inner voice," and yet they ask me for guidance. If they were really in touch with that "inner voice," they would feel no need to ask me the kinds of questions they do. I often picture them standing on the outside of their own interior castles, where their egos meet their souls, wanting so desperately to engage with mystical consciousness and yet so fearful of how their lives will change once they cross over the drawbridge. They sense how true it is that once you have had an authentic mystical experience, nothing is the same. Life immediately changes, for example, from an external world full of people and chaos to a sacred field of grace in which all of life has purpose and meaning. That you cannot understand that meaning is, quite frankly, irrelevant.

What is relevant is that such a mystical experience animates an inner power, an inner sense of the reality of grace and God that previously existed merely as "words in the mind." And words and images in the mind cannot heal; they are merely words and images. The people I know who have experienced healings told me that they were able to detach from their pre-existing images of God. Indeed, they managed to detach from everything—their wounds, their need to be right, their need to win, their need to know why things happened as they did in their lives. In doing so, they discovered that all they really surrendered was their fear, their darkness—and, much to their great awe, their disease. In giving up these things, they were given everything they needed, beginning with their lives. That was the pattern that I saw in all of the healings that I witnessed, the pattern that became the inspiration for this book. I realized that healing was not a matter of visualizations, sacred oils, processing wounds, lighting candles, and all the rest. Ultimately, healing is the result of a mystical act of surrender, an awakening that transcends any religion. It is an intimate dialogue of truth between the individual and the Divine.

Because I direct readers to leave their reason at the door, so to speak, and enter the realm of mystical consciousness—not just for healing but as a way of life—I chose the title *Defy Gravity* for the first edition of this book. The word *gravity* comes from the Latin *gravis*, meaning "serious" or "weighted"; thoughts and emotions with weight, in other words, generate emotional, psychological, and intellectual gravity. Mystics, by nature, defy gravity: a mystic is someone who "perceives" life through the eyes of the soul, who experiences the power of God rather than speaks or debates the politics of God, and who understands the reality of mystical laws—laws that I discuss in depth in Chapter 6.

The essence of the mystical path is to discern truth. As Buddha taught his disciples, you need to learn to distinguish illusion from truth, because your illusions will weigh you down—literally as well as psychically, it turns out. Your reason alone cannot defy gravity, because your sense of reason by its nature seeks logical proofs. You cannot ask your mind to be other than what it is: a reason-seeking instrument. You must draw upon another part of yourself to transcend the stubbornly reasoning mind that seeks vengeance for being humiliated or continually convinces you that you are entitled to more than what you have in this life. Such a mind is filled with toxins and it, too, needs healing. You must defy your mind, rise above it. You must defy gravity if you intend to heal or successfully navigate through any life crisis. But you must not wait for a crisis to motivate you. Learning to see life through mystical eyes while holding down a job and running a family, along with all the other business of living, reflects the true essence of what it means to live a conscious life.

We now stand at a pivotal moment of change in human history. Part of that change calls us finally to embrace our inner consciousness, not with words alone, but through understanding the profound mystical nature of life. I believe deeply that many people are more than ready to learn how to defy gravity in their lives—not just in order to heal from an illness or navigate a crisis, but as an integral part of everyday life.

Caroline Myss
Oak Park, Illinois

Chapter One

─── **BEYOND REASON** ───

Healing in the
Age of Energy

Y ou never really know how or when your life is going to change, and that's for the best. If someone had said to me, "Be on the lookout tonight, Caroline, because someone is going to experience a spontaneous healing in your audience," how would I have reacted? And at whom would I have looked? Would I have cast my attention to the two people in wheelchairs? Would I have looked for a sick child, because that's got a certain Madonna-and-Child quality to it? Would I have asked for a show of hands to count how many people were ill, just to see how many subjects were in the running? I don't know what I would have done. But a healing did happen that night while no one was looking.

The evening was part of a tour to promote my new book, *Entering the Castle*. It was planned as the usual type of tour event, at which I introduce the book, chat about it for a couple of hours, answer some questions, and then autograph copies. But that's not what happened on this evening. It started out that way, yet as I began to describe the "interior castle,"—the image Saint Teresa of Ávila used to beautifully describe the inner soul—I could tell that my words were not communicating its power or mystical significance. The people in the audience were simply not relating to the seductive power of their souls through words, and it was obvious that all the metaphors and analogies and poetic descriptions would only continue to fall short. In fact, lecturing about the nature of the soul grew more frustrating with each passing minute, as I could tell that for my audience, "soul" itself was just a mental concept, a word without an experience attached to it. How could anyone relate to a description of a mystical experience? How could I possibly tell these people to get enthusiastic about a place they had never experienced? Words cannot get you to experience Paris, can they?

I began to realize that my listeners were craving an *actual* mystical experience, or as close as they could come to one. They didn't want me to talk about the interior castle; they wanted to enter their own interior castles. I looked at this audience of more than 800 people and thought, "How am I going to do this without prayer?" Teresa was clear in her writings that the only way into one's interior castle is through prayer and inner devotion. But my experience through the years had consistently been that although audiences were comfortable with meditation, guided imagery, moments of silence, and even terms like the Divine, the Goddess, and the Great Spirit, mention prayer or God and feathers got ruffled. "That's too Catholic," I have been told on more occasions than you can imagine—and though I'm not exactly a fan of the Vatican, I do come from a Catholic background. As a result, I had never introduced prayer into my workshops, not even moments of silence or meditation.

That evening I had to confront this ironclad policy. I knew that if I simply told my audience, "Close your eyes, sit back, and listen to my words as I lead you into your castle," not only would I be dishonoring everything I knew about the mystical journey, but these eager people would also be denied an opportunity to experience something quite tranquil and authentic within them. I knew that the transformative link that drew a person "out of the mind" and into an altered state of consciousness, however slight and however brief, was prayer and that without prayer, the entire exercise into the castle—this metaphor of the soul—would be no more than a mental visualization. For me, that dishonored the very essence of the mystical experience.

To be clear, I differentiate between what I call a "mystical journey" and a "mystical experience." A mystical journey is an inner exercise scripted with language that is specifically soul-focused. That is, instead of saying, "Relax and breathe into your energy," as I might do in a different kind of guided meditation, I instruct people to "breathe into a field of grace." I direct them into their "interior castle," their inner soul, through prayer, not relaxation. I use the vocabulary of the soul and the sacred. A mystical experience, on the other hand, cannot be self-initiated. Rather, it is a spontaneous occurrence in which an individual is consumed into an altered state of divine consciousness.

So I told the audience that the journey into the interior castle required prayer and grace—not ordinary prayer, as in prayers of petition or repetition, but the type of prayer that withdraws your attention from external distractions and from your five senses. The audience was more than willing, and so, for the first time in my career, I led 800 people on their maiden journey into their interior castle.

As I continued the castle meditation exercise, the atmosphere in the room began to change. One way I can describe this is to say that it felt as if everyone had relaxed their shoulders and jaws at the same time. The tension was gone and its absence was palpable. I realize now that the collective sharing of prayer and opening to the experience of channeling grace had created a unified field of grace, generating a mystical atmosphere ripe for the experience of healing. A field of grace emerges when people come together in prayer or for acts of good intention, such as helping others after disasters. You can sense the absence of negativity in a field of grace, for example, and though it may not last long, the sensation that negativity has evaporated is akin to the absence of psychic tension, as if a soft harmonious breeze has filled the room. Everyone settles into an effortless place of calm and without being led into forming a chorus of breathing together, they silently unite into one whole breath. Such is the absence of negativity and rarely do people emerge rapidly from such inner tranquility. They want to reside in this grace as long as they can, not because they recognize it as grace but because for a small second, they are aware that they are experiencing a calmness that is not self-generated or contrived or imagined. It is a calmness that has been bestowed upon them and this is a calmness they will seek to return to again and again.

After the exercise, few wanted to leave their chairs, which is quite something in a room of 800 people. The silence in the room was not an ordinary one, but a soothing, healing silence that had penetrated deeply into the stressful minds and hearts of the audience, and they wanted to remain in this grace-filled quiet for as long as they could. Finally, I had to begin to sign books, so I thanked everyone, left the stage, and went to the signing table.

Hundreds of people lined up for inscriptions. It's impossible to have a conversation with everyone, even though I want to because I am so grateful to see each person. Precisely because each person in that line who has bought a book wants to say something to me or ask me a question, there is always a "bad cop," so to speak, someone who gently encourages people to keep moving. On this evening, when I was nearly done, a woman walked up behind me, somehow bypassing the vigilant bad cop, and said, "I've suffered with chronic pain for 20 years in my shoulders, my back, and my hands. I've never, ever been out of pain in all that time. I don't know what just happened to me or how it happened, but my pain is gone, and somehow I know it is gone forever. I thought you would want to know that."

She told me this while I was signing a book for someone else. I looked up to see her face. Shimmering with awe, she whispered, "Thank you," and left. I wanted to run after her and ask, "Who are you? Tell me more about what happened," but I couldn't leave the book-signing table. And then she was gone.

"HEALING IS REAL"

As the book tour continued, so did the healings. Sometimes they were immediate, as at the first event. Other times I received an e-mail from someone who had been at a lecture on *Entering the Castle,* then noticed that within a week or two or three, a condition that he or she had been coping with for some time was improving—or, in some cases, completely healed.

The following May, I took the bold step of offering a workshop in Austin, Texas, specifically for people who needed healing. The focus of this workshop was not to teach people *about* healing but for people who actually needed to be healed. The workshop was built around the teachings of *Entering the Castle,* as I had realized by then that healings occurred only within those specific workshops. I had reviewed the significant differences between the castle workshops and all the other theme-oriented workshops I'd offered, such as Sacred Contracts, Energy Anatomy, and The Science of Medical Intuition. At first it made no sense to me that the choice of any particular theme could create an atmosphere that somehow became a vessel for healing. Then I realized that the castle workshops were the only ones in which I broke through my own resistance and introduced the element of prayer as the means through which participants gained entry into their interior castle. Prayer draws a response from the Divine, and as I reflected on the relationship between prayer and healing, I realized that one of the many graces available to us through prayer is the grace to heal—a grace that renews our inner physical, emotional, mental, and spiritual vitality. During each of the journeys into the interior castle, I specifically offered a healing prayer, invoking the mystical quality of grace that is capable of melting through illness and shattering the rotting parts of the mind that hold on to old wounds decades past the point when they should be forgiven and forgotten.

The difference was prayer, but not just that I had broken my own rule against praying at a seminar. What mattered was that the workshop participants had broken through their own barriers of "political correctness" or even a kind of social arrogance on occasion that had prevented them from even acknowledging that they needed prayer in their lives. As I am quick to point out in all my workshops and books, I am not speaking about specific religions or any specific kind of prayer; I am especially not speaking about the Roman Catholic tradition of prayer. I have to point that out, because it is widely known that I am Catholic, although I do not write from a Catholic position. Prayer is a power that transcends the politics of any religion, as is the power of God.

At this point in my personal introduction to healing, I realized that healings were actually happening—that such things were not "New Age wishful thinking," as I had so often commented to myself. I determined then that I would always close my workshops with a guided prayer leading the participants into their interior castles for their own healing.

Awe is a hard state to describe. The realization that a room full of people praying within their interior castles—which is to say, praying beyond their boundary of reason—had resulted in actual healings filled me with awe in a way few events in my life ever had; I was truly awestruck. *Awe* is a marvelous word that has so much more resonance and complexity than its use in the cliché epithet *awesome* ever allows; it comprises wonder and dread, admiration and trepidation, often at the same time. I was finally witnessing the truth of what I had studied in grad school about mystics and healing, the reality of cosmic laws unfolding, and the way the experience can feel both humbling and exhilarating. That I would now put a sign out reading "Healing Workshop" represented my decision to trust in this awe: to trust that this was not just a passing ship in the night, that this healing grace would flow abundantly no matter who asked, no matter when, no matter where, and that no illness was too great a challenge for the power of grace. Was I really willing to step into those waters? Because even though I absolutely believe that you can be healed unto your final breath, I knew that not everyone would or could be physically healed. I had to ask myself if I had the stamina to cope with the disbelief and disappointed expectations of others who would not reach their goal of recovering their health.

After I sent out the notice of the Austin workshop, I considered what I had done. Perhaps, I thought in a moment of quiet sanity, I had become a bit too ambitious. It's one thing to teach a subject and watch as the field of grace it creates inspires a healing, but to actively pursue healing is an entirely different matter. You are now openly stating that you personally have access to knowledge that can potentially initiate healing—and that raises the responsibility bar several notches. I needed help, and so I asked a close colleague and friend, Steve Fanning, who is a professor of history as well as a gifted healer, to teach the workshop with me. Years ago Steve ended up bedridden as a result of an asthma attack that left him in an extended coma. The prognosis was that he would never walk again. But Steve healed himself, and through that journey he became a vessel for the healing of others. Within weeks our workshop filled to capacity with people struggling with every kind of ailment, from cancer to advanced diabetes to leukemia to HIV/AIDS.

On the first day of the workshop, as I looked at all of those dear, hopeful, frightened, precious people, I expected to be over-whelmed, but I wasn't. Instead, I felt a ferocious fury of belief take over: *Healing is real.* It went through me like a bolt of lightning. I knew I had to believe it enough for all of them. Steve had already been a healer-sage for years, so he was comfortable in his "mys-tical skin." That is, because of his own experience in healing a condition that he had been told was unhealable, Steve came to the realization that the interior self—in other words, the soul—is infinitely more powerful in its capacity to do the impossible than is modern medicine.

For me, this workshop proved to be yet another turning point, because it represented my growing comfort level with the arena of healing. This workshop also became the first of many provocative forums about the experience of healing. "What exactly is heal-ing?" one person asked on the first day of the workshop. "Can you tell just by looking at us who is most likely to heal?" That may sound like a show-biz question, but the fact is that people do think in those terms. No doubt part of that association comes from the idea that some people may be the "lucky" ones predestined to heal, or that those who are meant to heal somehow radiate a certain glow that can be intuitively perceived. Neither of these presump-tions is based in truth, needless to say, but I completely understand how hope can get mixed up with excitement, the end product of which is this almost childlike anticipation—"something" is surely going to happen to someone, right? Much to my surprise, I later discovered that several people were thinking that same question but were too shy to ask it.

With a question like that, I have to look beyond the surface, because what it implies about the psyche of the person asking could fill a chapter in itself. The question hints at a belief in the existence of a cosmic system of reward and punishment, a Council of the Fates that has already determined who is most likely to succeed at healing. The questioner may be symbolically saying, "If you already know whether I'm going to heal or not, then it doesn't make any difference if I try. So I can just stay the way I am." Or he may need proof of outcome before he will expend effort. If healing is not guaranteed, why bother at all? Questions like these and the many conversations that they generated ultimately formed the core material for this book.

Two remarkable healings occurred during the Austin workshop, each extraordinary in its own way (as if healing in and of itself is not extraordinary enough). On the last day, a woman grabbed my arm to get my attention. She was on the verge of tears, nearly hysterical. "Look at me," she said. And then, in a louder voice, she repeated, "Look at me! I can move my hands! I can walk! I could barely walk when I came to this workshop, and I could hardly open my hands. I've had crippling arthritis for over 20 years. Now you tell me—you tell me—if I leave this room, will I go back to being crippled?"

I wrapped my arms around her and felt her sobs right into my heart. Years of burning pain had evaporated, just like that. And movement had returned to her body, not completely fluid movement, but enough that she could open her hands and walk without support. I told her that I believed that the healing she had experienced was not something to be enjoyed only within this room. This precious woman was frightened at the thought of leaving the room within which she had experienced her healing, but with the help of two compassionate women, she finally did. As she walked through the doorway, she looked like a newborn chick coming out of an egg. She was free, but anticipating the return at any moment of the iron chains around her wrists, hands, hips, and knees. As the day progressed into afternoon and evening, she remained pain-free, and she awoke the next morning feeling even better as she took off for home.

I did not find out about the second healing until eight months later. I was leading another workshop when a young woman introduced herself and mentioned that she had made the trip there to thank me for her healing. She had come to Austin with a diagnosis of terminal brain cancer. Going to that workshop had been her last hope. Afterward, she had continued to pray every day in her "interior castle" for a healing. Within two months, not only was her tumor completely gone, but the damage that the tumor had caused to her neurological system had also repaired itself. Her marriage, too, had subsequently recovered from the trauma of her illness. Unlike those few astonishing healings that take place on the spot, most, like this one, occur over a period of time, but are no less extraordinary for that.

HEALING AS A MYSTICAL EXPERIENCE

I have since led many more workshops, in Austin and elsewhere, devoted to healing. My thoughts and observations have solidified to let me identify a set of beliefs that I am convinced support or detract from the healing process. By far, the most significant of the supporting beliefs is that healing is ultimately a mystical experience and not one that can be attained through the maneuverings of the mind. By mystical, I mean that a transcendent power consumed with divine intention is required to return us to complete health, particularly in cases deemed hopeless. It doesn't matter whether a person defines that transcendent force as God, the Spirit, or grace. The fact is that the body and the mind alone cannot disintegrate an army of cancer cells that has invaded multiple organs, whereas that highly refined spiritual substance that I refer to as grace, combined with the resources of the heart and the mind, can ascend to mystical heights.

Talking about healing within the context of a mystical experience can seem to imply that no matter what you do, in the end some divine force has already decided whether or not you are going to recover, again raising the question of whether anything you do really matters. Yet everything you do matters, especially when healing is understood within a mystical context. As we shall see, the mystical realm is not governed by physical laws, nor by cosmologies of karma, in ways that we are able to fully comprehend. That is, while karma is indeed a cosmic law, attempting to discern the karmic reasons for a particular illness is not unlike attempting to describe every beach in the world while gazing at one grain of sand. The sand is real, the beaches are real, but the grain of sand is out of proportion to the quest of understanding the size, beauty, and complexity of all the beaches. It cannot be done.

Further, in matters of life and death, inevitably the question arises as to whether there is a pre-determined moment of death for each of us. The option to heal in life suggests to me that each of our lives contains experiences that bring together certain forces with greater intensity. The "death and rebirth" archetype visits us all in small ways but sometimes it gathers momentum and sweeps through our life with great intensity, bringing several endings simultaneously; perhaps too many at once. In times like that, we may choose to cooperate with the cycle of death instead of the cycle of life, in which case we enter into the forces that lead us to our death. Conversely, we may choose to re-engage with the life cycle, to re-evaluate the purpose and meaning of our life and renew a commitment to living in a way free of the destructive patterns that have led us into this cycle. Such is the power of choice and the essence of the mystical cycle of death and rebirth.

Many of the great mystics understood how to work in harmony with the universe at a cosmic level, where the ruling order of life is governed more by grace and prayer than by the lower psychic forces. Instantaneous or accelerated healings, for example, can be better understood through "mystical reasoning" once you grasp the nature of mystical law. Mystical reasoning refers to a blending of your intellectual skills and knowledge with an awareness of the nature of the mystical realm. As a rule, we are taught early on to "choose sides," to focus our senses either on the external world, which is a tactile, physical reality, or to trust our interior world of highly personal, subjective, and intuitive experiences. Physical experiences can be proven and collectively shared, whereas subjective, intuitive ones—never mind spiritual ones—cannot. Numerous people have told me stories of having invisible friends or seeing apparitions of garden fairies or angels when they were very small children. Such encounters gradually stopped for all of them as they approached the "age of reason" (about seven), when we tend to retreat from what is referred to as the innocence of childhood into the far less enchanting domain of the mind. But those early years of enchantment, of innocence, remind us all that we were born connected to another way of perceiving the world. Somehow, through the centuries of our adoration of the mind, we've evolved in a way that has made our capacity to perceive through the eyes of the soul not only difficult to access, but also threatening to the stability of our physical and mental life.

Our powers of reason are, if anything, among the greatest challenges to our healing, because rationality insists on discovering an explanation for why things happen as they do, including why we become ill. There is rarely one explanation, however, for why a person falls ill or enters into a cycle of trauma. There is rarely a simple explanation for why we do or say anything, much less for the underlying complexities of why our health or our life falls apart. For all the many healing methods you can study and incorporate into your life, including various therapies and nutritional programs—many of which are beneficial, no doubt—the complete recovery of your health requires more than these options can individually or collectively supply. While they can regenerate your energy and make you feel better for a day or a week, your "energy" is not the substance that heals. Grace is what heals. And grace does not come from a diet or from working through traumatic memories of an unhappy childhood. Grace is provided abundantly through prayer.

Of course, when it comes to certain types of healings, sometimes more than just prayer is called for. For example, prayer cannot be expected to compensate for a lack of common sense. You must also adhere to your allopathic or complementary healing protocols—from medication to acupuncture—as well as to personal practices that enhance health, such as proper nutrition and sensible exercise. But you must simultaneously do what is called for from within: that is, forgive the past; accept what cannot be changed in your life; relinquish any personal agenda for how your healing should unfold; and be present to your life as it is right now. Although no path can guarantee a healing, you can place yourself on the path with the fewest obstacles. For example, most people struggle with forgiveness, precisely because it is against the nature of our reason to forgive. Forgiveness doesn't make emotional sense to us, much less appeal to our pride, although it might sound great in theory. Our reason and our emotions prefer the logic of justice, an eye for an eye, a hurt for a hurt. Forgiveness seems to fly in the face of that, as if we are letting the person who wronged us off the hook. But forgiveness is a mystical act, not a reasonable one. Forgiveness is a challenge meant to cleanse the windows of your mind, particularly those through which you can see only your need for personal justice. You can't see anyone else's pain through these windows, because, like mirrors, they reflect only you: you are the center of the universe, yours is the only pain that counts, and all that is just and fair should be based on what serves your life.

The mind may never be able to come to terms with forgiveness; by its very nature the mind is forever concocting strategies for ego repair and enhancement, particularly if you have suffered from a wound that included humiliation. Forgiveness represents a struggle not only between yourself and the person who harmed you, but between yourself and God. It can be an initiation into the level of perception where you begin to comprehend that individual justice, as such, can never really exist in its idyllic form within any society. The capacity to forgive is nothing less than the acceptance of a higher principle of divine justice, rather than earthly justice, as the organizing element behind the events of your life. When understood through the lens of this higher principle, events and relationships take on an impersonal quality. People's actions are driven by forces that have nothing to do with you, even though you might get harmed when you stand in their way. Or you might harm those who happen to be in your way—even if you care deeply for them.

Such a view does not by any means excuse us from responsible action or from seeking civil justice in matters that demand it. What this perspective does give us, however, is the knowledge that each action we initiate is never isolated, but part of a physical, emotional, mental, psychic, and spiritual continuum. Most often we are driven by reactions and unnamed forces within us, and it is difficult—exceedingly so—to maintain perspective on the impersonal complexity of our every action while engaging in an angry exchange with someone. Yet, think about how often, after an upsetting conversation, you have tried to explain your behavior by introducing bits and pieces of your history that had an influence on why you lost your temper in that moment. "Well," you might say, "I had a difficult childhood and an alcoholic parent, so it's not surprising that I behave this way sometimes. When you said what you said, it reminded me of all the times in my childhood when I was yelled at, and that's why I responded so angrily to you." In other words, you should be forgiven because your rage really wasn't "personal"; it was historical, complex, coming from a number of caverns within yourself. After providing a person with a litany of your problems, you fully expect to not only be completely forgiven for whatever you said or did, but sympathetically so!

Forgiveness is a transcendent force that releases you from far more than the individual with whom you have a painful history. Forgiveness releases you from an ego state of consciousness that clings to a need for justice built around the fear of being humiliated, based on prior experiences of humiliation. Forgiveness is essential to healing, because it requires you to surrender your ego's need to have life fall into place around your personal version of justice. I will present a detailed way to accomplish this level of forgiveness in Chapter 2, and in Chapter 6 I'll talk more about how it functions as a mystical law governing all of life. But one thing should be clear right now: You cannot reason your way through forgiveness. Forgiveness is an act beyond reason. You must learn to draw on another kind of power within you to carry out this transformation.

THE CHALLENGE OF HEALING TODAY

Although healing is never easy and perhaps never will be, two interrelated factors are largely responsible for redefining our approach to health and the human healing potential. First, we have clearly entered the "energy age" or the "psychic age," whose fabric includes our exploration of our psychic natures. Second, we have blended this exploration with an equally passionate pursuit of spirituality, and the result is an epidemic of spiritual crises mistakenly diagnosed as psychological sufferings.

Both of these subjects have a direct bearing on how we should approach illness today; specifically, that we recognize the spiritual crisis as an authentic crisis that is not the same as a psychological or an emotional crisis, though it may express itself through the psyche and emotions. Without this recognition, we often end up medicating a crisis that in fact requires not tranquilizers or sedatives, but spiritual direction.

Entering the Age of Energy

We now think of ourselves not simply as physical bodies, but also as "energy systems" that require various kinds of treatment. Our energy system is the harbor of our psyche, emotions, mental capacities, unconscious or subconscious mind, and spirit. All these aspects of ourselves require forms of treatment and care based on sophisticated philosophies of psychological integration. Further, their treatment must be harmonized with the healing of our physical body.

As if that's not a tall enough order, we have yet to fully understand ourselves as "intuitive" human beings. We have not established a clear-cut model of health and illness that maps out the relationship between the psychic and physical realms. We have yet to recognize that certain disorders originate as psychic traumas or with macro-psychic influences. By macro-psychic, I am referring to the effect of energetic pollution, a type of pollution that is impossible to measure but is nonetheless present and very toxic. For example, we now live in an atmosphere that is crowded with invisible technology. I imagine that if we could hear all the radio and Internet communications traveling through the air, we would go mad. But even though we don't actually hear and see all these transmissions and waves, we are psychically sensing this data as it is penetrating our energy fields. We tend to discount such things, because our five senses can't "reason" with that reality. The problem is literally beyond reason for our five senses, and so we dismiss it with the thought "If something can't be seen or heard or tasted or touched or smelled, it really can't harm us." In truth, we have yet to develop the intellectual or psychic mechanism to cope with what we are able to intuitively grasp, and so we dismiss the data from our intuitive intelligence, relying instead upon "scientific data" to be our guide.

But I suspect that these massive networks of communications generate an enormous field of "psychic free radicals" that do penetrate the subtle, porous energy fields of the general population. The long-term effects of the war in Iraq, for example, or the dramatic and (one might say) traumatic decline of the economy have certainly had a collective impact on the psychic health of the nation as well as the health of its finances. The stress people feel is palpable, bleeding out of their energy fields like a slow, heavy mist that fills the collective atmosphere with a sense of dread. The weight of these psychic free radicals is felt by everyone, from those already embracing intuitive consciousness to those who resonate to gut responses—people whose intuitive systems are just beginning to awaken. It is even possible that the quantum rise in energetic disorders—mood swings, anxiety attacks, the inability to concentrate, sleep disorders, ADHD, and perhaps even autism—is influenced by the spontaneous combustion caused by the intuition age colliding with energy technology.

We have not fully recognized the parameters of psychic health and well-being, as opposed to those of physical and psychological health. Our psychic and intuitive natures are not yet real enough to us to be a recognized factor in our health. No doubt that day will come, but in the meantime the absence of this vital bank of knowledge, and of the ability to accurately evaluate a psychic disorder—much less treat it—has placed many people in the risky position of medicating conditions that may require far more astute treatment by individuals skilled at recognizing stress disorders originating from the subtle and indeed impersonal field of consciousness.

Spiritual Crisis: A Reality of Our Times

Nor have we recognized the precise nature of spiritual crises, such as the "dark night of the soul," as very real suffering experienced by countless individuals in our society. Such a crisis is beyond reason; that is, the suffering of the soul does not take place within the mind, even if the mind gives expression to the soul's darkness. But if our suffering is anchored in the soul, how do we respond to that within a society where the sacred has no clinical authority? In the traditional setting of a monastery or ashram, the seeker on an inner spiritual pilgrimage would most likely have access to spiritual directors, mentors, or gurus—those who know the rigors of the inner path. This seeker would be told to anticipate the experience of the dissolution of her ego, done in darkness again and again.

Why is this happening now? For one thing, contemporary society presents us with ingredients unique to our time: easy access to refined sacred texts and spiritual teachings, inspiring an appetite for the inner life, within an atmosphere that encourages the pursuit of psychological and emotional integration and healing. When we open the vast territory of the psyche and soul, the inner world begins to consume the outer world. Without the keen eye of a trained spiritual director, it is easy to mistake the spiritual crisis that may develop in this way for a psychological problem.

Spiritual depression presents itself in much the same way as clinical depression—but not quite. The marks of distinction are crucial, yet hard for the untrained to recognize. They make the difference between interpreting the source of depression as a problem that may require medication or as a process of transformation that is best served by reflection, discussion of the stages of the dark night, and understanding the nature of mystical prayer. I have met many people who have been treated for depression and other conditions when they were, in fact, in the deep stages of a spiritual crisis. Without the proper support, that crisis becomes misdirected into a problem with relationships, a problem with one's childhood, or a chronic malaise. Spiritual crises are now a very real part of our spectrum of health challenges and we need to acknowledge them with the same authority as we do clinical depression.

Further, we have made the healing process exceedingly burdensome and complex. Today it is not uncommon to approach an illness as an engrossing and demanding new relationship, one in which the illness becomes a means to an end, a temporary visiting friend, a doorway to a new life as well as to past lives, the motivation to excavate every hurt feeling from the past, and the inspiration to begin the quest for meaning and purpose in one's life. Although it is understandable that an illness can inspire us to reevaluate what is important, dismantling the whole of our world at one time is a Herculean task that even a fully healthy person is rarely prepared to undertake. This kind of approach is also beyond ordinary logic and reason; it hints at being motivated by fear and panic more than by wanting to make only the essential choices. Healing demands that you focus on the elements in your life that require immediate attention and that are essential to your transformation to health—period.

The Global Factor and Health

Finally, we need to consider how global and psychic issues affect the quality of our health. Three major psychic pressure points are now a part of our lives, and they are here to stay. First, change has become instantaneous, whereas even as recently as a few decades ago we could take comfort in the illusion that we were not aware of events taking place in other nations. That field of blindness is forever gone. Second, all change is global in its impact and magnitude. We are now a planet made intimate by environmental concerns, weapons of mass destruction, fuel and food shortages, and interlinked financial markets. We have become an intimate planetary community, albeit an aggressive one. And there is no way of returning to policies of isolation or domination. And third, change has become profound in its capacity to affect individuals, families, communities, nations, cultures, and the environment. By profound, I mean that the changes we are now experiencing have external consequences beyond just introducing us to new technology. As a global community, we must now confront the disintegration of our planetary resources as well as extreme climate changes. Profound change means that no one shall be untouched by what is now taking place on our earth.

These are conditions of a new era, an age of interconnectedness with threads so tightly woven that each of us must now truly consider our role in this life as significant to the whole of life. Again, this may be a position that seems unreasonable to the ordinary mind, but consider that the fundamental tenet of "energy literature" is that thoughts and attitudes are an individual's primary power. So far that truth has been applied most enthusiastically to health and healing, but a truth cannot be contained to one area of life. If thoughts, attitudes, and beliefs are powerful enough to remedy an illness, should we not actively and with determined devotion focus our positive intentions on the healing of this planet? Psychic free radicals are a reality, the result of the debris of our collective negative thinking and unchecked emotions, because we have yet to raise the bar on how conscious we want to be of the invisible power that we command. Yet we cannot afford to be selective about this, applying positive thinking only to our personal health but not to the whole of life.

How much these global and psychic changes affect us remains to be seen, but that they do affect us is beyond question. Here, "reason" itself requires examination. As a species, we have relied increasingly on our ability to reason our way through problems to guarantee our survival. It has become routine to gather world leaders at global summits in order to resolve political or monetary problems or to direct sanctions against the policies of other nations as a way of coercing them back into compliance with the code of the global family. The creation of the United Nations was the first significant attempt at finding reasonable solutions to mounting catastrophic global problems such as hunger, disease, and poverty. We count on these gatherings—and the capacity of their representatives and other world leaders—to stay within the boundaries of good judgment and not commit the final foolish act of releasing global nuclear weapons upon the planet. It is beyond reason, at least for any sane person, that humanity could reach such a moment of absurd action, and yet we are now at that place. We are at the "beyond reason" point of our evolution, meaning that the type and scope of the problems we are now confronting cannot be resolved by a mere gathering of "reasonable" people around a table.

We cannot, for example, reason with Mother Nature. We cannot sanction our way through global warming or declare war on the melting ice caps in the Arctic in order to make them cease their melting. We cannot gather the dying bee population together, demand by law that they stop dying, and order them to continue to pollinate our plants, lest we suffer starvation from lack of plant regeneration. Reason has run its course when it comes to Mother Nature, and because we are all part of Mother Nature's life system, we intuitively know this to be true. We can all feel that there is a psychic pressure in the collective atmosphere, a type of shared anxiety that is both personal and impersonal, as if the atmosphere is pregnant with impending disasters, but yet our five senses tell us the world we live in looks the same as it always has. Only intuitively we know it's not the same. Everything about our lives is changing at light speed now, changing so fast that the world we wake up in is significantly different from the world we go to sleep in each evening. People are rising in the morning as millionaires, for example, and going to bed paupers. Many people who never thought they would have to confront being homeless now find themselves in exactly that crisis.

Today such mind-blowing problems are not rare. Indeed, these rapid-fire life changes have become almost commonplace. People in the midst of these crises would have considered such events unreasonable just a few decades ago. But the belief that life is a continuum of reasonable events with scripted and manicured outcomes is rooted in fear. What's more, it prevents you from imagining that you can accomplish anything that reason calls impossible, such as healing an illness others view as terminal. Achieving the impossible requires that you outwit your voice of reason and access the whimsical part of your nature that inherently delights in the possibilities of the imagination.

Consider that we are living at a major turning point in the history of humanity, a time of great crisis and great opportunity. It may be unreasonable to imagine that you can make a difference to a world in crisis based on how you undertake your own healing, yet I believe this to be true. It makes no sense to our logical minds that as we heal, the whole of life heals. Yet the power of one mustard seed can move a mountain; the power of one clear light does illuminate the darkness; the power of a person devoted to truth becomes a channel for healing grace that benefits all humanity. No matter what you heal within yourself, from a negative thought to a progressive cancer, the very act of healing has in some way made a difference to everyone on the planet. It is a truth that goes beyond the bounds of ordinary reason, but so does all mystical truth, and that is why such truth has the power to heal.

THE GRAVITY FACTOR

When I think of gravity, images come to mind of Isaac Newton resting under a tree while an apple falls from the branch above, symbolically containing the inspiration for the law of gravity. Newton, of course, is considered one of the pillars of the Enlightenment and the Age of Reason, overlapping periods that are variously dated from the 16th to the 18th centuries. Newton, together with his forerunners, including Copernicus, Galileo, and Descartes, and contemporaries such as Locke and Spinoza—among many more leading scientists and philosophers of this renaissance of thought—stood on the threshold of an awakening power of the mind that would reshape the Western world. European society underwent a shattering transformation as the result of this flood of reasoning, a reaction to both the superstition and the mystical mindset fostered by the medieval church. The Renaissance signaled the dawning of a new age, one that would reshape even the celestial myths about the nature of God. If the systems of heaven were orderly, if the earth indeed revolved around the sun, if laws such as gravity governed all falling objects in some kind of universal harmony, then God, too, must be a logical Being. Reason was the power to strive for, the ultimate inner quality of the human being.

All material things have a symbolic counterpart in the archetypal realm that imbues each physical object or force with meaning. This meaning can be understood by interpreting the effects of the object or force on the physical world. Another way to say this is that the law of cause and effect operates on many levels other than the physical. Emotional and psychic forces, for instance, also have causes and effects. In the realm of mystical law, however, although the law of cause and effect functions just as reliably as it does in the realm of natural law, it is far more porous, or open to influences that do not exist in the same way within the physical realm. Grace and prayer, for example, have the power to influence the dynamics of the laws within the mystical realm. Some mystics have been able, in effect, to "defy gravity" as a result of their knowledge of and trust in the authority of mystical law. Some are known to have experienced levitation while in ecstatic states—as was the case with Teresa of Ávila—or bilocation, the ability to appear in two places at the same time. (I will explore the mystical laws at length in Chapter 6.)

To understand how the laws of the universe, including the law of gravity, can function in symbolic ways requires us to train our minds to perceive beyond the limitations of reason and logic. First, we need to understand the word "gravity" through its other meanings, such as "seriousness" or "heaviness." Symbolically, we might say that Newton discovered the law of seriousness, the law of the relationship between reason and the symbolic "weight of thought," along with the conventional law of gravity. Certainly it can be said that Newton made a scientific discovery in identifying the law of gravity, but from another and far more intriguing perspective, the case can be made that Newton had a mystical experience in which he was given a glimpse into the essential oneness of the universe. He saw through the veil of ordinary sight this one day of his life to comprehend the functioning of but one of the physical laws—which he named the law of gravity—which reflects the constant mystical truth that "What is in one is in the whole." He saw "into the whole" on that one day in his life and noted that all things are subject to one law, related to weight and force. That he applied his mystical insight to science is just part of his task, but the mystical consequence was that energetic weight—psychic weight—began transferring more "seriously" into thought as well as science grew more and more into prominence, eclipsing the value of emotional and intuitive knowledge.

How do reason and the "symbolic weight of thought" translate into our ordinary life experience? It's really pretty simple. Think of a person whom you consider frustratingly unreasonable, because no matter what you say or how logically you present your position, this person becomes emotionally manipulative or hysterical or goes into attack mode. (Surely you can think of at least one person who fits that description.) Recall the growing rage and frustration you feel as you continue to make a genuinely logical, reasonable point, but get only responses that are self-absorbed and defensive as you realize that the other person has not heard a thing you've said. Now, let me go through this scenario with some "live footage."

A woman I'll call Sara married for a second time in her late 40s. The man she married retired six months after the wedding, while Sara kept working. Foolishly, she had not initiated the in-depth discussions of finances that couples should have prior to a midlife second marriage, although that might not have mattered anyway. Within a few months after her husband's retirement, he began to spend their savings in careless and outrageous purchases of things he'd always wanted. His rationale was that now that he was retired and married to a "working gal," he felt entitled to indulge himself during his golden years. Within a year, not only had he drained their retirement account of nearly $400,000, he had run up a sizable debt.

Now, family and friends told Sara, "Just talk to him. Talk some sense into your husband. Doesn't he realize what he's doing?" No amount of "reasoning" could have ever reached this man, however, as he was locked into his position of entitlement and his wife was locked into her position of logic and reason. Think of this lock-in point as a "gravity" anchor, a marker in the timeline of your life in which you freeze a part of your energy into "matter," weighing it down as a result of a bad experience, trauma, or an unfinished power play that is going to need resolution at some point in years to come.

The more "gravity anchors" you accumulate, the more emotional, psychological, and mental "weight" you take on. To put this in Newtonian terms, you become weighted down in the "gravity of life," unable to envision the higher altitudes of the mystical or spiritual life. These altitudes become tainted, almost by default, because you are so weighted down by negativity that the possibilities of what you can accomplish or become in the realm of the extraordinary begin to seem increasingly unrealistic and unobtainable.

Applying reason and logic to the nature of the soul or the nature of God is ultimately unproductive as well, because we are merely using our own version of logic to manage our unconscious fears. We may be trying to view God through the lens of our lack of faith or a need to endorse a personal faith. Or we may be looking for a way to control the element of randomness, which is the most feared characteristic of God. We wonder constantly, for example, "Does God strike the good as well as the evil? Or does God function according to the laws of earthly justice, punishing only those who do harm?"

These are "reasonable" questions that everyone asks at some point, but in truth there are no reasonable answers. No one really can answer such questions, no matter how much we would like to crack that celestial code. As a result of this uncertainty, we tend to believe that if we do only good things, we will be rewarded with the blessing of earthly security. If such behavior keeps order on earth, then surely it must work the same within the courtroom of the heavens, right? If not, how do we find the key to bargaining with the random nature of God? If we can't find the key, we can either return to the days of superstitious practices, such as hanging trinkets of protection around our neck and lighting candles for assistance, or we can just ignore this random force and pursue a life of holistic health practices in the hope that they will be enough. To be clear, reason is not a flaw in the human design. It's just that when it comes to finding a logical explanation for all things, the cosmic forces will eventually exhaust the reasoning mind with an endless supply of mysteries and inexplicable phenomena.

The Enlightenment initiated a profound advance in the emancipation of the intellect and, in doing so, did society a great favor in overturning the absolute power of state and church and liberating a culture profoundly influenced by superstitions. The Enlightenment gave humanity permission to ask questions with less fear of church reprisals and to pursue knowledge with the hope that the answers would change their way of life. No wonder the people of centuries gone by fell madly in love with the search for knowledge and truth. The love affair with logic, intellect, and science that began hundreds of years ago only continued to grow and gain momentum. Our own love of logic and order and our need to find an explanation for why all things happen as they do—cosmically or otherwise—come from these early forerunners.

Yet, as this love of reason and logic took hold, other, more intuitive abilities came to be shunned. Intuitive skills represented data that could not be proven, measured, or quantified, so intuitive reasoning was not to be trusted. How could it be? It was unreliable and subjective—all things that real science dreads. Scientific, medical, social, and military advances made quantum leaps based on practical knowledge. Intuitive and mystical reasoning were no match for the newfound contributions coming out of laboratories and libraries. The Western world shifted through the centuries in favor of the power of reason, while the intuitives and mystics retreated into positions of lesser social authority, if not complete silence. The great irony, of course, is that for all the advancement science was about to introduce, a vast amount of knowledge of the soul and the psyche would be lost.

It's easy to understand how the Renaissance also brought on the end of a great age of mysticism, in which mystics were influenced not so much by a passionate love of the mind and reason as by a passionate love of God and the soul. Many of the pre-Enlightenment mystics were great intellectuals, but they did not lose their mystical instincts while refining their intellectual capacities. They managed to reside with equal footing in both their exterior and their interior worlds, attaining a position of balance that no doubt served them well. In Europe, they included many great Christian mystics, such as Hildegard of Bingen, Julian of Norwich, Clare of Assisi, Francis of Assisi, John of the Cross, and one particularly dear to me, Teresa of Ávila. All were known for the richness of their interior lives, the legacies of which continue to bless and enlighten millions of people.

Many of the great Jewish Kabbalists and Muslim mystics were chased out of Spain and other parts of Europe during the Inquisition, but regrouped in the Middle East and continued to flourish there. Meanwhile, in Asia, India, and Africa, mystics of the Hindu, Buddhist, and Taoist traditions, under less pressure to "modernize," carried on those legacies and developed highly sophisticated systems of meditation, prayer, and integrated physical practices. Their particular types of mystical experiences "defy gravity." These mystics, in medieval Europe as well as Asia and the Middle East, had intimate and direct experiences of the Divine. They had visions and received express instructions on what actions to take and when to write about their inner spiritual life. Teresa of Ávila often saw angels in her visions, once remarking that she was visited by an angel, although she was unsure from which realm it came, as it did not identify itself. She also had frequent visions of Jesus, which she alluded to in her masterpiece, *The Interior Castle*.

As the Age of Reason progressed, the mystical experiences of these extraordinary people grew rarer. Certainly mystical events involving direct experience of the numinous persisted throughout the world, especially in the Hasidic and Kabbalistic traditions of Judaism, as well as among the great Sufi masters and yogis of the East. But in the West, they happened with less frequency. The onset of the love of reason somehow reshaped humanity's relationship to God and the soul, and it obviously had a profound effect on the connection that was once possible between humans and heaven. For all the blessings that come with sharpening our intellect and our capacity to be discerning, it is obvious that we compromise our profound interior connection to the sacred when we replace our capacity for mystical perception with a need to have what in fact cannot be had at all—a reasonable and logical universe.

What is abundantly clear today is that, for all our technological advances, we have reached the end of the Age of Enlightenment and Reason. Like the forefathers of the Enlightenment who stood on the threshold of a great turning point in human consciousness, we, too, are standing at the end of one era and the beginning of another. We are living in a turbulent world and, although societies have always known problems, the problems we face today are bigger and more powerful than we are. We cannot talk our way out of our crises; we cannot solve our financial, political, or environmental problems by mere paper legislation. The problems facing humanity have become "unreasonable." A global nuclear crisis is an unreasonable crisis. A global climate meltdown is an unreasonable crisis that we cannot buy our way out of. We must, it seems, shift to yet another realm of perception, a realm that is beyond conventional reason, in order to maneuver through the problems facing us. We must learn to think as the mystics did. We must learn to defy gravity. This requires developing our intellectual and creative resources as well as our capacity to perceive the world through the power of our soul. In this way, what is impossible in the physical world of reason and logic becomes completely possible in our world of grace, mystical laws, prayer, and divine companionship.

It is in our nature to defy gravity, to transcend the limitations of the reasoning mind and connect with an inner realm of mystical truth. We have always been on the quest for this truth; we have always been seeking a way to defy the laws that weigh us down in ordinary thought. From a Renaissance of the mind, we are now coming full circle to a mystical Renaissance. It's time to learn the truths that govern our interior soul.

Chapter Two

————— **THE FIRST TRUTH** —————

You Can't Reason with Illness, Crisis, or God

The need to know why things happen to us as they do is a gut survival instinct. Something feels so off when we are denied an explanation for events and experiences, especially when they redirect the course of our lives. The absence of an explanation makes us feel powerless, as if we had done something wrong but we just don't know what. Most people fall into this line of thinking, which reflects the belief that if you are good, bad things shouldn't happen to you. So if something bad does happen, Why? "What went wrong? What negative pattern in my mind or heart is the culprit? Surely if I find that current of bad juice and cut it off at the source, I'll be rewarded with health, right?" It can't hurt, but it won't guarantee a healing either.

The people who have described their healing process to me have many beliefs and attitudes in common. First and perhaps most elemental among them is the realization that it was essential to give up the need to know why things happened as they did. Most did not come to this realization easily, as this thought pattern has an entire belief system attached to it, including a belief in how the mechanism of good and evil functions and how God interacts with individuals at the behavioral level of life. This isn't as simple as giving up sugar or caffeine. Giving up the need to know why things happen as they do requires a belief in some higher order or power that transcends rational thought. To what or whom, then, you might ask, did you release this need to know why? One phrase used to describe this release is "surrendering to God." Others might prefer to call it surrendering to the Universe. Either way, such surrender is fundamentally a mystical act of transformation, not a rational or intellectual one. It is a leap into the unknown that defies reason and requires every ounce of courage you have. Jumping such a high inner hurdle wasn't easy for these people, but it was—and is—a necessary step.

NO NEED TO KNOW

Until you surrender the need to know why things happened to you as they did, you will hold on to your wounds with intense emotional fire. Your mind will want to heal, but your pride, anger, and emotions will remain caught up in wanting to make sure that the people who hurt you feel bad about what they've done. Or you may want to hurt them back. But rest assured, your emotional self will remain attached to the unfinished business rooted in feelings of abandonment and humiliation, of having lost something or been cheated. Your mind may do what's required for healing and go through all the prescribed steps, but your heart will never fully participate in the healing process. In the end, forgiveness is an act of release, surrendering the need for an explanation. From that perspective, forgiveness has nothing to do with the individuals who harmed you. It is the act of accepting that there is a greater map of life, through which flow many rivers of events and relationships, all interconnected. Forgiveness is your release from the hell of wanting to know what cannot be known and from wanting to see others suffer because they have hurt you.

In order to reach this place of surrender, the people I encountered had to recognize that the word "forgiveness" is all-inclusive, encompassing childhood pain, broken marriages, experiences of betrayal, unresolved differences in various relationships, business deals gone bad, misguided or impulsive decisions that harmed others, and personal acts of misconduct.

That understanding represents the first level of wisdom, the one at which you can see that you had at least some role in the unfolding of events—or that although you may not have had a direct role in creating an abusive situation, as in the case of childhood abuse or neglect, no logical explanation will ever suffice for why you personally were the victim. Certainly you will never uncover an explanation that actually heals the full measure of your pain, because reason simply can't penetrate the heart and soul that deeply. Given that fact, we must strive for a position that is beyond logical understanding, one that may even be transcendent. One man described it to me this way: "My mother was an alcoholic. I have more memories of her passed out on the couch than I do of her conscious. I hated her for years, and after I left home I didn't see her for almost 12 years. I returned home because I wanted to reconcile these memories, but found I couldn't, because she denied everything I brought up. When I became ill, I realized that the reason I had been angry all my life was that I felt cheated about not having a loving mother. I thought there was something wrong with me. I realized then that there was nothing wrong with me. My mom was a sad, empty, and disappointed person, but I have no doubt she did not want to be that way. There was no one who could help her back then. How was she supposed to get out of her pain? It had nothing to do with me, and in realizing that, I healed this deep, dark wound. She lived long enough for us to truly reconcile, and for this miracle I shall always be grateful."

The next level of experiences you cannot reason with are more cosmic in nature, because they are impersonal, part of a collective catastrophe, or because they are potentially fatal. And the confrontation with our own death inevitability calls us to review our relationship to the whole of our life—that is, matters related to the spirit or cosmos. This level, then, includes accidents and injuries; the death of a loved one; economic crises that are seemingly out of your control (like a stock market crash or a major recession); environmental disasters that take away everything you have; or birth defects in your children. At the high end of this spectrum is personal illness, which often elicits our greatest need to know why—specifically, why we must now confront the crisis of a disease that could kill us. Even if the ailment is the result of our own actions—diabetes caused by obesity, lung cancer from smoking—we still want to know, "Why me, and why now?"

Yet when the moment for surrendering our questions finally arrives, we don't go through the list item by item. Instead, those people who manage to heal release an entire mindset that takes the whole list with it. This represents a cleansing of the ego that liberates the embittered self. In its place emerges an inner truth that assures you that nothing was a mistake or an accident and that all things can be healed. Imagine viewing a garden on the far side of the river that is rumored to have the most fragrant flowers ever to bloom on earth. No matter how poetic a description of each fragrance someone might offer you, your mind would not be able to produce the experience of one of those scents, even for a second. To smell the actual flowers, you must enter the garden. Such an experience is beyond the grasp of reason; it is an act of transformation, or at least of sensory delight.

Giving up the need to know why something has happened to you will definitely count among the most rigorous personal challenges of your life. Everything about human nature craves an explanation for why events occur as they do. Our sense of reason is more than just an attribute of the mind; it is akin to an archetypal power that governs our capacity to ground our lives and balance the forces of chaos in the world. The power of reason connects us to the rule of law and justice, directing human behavior on that tenuous path of right and wrong. Surrendering the need to know "why" represents the release of an entire inner archetypal map, one that the ego relies on for its strategies of survival in a world we perceive as heavily influenced by the polarities of right and wrong, good and evil. To surrender runs counter to all your instincts of protection, grounded as they are in your need for personal safety. Your unconscious fear is that to surrender is to release the force of evil in your life without the rule of good to counteract it. We tend to believe, even unconsciously, that if we do good, bad things won't happen to us. We not only believe that principle, but we also honor and live by it. Yet healing requires you to relinquish your need for an explanation—why, for instance, you experienced a brutal betrayal, or why you must take on the arduous challenge of healing an illness or assisting a loved one who is ill. Understandably, everyone asks, "How? How am I supposed to let go of this need for reasonable explanations?"

Surrendering the need for an explanation represents a profound act of personal transformation. What you are releasing is your need for God or the heavens or the Divine to explain the events of your life in a rational way, as if the heavens operated according to the laws of our land and the rules of human interaction. Surrender represents a course correction of our belief that others are responsible for our life and, more to the point, for our pain and failures. It also represents a supreme act of faith that states, "With you, God, all things are possible, including my healing." In saying that prayer, however, you leave it to God to chart the course of possibilities for your healing. As the saying goes, all our prayers are answered, but sometimes the answer is no.

Yet how does one accomplish that profound degree of inner transformation? Like Alice tumbling down the rabbit hole, you need to identify what I consider the unreasonable voice of reason— that part of you that encourages you to feel sorry for yourself or provides you with a list of reasons to go on believing that your life will never improve or that bad things happen only to you. Although we are calling this the voice of reason, in fact it is a voice that you cannot reason with, one that can prevent you from healing and make you believe that nothing you do will ever make a difference. This is a voice that can destroy all hope and lead you into despair and endless cycles of depression. Then your pride forces you to justify your actions and anger, and all the time you know in your heart that you are wrong. So-called reasonable behavior is unreasonable precisely because it is so often driven by toxic emotions, and we end up using our reason to justify actions that are emotionally irrational, negative, and hurtful.

The voice of reason is, in the language of Saint Teresa of Ávila, influenced by countless inner "reptiles" that need to be exorcised, because they exert control over our ability to make clear and healthy choices. These inner reptiles can make us believe we are thinking reasonably when we are actually possessed by fear: the fear of poverty, for instance, or the fear of being wrong or rejected. Such fears can and do lead us to act in self-destructive ways. People possessed by fear can rationalize all types of behavior, from addiction to abuse, and actually believe what they are saying is completely reasonable. Inner reptiles are the demons of our "reasonable" mind: fear, pride, control, and our need to have the guarantee of a safe outcome before we act on our intuitive guidance. These are the "reptiles of reason" that each of us must discover within. Or, to say it another way, we must each explore the unreasonable side of the power of reason.

UNREASONABLE REASONS

The field of human consciousness acknowledges the crucial role of the spirit, as noted in the holistic body-mind-spirit template, which implies a divine presence encompassed within the human experience. And yet most people are unsure as to how the Divine expresses its influence. So we have to leave it to our imagination to create a variety of beliefs that may seem reasonable on the surface, but upon closer inspection are really a combination of superstitions and cosmic guesswork. Included among these beliefs are some real mystical truths that, when taken literally or out of cosmic context, are frequently misinterpreted. Unfortunately, although these beliefs have come to be seen as reasonable, they often end up doing far more harm than good. They reflect our need to find a logical rationale for experiences that take us beyond our ordinary boundaries of pain or fear, and, in doing so, to reestablish a sense of order, control, and direction in our lives. The following are the most common "unreasonable" reasons that I have consistently encountered in my work.

1. There Is a Lesson in This Crisis—I Just Have to Find It

The search for the one lesson behind an illness or crisis is rooted in the archetype of the "good student" or the "good child" who, upon learning the lesson, is immediately rewarded—in this case, with the return of excellent health or whatever else was lost in the crisis. The fault lines in this belief show that it is far closer to a superstition than to a faith-based conviction: First, the underlying implication is that the student or child was somehow bad and that the illness or crisis is a cosmic punishment. Second, the individual sets his or her sights on the search for one event, one wrongdoing, one bad thing that happened, instead of placing attention where it should be, on dysfunctional lifetime patterns that call for healing. This belief keeps us focused on the past as the source of healing. Healing becomes dependent on finding this Holy Grail of what one thing went wrong. I've seen people become obsessed with this search, which in itself only becomes yet another stress.

Is there any truth to this belief? Naturally, up to a point, since otherwise we'd never change our dysfunctional behaviors. The value in a lesson is gathering wisdom and applying that wisdom to the life you have today. What have you learned from your life? You look back to retrieve wisdom so that wisdom positions you not to repeat the same errors. Looking into your past in order to find information that gives you leverage to feel worse about your life or that allows you to feel entitled to make others suffer because you have suffered is a useless quest, much less a healing one. Wisdom is healing grace; not guilt, not fear, not the desire to go backward into agonizing over who hurt you so that you can tell them about it. Healing comes from gathering wisdom from past actions and letting go of the pain that the education cost you.

2. It's My Karma

All too often, I have heard people speak of their crises as tied to a past life or negative karma. Earlier, I mentioned that some beliefs are rooted in mystical truths, and karma certainly qualifies; but if any law could blow the doors off the well-guarded room of reason, the law of karma would certainly be it. Years ago I went to the ashram of Sathya Sai Baba in India, where I had a conversation with a longtime resident. Jake had a number of fascinating stories about whom Sai Baba healed and whom he did not. He told me that when he first began to watch Sai Baba, he assumed that the sage would heal the crippled children whose parents had brought them to the ashram. When this didn't happen, Jake was profoundly disturbed. He believed that "innocent" children should be healed; yet Sai Baba overlooked many of them, healing people without any apparent pattern of preference. Age, for example, didn't matter. Sai Baba was as likely to heal a very old person as a young person, despite the obvious fact that the young had more life ahead of them.

Finally Jake told Sai Baba that he was confused and wondered why he was not healing more of the children. Sai Baba asked him, "Can you see their karma?" Jake replied that he could not.

"I can," Sai Baba said. "The crippled child you see as innocent was once a judge who delighted in handing out brutal sentences to innocent people. The woman who is now his mother helped him in this cruelty." Then Sai Baba asked Jake, "Do you still feel sorry for him?"

"No," Jake admitted. "He deserves to suffer for what he did."

Sai Baba smiled at him. "Do you see why it's better that you do not know the secrets of a person's karma?" he said with a smile. "It is far better that you believe that every child is innocent and that even you do not deserve to suffer all that comes your way in life. Your heart is not yet able to see people's karma and still feel compassion for them."

Karma is real, but it is a mystical truth far more complex than we can grasp. Is there any way a belief in karma can serve a personal healing? If we believe in the existence of karma, then it follows that we must see the whole of our life, not just the difficulties, as threaded by its strands. Cosmic truth is not to be applied as a problem-solving device, but as a living philosophy or theology that covers every aspect of one's life, from the challenges to the blessings. The law of karma holds balance and fairness at its core, and if you understand that, you are bound to utilize the ingredients of your life in this present moment based on the principles of this same law.

3. Illness Is the Result of Negativity

We are a culture that reaches its conclusions based on simple measures, among them the pain-pleasure scale. If something causes pain, it's bad; all pain must be stopped immediately. Illness is painful, crises are painful, and so, based on this line of reasoning, we usually assume that the root cause of these conditions is fundamentally negative. That is simply not true. Sometimes a health crisis is one's highest calling in life, and in that case negativity has nothing whatsoever to do with it. For example, Helen Keller developed an infectious fever at the age of 18 months that caused her to go blind and deaf. Was this because of her negativity, or was it a necessary crisis that opened her path of destiny? We know the answer to that now, and even Helen Keller wrote that she viewed her blindness and deafness as essential to her calling in life.

Illness is often part of a person's destiny and not the consequence of negativity or stress. A friend of mine riding on a bus in Chicago sat across from a young man who had lost an arm and a leg in an accident. He noticed her looking at him and immediately struck up a conversation with her about how his accident had occurred. She commented that she found his attitude about his loss of two limbs remarkable, to which he replied, "That's exactly what I hope people would say. I think my job now is to make people appreciate their lives more." You may think that losing two limbs is a high price to pay for being a vessel of optimism in life, yet I am now passing on his grace to everyone who reads this story, which makes him an even more effective vessel of grace.

Negative emotions and toxic attitudes certainly influence our health, yet I do not believe that they cause our illnesses. Illnesses and crises are the result of many factors, from our lifestyle to our DNA to environmental conditions. The psychospiritual health of our interior life also plays a role. It is certainly true, however, that negativity interferes with healing. No matter how excellent the medical attention or other assistance we receive, negative attitudes undermine even the best support systems. No one can shed a lifetime's worth of fears and negative patterns in an instant. Nor is it essential to do so. It is possible, however, to invest your energy, your life force, in thoughts and beliefs that are positive and beneficial rather than those that deplete your health. Keep your attention in the present and don't let your imagination wander into the "future." You'll only scare yourself with old fears and end up in some dark, negative space. Instead, keep near you books or films or phone numbers of people who can lift your spirits.

Healing negativity does not require that you excavate every negative thought or emotion; instead, make a decision each day to find something of value to appreciate in your life, but appreciate it all day long. Or choose a positive thought and use it during your ordinary activities. One insight that completely changed the quality of my life came from the writings of Thomas Merton, from an entry in his journal describing a hot summer afternoon. He noted the color of the sunset and how the breeze bent the flowers and how the bulls were resting under the shade of a tree because of the heat. He focused his attention on the simplicity of nature, on all that was silent and beautiful, and he ended his journal entry that day with this sentence: "This day will never come again." I read that line again and again until I realized it had taken on sacred meaning for me. It had illuminated the ordinary in my life, the way I saw my family members, each day, and each one of my friends. Every time we gathered—and gather—together, I now think, "This day will never come again. I will never be here with you exactly like this again." That one sentence was an illumination of my soul, and nothing in my life has ever been the same since. That one insight has given "right proportion" to all matters for me, and I dwell in that thought the same way I dwell in a deep prayer. A thought-prayer like that renews my perspective and lifts me beyond ordinary thinking. It reminds me that no day of my life will ever come again. All lesser things fall into a different perspective when placed against a truth of such magnitude.

ON THE GLOBAL SCALE

Beyond the personal issues for which we want explanations, many of us also struggle with matters of social justice. Sometimes the desire for an explanation arises in response to global atrocities or mass killings, like all the school shootings in the nation. A woman in one of my workshops, for example, questioned the existence of God in the face of crimes against humanity. "How could anyone suggest there is a loving God somewhere in this universe when genocide happens on this planet?" she asked. "What kind of God would allow those things to happen?" You can't reason with global crises, accidents, or traumas any more than you can with personal illness. But you can transcend them; you can accept the reality of mystical truths that melt through the lesser beliefs we hold on to out of fear. Replacing fear with truth heals.

I recall so clearly one of those extraordinary moments. It occurred in a seminar at my CMED (Caroline Myss Education) Institute when a student asked a profoundly emotional question of my guest speaker, James Finley. A former Trappist monk whose spiritual director was Thomas Merton, Finley offers instruction in contemplative living with that rare combination of mystical wisdom and common sense that characterized Merton's writing. This seminar took place shortly after a tragic event in Baghdad in which terrorists had allegedly used two mentally handicapped women as suicide bombers, directing them to walk into a mosque during prayer time. More than a hundred people were killed, including, of course, the two women, who probably had no understanding of what they were doing. "How could any God allow such things to happen?" the student asked Finley. "How are we supposed to make sense of that?"

The room became silent in a way that told me everyone had at one time asked this question. Clearly moved, Finley composed himself and then replied in his characteristically steady, gentle voice, "We can't make sense of events such as that—nor should we. We can never reason away the reality of evil and it is a mistake to try. Evil exists. Unreasonable cruelties happen and some may happen to you."

He paused, and I thought he had completed his answer, but then he continued. "The next level of that answer is that you take what cannot be changed on the outside and you transcend it on the inside. You use the external crisis to transform you, past the point at which crises of evil, despair, or destruction can destroy you. You must become stronger within by building a capacity inside of you that can respond to the world around you with a much greater power, the power of love."

You must, in other words, use events that defy your reason to break through your reason. You could liken this to pushing yourself through the eye of the spiritual needle into a higher consciousness. This consciousness grasps the truth that, although evil cannot be eradicated, love and compassion in some way counteract its force. Illness and catastrophe are but two of the endless expressions of the fact that life is not a reasonable or controllable journey. Although events prove this fact time and again, our personal experiences still do not stop us from yearning for life to be otherwise. While we can tell ourselves that we live above and beyond the law of chaos because we are good people, such thinking is yet another facet of the unreasonable side of reason. Many of the things we tell ourselves are quite unreasonable, yet we cling to them, thinking that somehow a belief such as "That illness happens only to those types of people" will somehow protect us. One woman I know believes that she will never develop breast cancer, because she considers herself a medical authority on the disease and works with women who have breast cancer. As a therapist, she is brilliant, but the fears controlling her go beyond her reasoning mind and well into the depths of her emotions and unconscious. The decision to work with breast cancer patients is her attempt to reason with the illness, to strike a bargain with the demon itself in the hope that, in exchange, she will never become a breast cancer patient herself. Perhaps she will never see that her motivations come from the unreasonable side of reason, because on the surface her actions benefit others. We often trick ourselves this way, creating reasons for our actions that are substitutes for the real agenda that we don't want to confront.

Another woman stands out in my memory because of the concerns she discussed after learning that she had MS. Long before we get to the highlights of transformation and all the positive insights we may gain through the experience of having a disease, we have to deal with what the disease is going to do to our bodies and how that will affect our lives. Illness changes a person, and it can be difficult to speak about the more intimate issues that it automatically puts on the table for us, but this remarkable woman had the courage to address them. "My first reaction was that I felt like a failure for having become ill so soon after I was married. I had been married only a year!" she said. "I was overcome by shame, inadequacy, guilt, and the fear that my husband would find someone else. I mean, I was about to lose all my hair and my looks, and I realized that I would never truly be beautiful again. Why would he want to stay with me? What kind of life could I offer him now? One night I came up with a list of reasons why he should leave me and I told him I would be all right if he did, because I had failed him. You realize that my way of coping with my anguish was to create a list of reasons that released him from our marriage. He, of course, ripped up the paper, but I remained tormented and ashamed for being ill and disintegrating through chemotherapy. Eventually I pushed him away because of shame. I could not bear to have him see me like this. So I ended the marriage. I could not reason my way out of my own thinking, my own shame, even though I so desperately wanted to get beyond it. My fear of feeling humiliated because of this illness, as unreasonable as you may think that is, had more power over me than my strong desire to save my marriage."

Healing demands that we dig deep into the unreasonable side of our nature, because that's where we discover what can block our healing process. A man named Bob who healed from skin cancer told me, "I never saw myself as unreasonable at all. In fact, so far as I was concerned, I was the only reasonable person I knew. I was actually completely unreasonable, because I could not handle change of any kind or anyone challenging my opinions. It was the stress of trying to keep everyone and everything under control that eventually brought me down. I'm convinced of that," Bob said. "I finally gave it all up. I saw very clearly that if I was going to live, I had to let everyone else live the way they wanted. I had to let go of them and my need for authority. It seemed like the most unreasonable, impossible personal transformation until I was faced with death, and then I thought, 'Whatever it takes.'"

CHARACTERISTICS OF REASON

As you read the characteristics of reason listed below, personalize them. Think of reason as an archetypal instinct, like emotions. The task is to identify how your particular consciousness functions within your natural instinct to find and to have order and logic in your life.

The following descriptions serve as "voices of reason," illuminating the ways the archetype of reason instinctively functions in all of us. After reading each description, spend some time answering the questions that follow it, but not with a simple "yes" or "no." The answers you give reflect much larger patterns, showing how you have structured an entire base of power. When something you consider unreasonable happens to you, that unreasonable occurrence also threatens an entire substratum of power. We seek control over others, for example, so that they do not do unreasonable things to us that could, in turn, disempower our life. So give serious attention to these questions, as they are meant to take you into places of deep inner reflection.

1. Reason Is Reason-Oriented

Reason seeks a logical cause for things happening as they do. Intellectually, our instinct to attribute causes to certain events motivates us toward paths of knowledge and discovery. Applied to our personal lives, however, it can compel us to seek personal justice or even vengeance, negative goals that can become obsessions. Ask yourself these questions:

- Do you seek reasons why things happen as they do in your life?

- In what areas of your life do you most often need reasons?

- Are personal resolutions essential to your health? That is, have you ever held or are you now holding on to any mental or emotional unfinished business that is rooted in a need to know why something happened to you? Can this really be resolved? If so, identify that path of resolution.

2. Reason Collides with Intuition

Reason relies more on the information supplied by your five senses than on your intuition. It likes the information to be tangible, provable, reliable, and well tested. Facts, figures, and practicality rule the day for reason. At the same time, you know that emotional, intuitive information and spiritual guidance are equally valid. Here lies part of the problem: When you're calm and centered and the outcome of a decision doesn't have life-changing consequences, you trust your intuition. You are especially intuitive when it comes to others, because the consequences of those "intuitive hits" do not affect you personally. But when you're frightened, or when the decision involves money, power, or your personal relationships, you want "proof of outcome," so you are more likely to retreat to information derived from the world of facts and figures. You receive intuitive guidance continually about your home, finances, business deals, personal and professional relationships, and children—the micro-details that make up your day-to-day life. This is your "survival instinct" at work and it operates on automatic pilot, constantly transmitting micro- and macro-instructions to you, including such messages as "Don't eat that," and "You need to exercise," and "It's time for a checkup."

This intuitive system is highly attuned to your emotional, psychological, and physical health, which is why I refer to this guidance system as the survival instinct. It is also the instinct most ignored, no doubt because the voice is so constant and so full of common-sense instruction.

Learning to work with reason and intuition in tandem requires you to separate from the unreasonable voice of reason that harbors all your fears. Your reason and intuition transmit a perspective, a "hit" for every choice and decision, from the seemingly most insignificant to the ones you consider most important. Sometimes your reason and intuition are in harmony, but when they are not, ask yourself whether you ultimately trust what you can touch and see or what you sense. I've met countless people who have said, in one way or another, "I know I'm supposed to do something with my life, but I'm just not sure what that is." These people often end up with psychic illnesses such as concentration disorders or migraines, the result of guidance overload or "psychic combustion," because they are filled with creative vision and drive but simply cannot get their reasoning powers to cooperate with an intuitive leap of faith. They must see, feel, touch, smell, and hear the signs of success before they make a move. Because they must have a guarantee of safe passage to their higher potential for fear of failing, they do nothing at all.

Having your intuition held prisoner by your reason in this way can create great despair, depression, anxiety, and chronic fatigue, among other energy disorders. If your illness has its roots in a reason-intuition dilemma, a creative solution must be introduced into the healing process. Just the act of acknowledging the reason-intuition dilemma advances your healing, because it begins the critical process of consciously ending the fear you may have of hearing your own inner truth. Without that creative step, the other healing modalities you try will have only minimal effects.

- What excuses does your voice of reason give you that allow you to act consciously against your intuition?

- What are the circumstances most likely to make you require "proof of outcome" before acting on a decision?

- How often do you betray your intuition because of unreasonable reasons?

3. Reason Strives to Protect and Defend Its Fears Rather Than Heal Them

We build much of our lives around our fears. Review all of the elements of your life, from your relationships to your occupation to the way you dress, through the lens of this one question: "How much of my life is organized around my fears?" You will find that your fears permeate everything. Sometimes we inherit fears from our parents or ethnic group, sometimes they enter our lives through experiences, and sometimes we are simply born with mysterious phobias that seem to be rooted in our psychic DNA. Yet many of us will defend our fears as if we were defending innocent children. "I can't help it, that's just the way I am!" "I almost drowned when I was a child and ever since then I've been afraid of water." Or worse, the claim that certain fears came from a past life and they are thus here to stay. And that's that. The fears are in place, never to be questioned, challenged, or exorcised. Identifying with fear patterns as a part of who you are, or as a way of proving that you had a trauma back in your youth, is yet another expression of the unreasonable side of reason. People sometimes perceive my disregard for their fear patterns as unsympathetic and harsh, when in fact my choice not to support the authority of their fears is motivated by a desire to help them heal. Why would I encourage what I consider to be a form of psychic possession? Any time the psyche is controlled by something other than the healthy, conscious self, a form of possession is at work. When a fear has more authority over your actions than you do, you are possessed by it, and it can cause you to behave outside the boundaries of kindness and love.

- What fears exert an unreasonable control over you?

- How deeply have you challenged your unreasonable fears?

- Are you someone who caves into the authority of
  a fear? If so, why do you do that? And how do you
  cope with the consequence of living under the
  authority of a fear? Inevitably you will transfer your
  anger for having done that to someone else; thus,
  who do you punish as a result of being held captive
  by your own fears?

4. Fears Are Powerful

Fears are powerful, particularly because they are unreasonable and often rooted in superstitions. Indeed, many penetrate well beyond the parameters of our reasoning mind, gaining a foothold deep in our unconscious, where they morph into irrational beliefs. I have yet to meet a person who doesn't harbor at least one superstition, even if it's the habit of knocking on wood for luck or protection from "evil." I've tried to get people to suspend their superstitious "good luck" habits for the duration of a workshop, just as an exercise in being reasonable, without much success. "What do you think will happen to you if you remove your good-luck charm?" I asked one woman. She laughed and said, "I don't know, but I sure don't want to find out." Is that faith or fear? I don't believe that it's disrespectful to challenge such thinking. Superstitions demand challenging, because they are ruthless in your unconscious, like dark spells that hold you prisoner to irrational fears. Many of the people in my workshops ask not to participate in the exercise, although they laugh about wanting to be excused. The fact is, however, that they cannot get free of the hold of the unreasonable side of their reasoning mind, which has them completely convinced that the forces in this universe are commanded by knocking on a piece of wood or hanging talismans around their necks (wearing garlic "necklaces" in medieval times to ward off vampires comes to mind).

Here's the bottom line: Fear patterns block healing, especially fears that are based on nonsense, superstitions, and irrationality. You are always receiving guidance on how to proceed with your healing, and just as often you may repress that guidance by claiming you are afraid to act on it.

- Identify three superstitions that have authority over you. By superstitions, I mean wearing talismans for safety or knocking on wood for protection. Reflect upon what your superstitions are and write down, actually name, what the force is you are attempting to protect yourself from. Is it evil? The devil? Negativity is not a "thing" as such; the source of negativity is your real object of fear, so what is that object?

- Do you believe in evil? Is that a real presence for you? Do you avoid talking about evil?

- Do you consider your fears to be reasonable or unreasonable ones?

5. Reason Collides with Forgiveness and Pride

Humiliation ranks among the most difficult personal injuries to forgive; for many people, being humiliated is the most painful and unforgivable experience of their lives. Humiliation robs us of our primal power of self-protection. It is a violation of the survival instinct, in that we feel we have failed to protect ourselves from one of the most painful of all personal traumas, and the consequences of feeling vulnerable to personal humiliation are devastating. The trauma of being deeply humiliated early in life can be so consuming that we grow up fearing that interacting with anyone will ultimately lead to being humiliated again. To forgive an act of humiliation—much less a number of them, as in multiple incest experiences—makes no sense to the reasoning mind that views matters through the lens of innocence and retribution. No matter how many times we recognize the logic in forgiving and moving on by reminding ourselves that holding on to our injuries is an act of self-injury, our reason demands justice, and perhaps vengeance. Many people are loath to admit to a desire for vengeance, a desire to hurt others as much as they have been hurt, especially since so much of therapy is directed toward examining the client's hurt. But the need to strike back is essential to the archetype of justice as we honor it. That archetype represents an inherent need in us for fairness, a sense of "an eye for an eye," which also includes a feeling that we must give fairly to those who give to us. Justice is not only about retribution. This deeply rooted sense is also about fair play.

The need for justice and retribution underlies the American legal system, and this subtle thought-form is active within our psyche. The introduction of forgiveness is shattering to the entire archetype of justice as we know it, especially if we are accustomed to seeing ourselves as innocent and humiliated. This is where pride can inject a most commanding—and unhealthy—presence. Pride mixed with the fury of humiliation can make us more unreasonable than we ever realized. Divorce cases are classic settings for such an alchemy of emotions. To introduce the need for forgiveness into a psyche craving justice often results in the "victim" seeking yet another therapist, just to work on getting to the point where she can tolerate the required healing solution—because forgiveness is essential to healing. And the burning rage within us is only more proof that such poison needs to be released from our body, mind, and spirit. Yet reasoning our way through forgiveness is generally useless.

Forgiveness is a mystical directive, not a rational one. The impulse to forgive comes from a part of you that often is in direct conflict with how you feel or think about the person in question. The fact that you are in conflict about forgiving someone is in itself an indication that some part of you wants to forgive while another part, usually the ego, remains locked into the history of your wound. Every part of your mind and emotions will battle such a directive, because the ego needs to have its day in court. We will examine forgiveness as a mystical principle in a later chapter, but suffice it to say here that reason will partner with pride to produce grand arguments for why you are entitled to maintain your wounds, however you acquired them. Some people have had horrendous childhoods or brutal personal experiences in their adult lives. These injuries need to be witnessed by someone worthy, because witnessing with respect grants dignity to a person's wounds, and that is essential to the healing process. But remaining in the psyche of the wound, no matter how deep, is like setting up house in a cemetery for the rest of your life. Your wound is a tomb that you continually visit, filled with stale psychic air that consumes your life force more and more each day. Psychic tombs are costly to maintain. Forgiveness unearths you from keeping a constant vigil at the tomb of your wounds.

- What reasons do you give yourself for refusing to forgive someone?

- How many of your wounds have come from humiliation and pride?

- How many of your physical and emotional stresses are the result of your fear of being humiliated, or of power plays you are involved with because of your pride?

- If you knew that the stress of a conflict was weighing against your physical heart, increasing your blood pressure, or putting you at risk for a stroke, would you immediately act on that information and settle your disputes?

- What is more important to you, maintaining your pride or your health? That is, which one controls your actions?

6. Reason Needs a Reason to Live, but Logic Alone Can't Provide That

A great paradox of contemporary therapy is that it cracks open so many crises of the mind that can't be healed with the mind. A reason to heal will never be found through mind therapies; all the mental work in the world cannot make a person want to live. The absence of a connection to life, which is more common than most people realize, is a psychological crisis as well as a spiritual one. Having a reason to live—to gather your courage to take on

49

the rigorous journey of healing or of rebuilding your life after a crisis, such as the death or loss of a beloved partner—comes from the soul.

When we hit bottom and recognize that we have lost the "will to live," words alone, even spirited pep talks, are not much help in bringing us back to life. This type of crisis, rightly called a spiritual resurrection, requires the intervention of grace and prayer. Reconnecting to one's reason to live, to the meaning and purpose of life, is a mystical experience, not a rational one. It is a deeply interior moment of revelation in which one reengages with the grace of life and a profound knowing that all life, including one's own, is of great value, transcending work or money or status. That we often need to be brought to death's door to realize this is unfortunate. But in the end, only grace can mediate such a transformation of our fundamental nature.

- What gives you a reason to live?
- How much of that reason is dependent on others?
- Reflect on what it means to be "alive," to have the gift of life. Is life alone enough of a reason to want to live?

WHAT HEALING DOES NOT REQUIRE

Healing does not require that you master the unreasonable side of your reason. Nor does healing require inner perfection of any order. A common trait shared by people who have healed is that they cease being unreasonable in ways that no longer matter in the greater scheme of life. Against the scale of life or death, how important is winning an argument? How important is holding a grudge? How important is anything other than how well we love others, how deeply we regard the value of the gift of our life, and what we do with our life that makes this world a better place?

With these questions in mind, we turn to the next truth that has a profound role to play in your healing or in surviving a crisis, and that is the need to connect with a sense of meaning and purpose.

Chapter Three

—————— **THE SECOND TRUTH** ——————

Connect with Meaning and Purpose

The quest for meaning and purpose is one of the most profound rituals common to all cultures in some form, extending back even before the advent of written language. It marks a transformation of consciousness from the self-centered ego to a Self that is empowered by inner or spiritual resources. From the worship of the Mother Goddess that predates recorded history, through the earliest cultures of Mesopotamia and the rich mythologies of the Romans and Greeks, the ancient spiritual texts from a multitude of traditions reveal that human nature has this fundamental design: we are made to pursue the mythic course of our own lives, to seek out and follow our own greatest quests.

This desire we all share is an archetypal appetite to transcend the ordinary, because along with the burning need to shed our limitations we are also discontented with the mundane aspects of our life. We are predisposed to find the normal and ordinary uncomfortable, even to disdain it if it becomes overbearing. We may not speak about this truth directly, but we constantly project its consequences into our world. That is, we project this disdain of our ordinariness onto other people and conditions in our lives that seem unable to protect us from humiliation or failure. If our negativity is blended with feelings of helplessness, we can become destructive by externalizing our struggle against a demon that resides within: for example, the need to feel superior over others or to bully others or to exert other forms of control often comes from a desperate compulsion not to be controlled by ordinary rules and authority. Or we might spend our lives running away from ourselves, always believing that something outside of ourselves is the solution to this bizarre inner sensation of discomfort.

And yet the solution is not to be found in the physical world, because the material domain is by its very nature imperfect, transient, unsatisfying. We may find a temporary solution, but eventually the core of our suffering will reemerge in the new setting. The deeper truth that we must ultimately confront is that the healing of the inner self that is required to release us from these depths of suffering and despair—and make no mistake, feelings of inadequacy and constant emptiness are a suffering—is more than an ordinary healing. For suffering like this to end, you need a spiritual transformation. This is a mystical truth, one that is beyond ordinary thought and reasoning. Like so many truths, its value and power remain hidden until you need such wisdom to survive a personal ordeal or a health crisis. Then, turning within to look for the greater meaning of your life becomes a quest that often leads to profound inner transformation and personal healing.

Not surprisingly, the archetypal heroes of all cultures are figures who have accomplished precisely this inner journey. Ancient figures such as the Mesopotamian king Gilgamesh and the Greek warriors Hercules and Ulysses mapped the Hero's journey by confronting obstacles of darkness, achieving the liberation of their willpower from all earthly forces, not least their own fear and doubt. Many other mythic figures and legends have continued to appear in Western culture, such as King Arthur and his Knights of the Round Table, because people need heroes who are able to transcend and defeat the ordinary. Within the realm of the ordinary resides a darkness that thrives on our fears about survival. The fear that we cannot survive in this world, that we cannot provide ourselves with food, clothing, and a roof over our heads, is the weakest link in the human psyche. Snap that fragile link and we find it difficult to maintain a belief in our own destiny. And, so, we are drawn to icons who have completed a journey that in some way we know we are on as well. Mythic or real, they have mastered an inner power; they know their destiny, and they are guided by an illuminated code of inner truth. They are among those who dwell in their highest potential. This is the aura that draws people to them through the centuries, fantasizing about achieving such a clear sense of identity and the power that emanates from such refined self-esteem.

Although mythic heroes fulfilled human fantasies of romantic and earthly pursuits, teachers such as Jesus and Buddha offered role models for spiritual perfection, drawing on the same appetite for attaining inner authority over external obstacles that drew people to mythic warrior-heroes. Jesus and Buddha were, of course, real, but the perfection they came to represent grew to mythic proportions after their deaths. They awakened the interior journey as each taught in his own way that the truest path on this earth was the one that led you toward, not away from, yourself.

The illuminated path leads toward truth, not illusion. Purpose and meaning are jewels to be found, paradoxically, through shedding what does not qualify as having purpose or meaning. Things of this earth become problems and burdens only when you believe they have more power than your soul and your destiny. Acquiring material objects can never qualify as a spiritual destiny because there is nothing inherently sacred in such a life path. Only fear makes us live to acquire. Buddha instructed his disciples to shed those illusions, because they were burdens that interfered with enlightenment—being in harmony with your inner light.

HEALING AND THE QUEST FOR MEANING AND PURPOSE

Whether we realize it or not, all of us are on the quest for meaning and purpose. We may externalize our journey through adventure as in the archetype of the Hero, or internalize it as the expression of a personal or spiritual choice. Yet no one can slip through life without confronting the need to know: "What is my purpose?" Some pursue that purpose indirectly, through struggling with commitment issues in relationships, for example, or through an inability to put down roots for fear of missing out on something better down the road. Many people have told me that they feel as if something is missing deep within, as if a part of them had been deliberately withheld prior to their birth. The yearning for that missing piece becomes a black hole that drives them to wander from place to place, from relationship to relationship, or into a life of addiction or high-risk behavior.

We have made this archetypal sojourn far more complex in our modern world than it was in earlier times, because we have made the need to find meaning and purpose tantamount to a life-or-death struggle. During the formative years of the holistic movement in the 20th century, the search for the essential self, which is another way of defining the purposeful life, intersected with increased interest in health and healing. So many of the people who have approached me for guidance about a health or life crisis say the need to find a deeper purpose is key to their survival. Some even believe that the very reason they have survived accidents and heart attacks is that they have yet to fulfill their soul's purpose and have been given a kind of "second chance."

The association of meaning and purpose with a health or life crisis suggested to me that many individuals must have experienced an absence of meaning and purpose prior to the crisis. When I asked them about this, most agreed that their life lacked a definitive sense of spiritual purpose prior to their particular crisis, adding that they had not reflected on the core questions about their mission until illness or catastrophe forced them into a life review. I found this curious for a number of reasons. To begin with, many of the people who come to my workshops and lectures or ask me for guidance have been part of, or in some way influenced by, the holistic health movement or what is loosely termed the "consciousness culture." Because that culture is saturated with spiritual literature and holistic practices covering every aspect of life—from nutrition and exercise to meditation and prayer—my encountering so many people who admitted that they felt devoid of spiritual purpose struck me as more than ironic. How was this possible?

But the more I thought about Western culture in general and our love of all things reasonable and rational in particular, the more predictable it seemed that so many people would admit that they had no precise idea what their spiritual purpose was. And when they did have an idea, they defined their purpose as their ideal occupation, which would reward them financially while affording them plenty of free time in which to grow spiritually—and then retire early. Meaning and purpose had become synonymous with achieving one's highest potential in both a material and spiritual sense; this was something you could choose or create, thereby controlling its impact on your life.

In such a mindset, the revelatory processes of the deeper essential Self cannot be felt or recognized. People who reside mainly in their minds, that is, in the world of reason, believe that it is possible to do something or find something that will make everything better. The rational mind often discounts signals from the intuitive system telling you that you now need to turn your attention to a different area of your life. The reason for dismissing such signals is that they often portend dramatic life changes. A conflict then arises between your reason, which is determined to hold you to the familiar, and your intuition, which wants you to become curious about unexplored possibilities.

At this crossroads where reason and intuition collide, the quest for meaning and purpose often intersects with a health or life crisis of some kind. Psychologists have named this turning point the "midlife crisis," as we tend to enter this confused stage sometime after turning 40. Its most obvious symptoms are depression, anxiety, a sense of hopelessness, detachment from ordinary life, and the development of chronic physical and psychological disorders.

Although many people I meet consider themselves "intuitively sensitive," when it comes to making major life decisions that involve risk—and risk is the operative word—they admit that they are unable to take the leap and follow their intuition. Further, many of them believe that a meaningful life is the ideal, but one that few can attain without going through some type of ordeal. Because so many people believe that a meaningful life comes at the price of all that they have acquired in the physical world, it strikes them as unreasonable that they can attain a meaningful life through intuitive guidance without having to risk their material security. Illness is one such ordeal that has often served as a catalyst through this passageway of confused values. Another is the breakup of a marriage or a financial crisis. Sometimes it's hard to tell if the crisis occurred because a person needed to move on or if the person realized during a crisis that in order to heal from the situation, a transformational decision would have to be made. Either way, what is apparent is that events frequently make decisions for us that we would otherwise never be able to make.

Karen's Story: One Woman's Breakthrough

Karen had the pivotal experience of reaching the breakthrough moment, that transcendent calling of grace at which you are presented with a life-changing decision either to pursue your deeper purpose or to retreat into an even more irretrievable place of despair. This mystical experience is almost visceral in its force and clarity, so unmistakable is the divine call to follow your interior path. Karen told me that she would not have been willing to change a thing about her life without the motivation of a crisis, even though she knew she was not happy. "My life was not in good shape before I got sick and I knew it," she said.

> I knew I was depressed and not doing things right, but quite frankly I wanted someone else to make my life better for me. I kept getting angrier and angrier about my life, telling everyone what a mess my finances were and how difficult my kids were, hoping someone would come in and rescue me. Then I just got to the point where I couldn't

get out of bed, first one day and then the next. I started taking antidepressants. Finally I ended up in a hospital. I only had one visitor the entire week I was hospitalized. At first I felt very sorry for myself, and then I realized I've always only felt sorry for myself, which is why no one was coming to see me. I started to think about my life, what I was doing, the type of person I was, and I realized I had no purpose whatsoever. My kids were almost adults, but children are not enough. I was still me, and I had no sense of who I was or why I was alive. I knew right then I had to make a decision to step into my life or my life would permanently step away from me. That was my breakthrough moment. I began my search for who I really was and where I belonged in this world right then and there, and somehow I knew immediately I would make it.

Our need to connect to a sense of meaning and purpose is essential. I have interacted with many people who credit discovering a sense of meaning as their primary inner resource of healing grace; I could almost say that this is our most important need. Therefore it is crucial that we examine our relationship to the mystical search for purpose and how it shapes our journey, not only for our healing, but also for our lifelong health. To help you relate more intimately to this subject, here are some basic questions to explore:

- What makes connecting to my meaning and purpose a healing experience?

- What gives my life meaning and purpose?

- How do I personally make this connection?

- I find that I cannot relate to any sense of meaning and purpose in my life because _____.

POWER: FROM GROUND LEVEL
TO MEANING AND PURPOSE

As I have often written, power is the fundamental ingredient of the human experience. Every action in life, every thought,
every choice we make—even down to what we wear and whether
we are seated in first class or coach—represents a negotiation of
power that we engage in somewhere on the scale of the power that
constitutes life. Power expresses itself as the psychic force of which
you are most aware: who has it, who doesn't have it, what type of
power you are dealing with, what type you want—and what you
have to do to get what you want. The acquisition of power com-
mands you more than you realize. Power manifests in countless
forms: physical, emotional, mental, psychic, and as the healing
power of grace. Like ice melting into water and then evaporating
into steam, power follows a similar dynamic of expression from
coarse to fluid to subtle. You are a vessel of power, and whether
you are controlled by dense power that weighs heavily on your
body and mind like ice or flows easily through you like grace-filled
mist depends on the refinement of your interior consciousness.

Does power have meaning and purpose? Not in and of itself.
But power in all of its countless expressions is the impetus behind
our every move in life, from the power to receive or reject love, to
the power to acknowledge or deny the value of another human
being, to the power to give or destroy a life. Every one of our
biographies can be written from the perspective of our relationship and history with power. And in writing that work, we would
be able to cover every detail of our life's journey, including who
encouraged us, ignored us, inspired us, humiliated us, loved us,
instructed us, and befriended us. We are creatures who thrive on
the many expressions of power. It is our common substance, as
common as air and water.

The impulse to direct our power into physical expression—
through creativity, sexuality, communication, and all other means
that secure our survival—is primal. This power has other names,
among them life force, energy, prana, chi, and, within the Western context of the sacred, grace. How wisely we use this power has

a governing influence on our health and other aspects of our life, including the quality of our relationships with others and with ourselves—perhaps that most importantly of all.

Our intuitive senses are yet another expression of power as it shifts from the obvious manifestations of physical forms, such as status, money, property, political, and social power, to inner authority. Interior power is the province of the Self, power that is unseen, mystical, and of no practical value in street currency. And yet we are all born with an uncanny sense that it is our interior Self that is our most valuable, our most powerful treasure. How well we refine this inner power determines whether the external crises of our lives will "make or break us," as the saying goes.

Early in life, we instinctively assess what we need in order to acquire and maintain power. We instinctively know, for example, that we must learn how to survive, so the first level of power that we cut our teeth on is physical power. In keeping with the well-choreographed rhythm of life, the first expression of our intuitive voice is our gut or survival instinct, which communicates certain basic truths about how we need to interact not only with life but also with each other, all aimed at learning how to manage the delicate force of our individual power within the social fabric. I remember clearly, for instance, watching my brothers and the other young boys in my neighborhood when I was growing up competing for snow-shoveling "clients" as soon as enough snow had covered the ground. Some of those boys were only eight or nine years old, but already the competitive entrepreneurial instinct was up and running in them. They weren't braving the cold weather and Chicago snowstorms because their fathers had ordered them to go out and earn a few dollars. These boys were in a ferocious competition with each other. It was a race to the finish line, and the finish line was springtime.

No one really had to tell these boys about another rule of life that comes encoded in our tribal DNA, like an impulse that automatically makes its way into our consciousness when the time is right. They just knew that they had to play fair with each other, that they had to honor their word in all their business dealings or the rest of the guys would hear about it, and that, aside from the social humiliation that would cause, it was just plain wrong to break your word. Who said so? Well, it just was. And they all knew it—as we all do. No one has to tell us that.

No one really ever did have to tell us that breaking our word was an inappropriate use of power or that stealing another's client, from the snow-shoveling days of our youth to our seasoned professional lives, was wrong. We were all born knowing certain truths about how to live cooperatively with each other—how to, in other words, manage our power in such a way that we did not and do not violate the well-being of others—and knowing that if we do cross those lines of integrity, we had better be able to come up with a good reason. Like my brothers and their friends from years ago, we, too, grew up learning how to survive in the physical arena of life and understanding that society functioned most effectively when all things were done for good and proper reasons. We learned that everything we did had consequences; everything we said and thought and did set in motion some system of power for which we were responsible. We have all lived through some version of learning these basic rules of ground-level power.

But there comes a time in most of our lives when ground-level power ceases to satisfy our sense of completeness. And so we begin to redefine our concept of power, taking it to a more subtle level. Power becomes the ability to manage our own time, to have dominion over our own space, and to openly state our own needs. Power becomes an inner substance, a personal force, an expression of self-esteem. This realization can be among the most exhilarating, liberating moments in our spiritual journey, because it is the classic passageway into the process of individuation. From this process emerge the questions about our place in life that inevitably awaken the appetite for purpose and meaning.

It's also possible to arrive at this same crossroads of power and the Self and interpret the moment as your last chance to get what you want before life forces you to make decisions that will "disempower" you. For example, I've often listened to young women remark that they want children, but "not yet." They are not yet ready to surrender their present reality, in which they are free to make choices as single women, and which would have to be permanently released upon choosing the experience of motherhood. At that point a woman's values and priorities are transformed from those that were more self-oriented to ones that are devoted to another human being. A mother's love for her child becomes all-consuming. Clearly this marks a shift in a woman's relationship to power in that the woman-turned-mother can never return to the values of the childless woman. Her sense of power comes through expressions that were never before animated in her, nor could they possibly have held any power before she became a mother. For example, the Mother Bear archetype becomes a very real power code in a mother, who will literally give her own life for her children and take on opponents three times her size when her "cubs" are threatened. Power rises in these mothers that comes from some wildly rooted earth reservoir that only Mother Bears have access to, but only when they really need it. Otherwise they are ordinary moms with ordinary body strength.

In the rare instances in which I have met women who did not feel comfortable in their "mother" skins, most have said that they became mothers too soon. They were not ready to give up the power of having their own time and space and attending to their own needs first. Most of all, they were not prepared to relinquish the power of being first, even in their own lives, because it was exactly that power that made them feel they had authority and control in their lives. For them, personal control and the freedom to choose what to do and when to do it represented the ultimate type of power, and all that evaporates with the birth of a child.

Perhaps, a few have commented, if they had waited, they would have been able to take on the responsibilities of motherhood with less resentment. They felt that early motherhood had cheated them of the opportunity to discover more about themselves, about who they could or should have become. Motherhood had not empowered them but rather had made them feel disempowered, as if they had sacrificed some unused portion of their personal power that they would never have again. They were missing the opportunity for something better—but what exactly was that? Not one of them could specifically say, because this mythic journey of self they mused about was beyond their reason. It clearly wasn't rooted in any lack of love for their children. None of them commented that they would exchange their children for freedom to venture into the unknown. For them, this missing piece represented an escape from the ordinary. They felt that their "timing" with destiny was off a notch, although they had yet to encounter circumstances serious enough to challenge the limitations of their present circumstances. But whatever the circumstances, one's encounter with the crossroads of meaning and purpose is a matter of "when the time is right," and that time is often introduced by a health or life crisis.

A DEEPER LOOK INTO MEANING AND PURPOSE

The quest for meaning and purpose is much more than a midlife crisis, in which one sets about finding a second career or another romantic partner. It is an inherent yearning to become a whole person, liberated from the fears that pervade the heart and mind and take control of one's life force: fear of being humiliated, of failure, of disapproval, of poverty. These fears prevent you, most of all, from being honest about who you are, not just with others but also with yourself. I am convinced that the deepest desire within each of us is to be liberated from the controlling influences of our own psychic madness or patterns of fear. All the other things that we battle against—the disdain of ordinary life, the need to control others rather than be controlled, the craving for material goods as a means of security and protection against the winds of chaos—are external props that serve as substitutes for the real battle, which is the one waged within the individual soul. Not until you turn to face yourself head-on, confronting one dragon-sized fear at a time, can you truly come to know what it means to be empowered and liberated at the same time. Simply put, the meaningful life emerges from the choice to become congruent with your intuitive nature. As the spiritual masters have always taught, the place you are seeking is within you.

When faced with the necessary choices that shift the direction of life from "more of the same" to a course with meaning and new possibilities, not everyone can go the distance and become congruent. As attractive as inner empowerment or healing might seem, making the choice to move from being ill or in crisis to being on the path to personal transformation requires courage, because it raises the bar on the quality of your personal choices from that point onward. A man in one of my workshops whom I'll call Carl stated emphatically that he did not want to be "more conscious" than the people around him. From Carl's perspective, that placed the burden of behaving more consciously always on his shoulders while "all of them get to do whatever they want and never say they're sorry. I'm not ready to always be the forgiving one and always be the one looking for the higher meaning in things. I'm entitled to my anger and resentment as well, and I'm not ready to give up being hurt when they step out of line." To my amazement, the audience applauded Carl's comments. I then asked him if he felt conflicted, knowing that he had sufficient awareness to make a positive contribution to the problem instead of a negative one. I pointed out that to consciously infuse negative energy into a situation, knowing the consequences, seemed a most unreasonable personal choice.

"I know that it's not reasonable to think I would deliberately choose to be negative, especially with my own family," Carl replied. "But in those moments when tempers are flying, all I can think about is that I want to win the argument or get them to see that they don't appreciate me. I'm not ready to reward them by becoming more conscious and more forgiving than they are. That would be just one more thing they would never be able to appreciate in me."

To be clear, Carl's greatest conflict came from his deep attunement to his intuitive self, which longed to live more congruently. He was living on the cusp, thinking about what his life would be like if only his wife would open up to his newfound interest in the healing arts. A successful pharmaceutical salesman, he believed that complementary healing could help people far beyond the capabilities of conventional drugs. At the same time, his wife found his interest unreasonable, because she viewed that field as a gathering of cult practitioners barely able to earn an income.

The power plays that characterized Carl's marriage were the result of his wife's refusal to join him at seminars on personal development and healing. He was incubating a new vision for his life and he wanted it to include her, but gradually she was fading from view. She could feel this, but her way of clinging to their dissolving union was to criticize everything he had become interested in rather than join him.

I could see that Carl was suffering constantly because he could feel that other life emerging within him. And no matter what he said or did or how many arguments he got into or avoided, I knew that eventually he would reach the crisis point and have to choose between his old life and the new. More to the point, his new life would ultimately choose him, but I was doubtful that it would include his wife.

There is nothing easy about initiating profound change, especially when a crisis may have left you lacking personal strength or resources. I know several people who had very clear intuitive hits about what they needed to do to heal, for instance, but they just could not make those choices. One man who developed colon cancer realized during the recovery from surgery that if he returned to his job, he would inevitably suffer a second bout with cancer. During his time at home, he felt desperate about quitting, which is why he contacted me. He felt he was being "assaulted" by guidance, yet he was unable to act on it, because he needed to know exactly what to do next. The idea of quitting a job with nothing else lined up struck him as even more unreasonable than following guidance that was so strong it often woke him up in the night. Whether that guidance was psychosomatic or his own soul forewarning him that he had to release a life of chronic disempowerment, this dear man did return to work, and he passed away two years later from a second episode of colon cancer.

Without a doubt, grace works most effectively through precisely the kinds of choices that take the most courage but perhaps make the least sense, because these are the choices that demand the most of your soul. The search for meaning and purpose becomes a healing passageway because of what it represents—an opportunity for you to make the transition to an interior base of power.

THE HEALING CHOICE OF TRANSFORMATION

It is a rare person who can pierce the veil between ordinary life, consumed with matters of physical survival, and pursuit of the empowered path of purpose and meaning unless he or she is motivated by a crisis. Most often we require the failure of some system of power that we rely on before we take action. Several kinds of crises qualify as power breakdowns—the end of a relationship that we had counted on going the distance, losing a job we had thought was secure, or confronting a serious illness. My experience as a medical intuitive has taught me that, because our power is so intimately involved in every aspect of our health, from our physical bodies to our belief patterns about ourselves to how we see God, and because illness and accidents are what bring us to examine our own mortality, the desire to heal is the deal breaker that can open the floodgates to that other life. I know this to be true from personal experience.

Before I moved away from my home in a Chicago suburb years ago, I had been living in an area rich with ethnic restaurants, art galleries, and coffee houses. I couldn't imagine being anywhere else. Then all of a sudden everything within me came to a standstill. I had no idea what had hit me, but it hit hard. I became nearly dysfunctional, barely able to get up in the morning and shower. Waking up one day, I thought, "I hope I am merely remembering this life and not still in it." Then I opened my eyes and saw the blue wall of my bedroom (I still can't stand that particular shade of blue), and I was overcome with despair but could not identify why. I realized that I was sinking into depression, a state I had never experienced before. No matter what I told myself, I could not stop it. I could not retrieve myself, my accustomed optimism, my sense of hope.

I went for a walk with my closest friend one evening that summer and opened up my heart to her. "My spirit has begun to leave my body," I said. "I can feel it. I have begun to die. I know it. If I do not do something, I will become terminally ill." I went to see my mother and told her something similar, but a bit less dramatic. I also said a prayer, asking God, "What do you want?" Within a short time, two people I had recently met at what I considered a somewhat bizarre workshop phoned and invited me to join them in a publishing venture. This would involve moving to a town of 800 people in New Hampshire, a state I had never even visited. Had I had my health and my wits about me—in other words, my reason—I would have said no. I would have envisioned myself living alone in a tiny house, in a ridiculously small village in the middle of nowhere, trying to start a business with two people I hardly knew. And, with that vision in my head, I would have said, "No, thanks." But I also knew I was dying—not literally, but energetically. As I have since witnessed many times through my work, long before the body breaks down, the spirit slips out inch by inch.

Without thinking, I said yes. It was one of the most unreasonable choices of my life, one completely motivated by a desire that I did not even know I had in me: the desire to live. This desire, stronger than the will generated by the conscious mind, comes directly from the soul. This is the one that pierces the veil. There is no negotiating with this force. You either jump in all the way or you don't. And you often end up exactly where you never thought you would be, if you thought about it at all. When I told my dearest aunt that I was moving to New Hampshire, her response was, "New Hampshire? Oh, yes, that's one of those tiny New England states. What on earth? Who lives there?" Well, I for one soon did.

People who have credited their healing to connecting with a life that holds more meaning and purpose have similar stories of finding themselves on adventures that they could never have imagined before they became ill. Prior to their illness, they were not empowered enough to make the kinds of choices that now define their lives. As with so many people, their illnesses also represented a breakdown of how they related to power, and through having the courage to examine their choices and beliefs they were able to part the veil and discover another path. In sharing their stories, I am adding commentaries about the way our relationship with power affects our health and our concept of what we view as reasonable.

Paul's Story: A Transformation to Inner Health and Wealth

Paul was a classic 1960s child, someone who liked to say, "I can't remember the '60s, but I hear I had a good time." Ironically, Paul emerged from those years, dusted off the drug residue, and became a wildly successful businessman. "Computer technology was second nature to me," he said. "I was at the right place at the right time, again and again." Paul turned his computer capital into real-estate capital and ended up a very rich man. "Life was perfect, but as all perfect stories go, I kept thinking, 'When is the party going to end?' And then I developed a tumor in my chest. I never even knew you could have a tumor there."

Paul's treatment included surgery, chemotherapy, and a substantial recovery time. The tests indicated that the cancer had metastasized, and although the doctors were hopeful that the chemo would be successful in sending his cancer into remission, there were, of course, no guarantees. Recovery time was the beginning of Paul's life examination. Until then, everything had gone as planned or even better. He had surrounded himself with the brightest computer wizards, because he could afford to pay them and he loved their eccentric personalities. Every one of his investments made money, whether in real estate, ideas, or office personnel. The only place things didn't go smoothly for Paul was in his intimate relationships. After three failed marriages, he found himself recovering from cancer in an empty home. For all of his success as a computer wizard and business man, Paul was a dismal failure when it came to matters of the heart.

"I didn't have any respect for emotions or feelings, to be honest," he said. "They irritated me and always made me feel manipulated. Looking back at who I had been in the 1960s, I have rather vague memories of always talking about my feelings and little else. But I shut that off when I decided it was time to go to work, because feelings don't produce profits; they interfere with profits. I lived by the creed that feelings clouded my judgment, and if someone became emotional, as all my ex-wives had to be in order to get my attention, I dismissed them as hysterical. I drove them insane. I see that now, but I also see that this was about maintaining my position as an impenetrable power figure. I couldn't bear to be thought of as a vulnerable person. Women are vulnerable, children are vulnerable, employees are vulnerable, but not me."

Sometimes it takes the right comment uttered by the right person at precisely the right moment to initiate a profound change. In Paul's case, his lead computer geek, Sam, did just that. Visiting him one evening, Sam asked how things were going and Paul said, "Just fine." To which Sam replied, "Hey, why do you think you got a tumor in your chest? Think it's because you have so much extra room in there? I mean, you're like the Tin Man in *The Wizard of Oz*, right?"

The song "If I Only Had a Heart" started to play in Paul's head over and over again, he recalled, the way "100 Bottles of Beer on the Wall" does on a bad day. He wondered if that was the way people saw him, as a heartless, mechanical man. The more he reflected on that, the more he realized he was terrified of his emotions and of being close to others. His entire definition of power was predicated on being a "human computer." A few days later, Paul sent word to his staff that he needed some time alone. He took his phone off the hook and spent the time reflecting on one question, "How do I feel about my life?" He realized he was lonely, empty, and terrified of dying alone.

"I will never forget that moment," he told me. "I was staring out my window looking at the ocean, thinking about the fact that I might not be around much longer. I looked around my house— my big, highly outfitted house—and thought, 'All this and none of it can help me now. What the hell good is it?' Suddenly I felt as if I were being given a choice to become a different type of person, to become human again, or maybe human for the first time.

That's the only way I can explain it. I started to weep from grief. The memories of all the hurt feelings of my past marriages rose up in me as fast as an attack of nausea. I saw the faces of my ex-wives, all of them trying to save our marriages. I realized how much they loved me, although why, I couldn't figure out!

"The guilt I felt nearly crippled me. I could not stop crying, grieving for what I'd so easily abused and how I'd rationalized my behavior at the time. I gave myself permission to do anything I wanted, because I was the one making the big bucks and paying all the bills. I would tell them, 'If you don't like it around here, leave.' And, of course, they did. And then I told myself I didn't care, because someone with money can always find another partner. But you can't always find love again, or someone to be there when you are full of cancer."

During that period of silence, Paul made a new plan for his life. He decided to hire a new company president to give himself time to ask, "Where to from here?" Among various personal changes, Paul became more approachable and more respectful of his staff. He also became more respectful of life in general, seeing it not as something that served him but as something he would be grateful to serve, should he recover his health. Paul poured as much dedication into discovering his interior life as he had into computer technology and diagnosis.

Today his health is better than ever, as are his relationships. Paul sees the world as a place to give to and not take from, a place of living beauty and wonder, not just of potential sales. He could not have imagined any of this prior to this illness. That would have been beyond rational analysis for him. Paul continues to be materially successful, having discovered that the meaningful life does not require a vow of poverty. Doing for others is now as much a part of his professional life as earning money had been. "I hate to say this, but I fit the character of Scrooge and not just the Tin Man," he told me. "I feel I was shown my potential future and given a chance to heal, but it required that I become a loving, generous person. I think about that constantly now, because if those were the conditions upon which I healed, what does that say about the essence of this universe? Is this universe—is God—essential love? For me, the answer is yes, and that is the greatest 'beyond reason' truth to come out of my personal journey."

Ann's Story: A Crisis of Personal Management

We often envision financial abundance as providing the freedom to make certain liberating choices. At the same time, many people view the acquisition of wealth as the antagonist of consciousness, assuming that the individual who is focused on money is spiritually lacking—an association that comes from a deeply rooted belief that to be a good person, one cannot venture into financial waters. Our culture has never come to terms with its conflicting beliefs about God, money, and financial abundance. Some variation of this conflict exists in most people I have encountered in my work, regardless of their financial comfort zone. It can certainly be a major factor in whether or not they can make the leap into becoming congruent with their intuitive selves, which for me defines the meaningful life.

I've had conversations with many people who, while facing the most serious health or life crisis, remain in a toxic situation because of their financial fears. Sometimes money matters need to be taken seriously, of course, but so often people are so possessed by their need for physical safety that they start believing that the most reasonable choice is the least risky one. A major reason why people do not heal is that they look for only the safe routes to recovering their health, despite the truth that genuine healing rarely takes a safe path. By safe I mean the path that introduces the least amount of change to the exterior field of one's life. But healing is often an all-or-nothing experience, even if that all-or-nothing is expressed at the level of shifting the toxic dynamics between certain relationships. That is, you should not view becoming more in harmony with your intuitive nature as depending on economic security or on how well others might receive your awakening to a healthy emotional life. Many people believe that if they first become economically secure, then they can "afford" to listen to their intuition. Only then can they figure out what they are really meant to do in this life. Yet money is irrelevant to your capacity to interact with the world around you through values that are empowering and aligned with truth.

You do not have to have the money to leave home, or the wherewithal to set the world on fire, to experience the profound mystical transformation I'm talking about here. Such a moment of inner illumination can and does come to many people who remain with their families, and as a result of their extraordinary personal journey, everyone is graced. Such was the case with Ann, who suffered disabling back pain. To relieve the pain, she had surgery on her spine, which unfortunately did not help. Her healing did not take place until she was able to transform her need to be the controlling force in her family and work environment. And in the process, she discovered the "meaning of meaningful," as she put it.

Ann's first language was control, and because she had style and charisma, her methods of control were especially difficult to challenge. She was always the one to take charge of organizing everything and everyone, and since most people prefer to be organized rather than to do the organizing, she was generally a welcome force. Although Ann worked as a personnel manager at a major department store, she viewed her real occupation as imposing her opinions on all the employees.

At home, Ann was even more controlling with her husband and children, insisting that the house be run her way, on her schedule. She was not at all physically or verbally abusive, but neither was she approachable when it came to negotiating the house rules. As her two sons grew into rebellious teens, Ann's family began to fall apart. It seemed as if all three males, her husband and two sons, simultaneously staged a strike. No matter what she said, no one was listening to her anymore, and she soon discovered that she was powerless.

Ann's back pain had begun when her sons were toddlers, but not until they reached their teenage years and began staying out all night did the pain hit the crisis level. Her marriage at that point had become little more than two people sharing a house and bills until the kids were old enough to leave home. Finally, Ann went for disc surgery, which left her practically helpless during her recovery at home. Still giving orders from her bed, Ann found herself seething with frustration at how slowly her sons responded to the orders she was giving about how to take care of the house and prepare the meals. One evening, she exploded at her older son, saying, "I can't stand the way you are treating me! Can't you see how helpless I am?"

Within half a breath, he fired back, "And can't you see that Dad's going to leave you? That you broke up our home? Can't you see that we can't stand it here, either?"

Ann said that his remark went straight to her heart. She felt a shattering from within, like glass breaking apart inside of her. "Oh, my God, Stephen," she said. "What have I done?"

"In that instant," Ann said, "I saw my family as the most precious thing in my life. I realized that I was so afraid of losing them that I had tied them up in rules and regulations so that they wouldn't stray from me, and now they wanted to run away as fast as they could. I asked my son to sit down and talk to me, to tell me about his feelings. His brother walked in a few hours later, and then my husband. We ended up talking all night long. My husband and sons made me breakfast in bed and we all cried that morning, as if we had found each other for the first time. I felt as if I were being released from some dark place, as if I'd been under a spell that made me see only abandonment everywhere. I kept using all my energy, all my power, controlling everyone so I wouldn't ever be alone—and suddenly I was going to be completely alone. The irony of that realization broke me wide open. I told myself I would never again do that to my sons or husband, and I meant it. I broke out of some dark way of being that controlled me like a puppet. Now it was gone and I knew these three men were the most precious people in the world to me."

Ann's back pain began to improve with increasing speed in the following weeks. She resigned from her job with the intention of looking for another one, because she felt a fresh start was in order. As part of her healing, Ann ventured into the world of yoga, acupuncture, and energy medicine. She is now entertaining ideas of returning to school to study complementary healing, something she would never have considered prior to her health crisis.

"I had no interest whatsoever in healing," she said. "But aside from that, what possible position of authority could the field of health offer me? I was someone, and perhaps I still am a bit, who is driven by the need to achieve in the outside world. Before, I thought that my family should feel only gratitude for my ambition and the financial support it was bringing in. I saw them as unreasonable and unappreciative. Now I wonder what I was thinking or feeling that I saw only my life as so important. It's amazing how reasonable you can make something that is, in fact, so extremely unreasonable just because it suits you at the time."

Ann's back is not fully recovered by any means, but she realizes that it's much better than if she had not changed. "I'm no longer stiff, angry, tense, or constantly worried about getting my way," she concluded. "All that pressure is gone, and my back knows it. I also know that I would never have understood what you were talking about had you tried to reason with me about tension and back pain before, because I simply would not have wanted to get it. I wasn't ready. You have to be ready to live more deeply. It's not something you can just talk about. It took excruciating pain to make me willing to examine the path my life was on."

YOUR PERSONAL JOURNAL: EXPLORING MEANING AND PURPOSE

Just as Ann and many other people discover, the search for a rich and meaningful life has always been a "quest" as opposed to a gift or a given. We are in charge of how deeply we want to understand the events and relationships that fill our lives. Meaning and purpose are gleaned through the questions we pause to ask ourselves about why we do what we do. And beyond the questions, we must then chart a course of action that expresses in physical form the deeper truths about ourselves that we articulate in exercises such as these. It is not enough to "live on paper" or live in your thoughts. Healing or transformation must move from thought into form, from idea into action. Too many people remain in the thought-form world because it gives the appearance of change, but in truth nothing ever changes without part two of the equation, which is courageous choice. Consider the following questions as examples of those that you should reflect on as you contemplate what gives meaning and purpose to your life. Set aside a portion of your journal and expect to revisit these questions over a period of days or months, even as you continue reading. Don't rush your answers, and be prepared for them to change as you address the questions from new perspectives each time.

- Observe how you spend your time during the day: How much of what you do contributes to a sense of meaning in your life? What specifically about that occupation generates a sense of purpose?

- If what you are doing holds no sense of purpose for you, then you are presented with a decision as to how to proceed, beginning with the question "What do I need to give to others at this stage in my life in order to feel useful?"

- List your life priorities, then put aside that list and write down the list that actually governs your actions: work, schedules, meetings. How often do you say, "I would love to if I only had the time"? Name the things you would love to do if you only had the time, and include people with whom you would spend some time.

- Would doing what you love and being with people you love improve the quality of your life? Many people postpone taking time out of their busy schedules for occasional lunches or dinners with loved ones or old friends, telling themselves that it's impractical or unreasonable, given their workload. But that's precisely why you should perform these

outrageous acts of love. Challenge that voice of reason in your head that always tells you to avoid the
spontaneous and the intuitive. Listen to and follow
that intuitive voice every now and again. Learn to
trust that voice.

• Write down where your imagination takes you
  when you think about your life. Imagine another
  life pressing against the thin veil between your reasonable self and your wild, unreasonable self, the
  person you imagine yourself to be "if only . . ." If
  only what? What do you imagine? What can you
  feel in that orbit of possibilities that surrounds your
  physical body? You might well think, "Oh, I could
  never do that, not really," because what you imagine seems unreasonable to you. But who knows the
  person you have hidden inside, the person yet to be
  tested or set free on that archetypal quest for meaning and purpose?

• If you have been inspired to reflect on the meaning
  of your life because of an illness, think of the illness
  as a passageway that has broken all connections
  with past wounds and negativity. Your attention
  needs to be focused in the present, on who you are
  today and what you have to contribute as a source
  of creative wisdom in your world.

• Reflect on all that you have learned in your life—
  not what you've done wrong or who has hurt you.
  Wisdom is the key ingredient. Collect your wisdom
  with your prayers and in your meditations, like col-
  lecting apples in a basket. And then envision the
  unfolding of a path to the way you can best use
  this wisdom. Nurturing this spiritual vision creates inner alchemy that supports the healing of the
  physical body.

The quest for a meaningful life has many forms of expression and many motivations. Illness and personal crises are but two of the reasons why you may be motivated to reconsider the purpose, values, and direction of your life. This quest, as witnessed by the stories of Paul and Ann, can take many forms. By far the most arduous type of quest, however, is the one that Saint John of the Cross revealed in his renowned work "Dark Night of the Soul." For many people, the experience of becoming ill and the long road to recovery has served as a kind of "dark night." For some of them, the dark night was exactly what they needed in order to heal. This is yet another of those "mystical mysteries" that is beyond reason, and it will be the subject of our next chapter.

Chapter Four

THE THIRD TRUTH

Courageously Navigate the Dark Night of the Soul

I've written extensively about archetypes and the roles they play in our lives. Although I usually speak of archetypes as personifications of certain patterns of human activity and identity—such as the Child, Mother, Warrior, Hero, Victim, and Saboteur—I also see them, as Carl Jung did in first describing them, as impersonal forces such as Good and Evil or Death and Rebirth. All of life's universal journeys include the archetypes of Death and Rebirth as well as the Hero's Journey. The journey of healing is no exception. As with the other journeys, the individual seeking to be healed is an initiate hoping to qualify for renewed life who is unconsciously guided through a natural progression of stages. The journey begins with the need to find a logical explanation for why an illness or a crisis has occurred. As an illness or crisis becomes more real, which is to say, as the illness or crisis begins to infiltrate the seeker's ordinary world, he or she automatically begins to think about what is of genuine value; this emotional stage is when the examination of meaning and purpose becomes most significant. Eventually, the experience of illness or crisis will penetrate even further, beyond the mind and the heart. At some point, each person will enter the essential stage of the healing process that is best described as the "dark night of the soul."

Most of the people I have met who have healed from an illness or made it through a life crisis not only experienced a dark night, but also found a way to navigate this harrowing passage. All of these people found themselves in the depths of profound inner darkness, feeling completely helpless and abandoned. All of them found a way through, or, as more than a few have put it, were shown a way through. Describing this stage, a man named Roger, who suffered from cancer, said that the worst time of day for him was evening, as the sun began to set and people were going home. His habit had long been to go out with friends after work, but he could no longer do that because of his illness. His depression felt most oppressive in the evening, as if emptiness and despair had become his dinner companions.

One evening, Roger started to weep, saying to himself, "I can't do this anymore." Then he heard a soft voice utter the words, "Yes, you can heal this illness." He did not know where the voice came from but instantly he felt calm, centered, and in touch with a sense of hope for the first time. "I hung on to the feeling of hope with all my might and it grew stronger each day," he said. "I kept reliving that experience again and again and again. I knew that voice didn't come from me, from my own mind. It came from some other place, maybe heaven. All I know is that once I had hope and practiced my own version of spirituality, I stopped feeling sorry for myself. I stopped fighting what was happening to me. And after a while, I began to feel better. No one expected my cancer to heal, but it went into remission and I've been fine ever since."

I often hear people speak about going through a dark night. It's a common phrase that many people use when describing what it is like to endure a prolonged state of depression or isolation, for example. Most of these people, including many of those I met in the course of my healing research, were unaware that the term "dark night" refers to an experience of transformation first articulated in a poem of the same name by the 16th-century Spanish mystic Saint John of the Cross. Whether they had heard a reference to the phrase without recalling it or absorbed it from the collective unconscious as the dark night, which is possible as the "dark night" has become an archetype of soul transformation, really makes no difference. That so many people are now using a mystical phrase to describe their psychological or personal crises does not surprise me, because this classic experience, once contained within monastic walls, has evolved into an experience equally suited to the consciousness of our times. It is important to note, however, that the emotional and psychological crises that are the hallmarks of the mystical path can feel much the same as ordinary psychological stress, even though the guidance required for someone experiencing them on this path is quite specific. While clinical depression is frequently treated through therapy and medication, medicating the spiritual crisis of the dark night of the soul would be counterproductive in the extreme. The dark night is not an experience to be "treated," but one to be examined and understood as a progression of self-realization and illumination, in the deepest sense, of what it means to come to know one's inner self.

Several factors have influenced how the dark night of the soul has become part of the fabric of what I have called the consciousness culture. First, our culture has become wide open spiritually and psychologically, and we pursue our inner development with vigor. Just as importantly, we now have easy access to once-arcane sacred literature from all traditions. And we have introduced into our lives spiritual practices, including many forms of meditation and yoga, that were at one time restricted to serious practitioners in ashrams and monasteries. All of these social changes reflect a society that has awakened to its interior life.

Without a doubt, however, one of the leading reasons that the mystical experience has made its way into our contemporary culture is directly related to the healing-centered orientation of the human consciousness movement. Over the past 50 years, many of those searching for more conscious ways to heal were interested in learning how to harness healing power so that they could heal themselves or others. Though many people were motivated by a genuine interest and passion for healing, stepping across this threshold into the mystery of the inner Self, even for the sake of healing, was nonetheless also a passageway into the soul. Few, it must be said, were interested in pursuing healing because it was a path toward mystical illumination. Yet this need to experience the power to heal elevated the interest in healing to the level of how healing works in harmony with mystical laws as well as with physical laws and it was precisely this "unlocking" of mystical laws that required a deepening of our collective spirituality, individual-by-individual, group-by-group, nation-by-nation. The seeker, though in search of healing knowledge, was unknowingly also knocking at the door of mystical transformation.

In a mystical experience the individual moves past the gates of reason and into a direct encounter with the nature of God. In that same way, the desire to channel the power to heal elevated the experience of the healer to mystic levels. The healer calls on a divine force—a force that is beyond reason—to interfere with the laws of nature on behalf of the person in need of a healing. The person best known for doing this type of healing is Jesus, the greatest cosmic healer in history.

The belief that the spirit within us is capable of regenerating the physical body is based in truth. The spirit can heal the body, the mind, and matters of the heart. Not only can you heal yourself, you can also channel healing grace to another. How this healing occurs is a mixture of mystery and "mystical reasoning," by which I mean that healing can be understood as the natural consequence of nurturing a spiritual consciousness. We need to realize that there is a natural order to the systems of life that is essentially harmonious; the laws that govern the universe are constant and function according to a code of harmony and balance. Those laws thrive within us as well as around us, both at the microcosmic level and at the macrocosmic level. In the sphere of healing, as you acknowledge and come into harmony with the laws that govern you, the result is balance. And that balance fosters a healthier system within you, to such an extent that you can recover your health. The mystery is that in some cases, as I have seen, people are able to recover fully, even after conventional medicine has stated that their illnesses cannot be cured. This is because the doctors were treating the illness from the outside in, instead of from the inside out. In some sense, that's all those doctors can do, because no mere physician can control how anyone navigates the dark night of the soul or handles obstacles such as forgiveness or anger. These are the "interior unknowns" that physicians and therapists have no way of calculating, any more than the patient does. Ask people how long it will take them to forgive someone and the likely response will be, "I don't know." This element of mystery added to mystical reasoning allows extraordinary healings to occur, because the spirit naturally generates the grace to heal the physical body, just as it is natural for the body to activate its own healing system the instant it has a crisis.

The healing journey, then, consists largely of achieving balance so as to allow grace to flow. We are made ready for that healing grace in a way that is similar to the way the archetypal Wounded Healer is prepared to heal others by first being given a wound that molds him. The experience of the dark night is one such wound that prepares the way.

THE HEALING JOURNEY OF THE DARK NIGHT

In order to appreciate the formative journey of the dark night as a part of your personal healing, you need to understand its basic structure. The setting that played a role in leading John of the Cross to compose his poem "Dark Night of the Soul" was probably also the catalyst for his mystical transformation. And it is emblematic of the kind of life crisis that is one of the most terrifying to confront—being powerless within a circumstance that you know to be completely unjust. John of the Cross (1542–1591) was a Spanish Carmelite who, at the age of 25, served as spiritual director for Saint Teresa of Ávila. Teresa enlisted John in her vision of reforming the Carmelite Order of Spain, but his attempts at reform incurred the ire of his superiors. In December 1577, after his refusal to follow his superiors' orders, but more likely because of his attempts to reform life within the Carmelites, John was taken prisoner by his superiors and jailed in Toledo. There they imprisoned him in a four-by-eight-foot space under a staircase, a space that had once been used as a latrine. John was taken out daily for beatings in front of the community during its noon meal. He was starved, humiliated, and forced to endure the cold without sufficient clothing. This torment went on for nine months before he managed to escape, seeking refuge at Teresa's convent.

During his imprisonment, while starving, bruised, and nearly dead, John of the Cross nonetheless broke through his despair in a moment of illumination, realizing that he had to transcend his circumstances by shattering his ordinary consciousness or else he would be consumed by the weight of injustice and torture. As a Catholic mystic, this meant that he had to choose love and forgiveness in the presence of oppressive hatred, lest he be destroyed by becoming hate-filled himself. Recognizing that he was incapable of reaching such an intensity of love on his own, John prayed to be filled with the love of Christ. Somehow, he experienced a profound breakthrough of love in the midst of despair, injustice, and personal anguish.

During this time he wrote his "Spiritual Canticle," based on the Biblical Song of Songs, in which he expresses his love for Christ using the metaphor of the mutual love of a bride (the soul) and bridegroom (Christ). This he composed on paper that was smuggled in by one of the friars guarding him. Some years after his escape, John wrote his renowned poem "Dark Night of the Soul," as well as extensive commentary on the poem (albeit unfinished at the time of his death) in which he detailed the progression of the dark night and identified the signs that indicate when one is entering it. Although John wrote 500 years ago about a deeply mystical journey, the archetypal template that he describes for how and why an individual experiences the dark night remains intact, in particular for those who have actively pursued any form of inner healing or a personal spiritual path.

When we apply the template of the dark night of the soul to healing, it becomes a brilliant mystical map that clearly distinguishes the domain of the ego from the soul. This same road map also provides a way of understanding the dynamic of healing. The difference between the domain of the senses and the soul, as John of the Cross describes them, parallels how our ego drowns in the experience of humiliation and how the soul then takes that action and examines how it has given us a desire to make another person suffer because we have suffered. In the depths of our soul, we discover our true source of pain, which is our desire to cause pain because we have experienced pain. We feel entitled to a reward because we have suffered and if that reward is not forthcoming, either in the form of special treatment or acknowledgment or a life made easy in some way with certain privileges, then we will make someone suffer for lack of those entitlements. And even if we consciously do not want to make another suffer, we will find someone to punish just the same because from pain, we expect to be rewarded, we expect acknowledgment. And if that is not forthcoming, we will punish someone—oh yes we will.

In the vast, deep, secret, and silent recesses of our soul, we discover why—why do we desire to put another in pain, to transfer our suffering to another? Why are we compelled to hand it down to another generation, from parent to child, from nation to nation? The ego cannot address this. The night of the senses, the night of the ego, will only give us reasons that justify our actions. To truly heal, we must go past our ego and into the depths of our soul, into our dark passions, examining the source of our actions and choices in life. Seeing how John's work distinguished the domain of senses and action from the realm of the soul and its passions lifted a veil from the face of a mystery that I had been exploring for years.

The Active Night: The Breakdown of the Senses (Ego and Reason)

The dark night of the soul progresses in two stages: the active and the passive nights. Each stage is distinctive in its characteristics and purpose. John of the Cross describes the "active night" as an experience during which the physical senses are broken down. By senses, he is referring to the forces of reason, logic, the mind, and the world of order as you know it. For what reasons would such an experience be necessary? The breakdown of the senses is a crisis of power or powerlessness. As the traveler through the darkness, you find yourself in circumstances that you are unable to bend, mend, or break. Instead, the circumstances seem more powerful than you.

Sometimes we feel an absence of emotion when we enter a darkness so penetrating that no emotional heartbeat seems present in the body at all. John of the Cross described this stage as one of purification, one of the five classic stages of mystical experience as described by Evelyn Underhill, one of the first and foremost scholars of mysticism, and others. During the stage of purification, in the words of John of the Cross, we encounter the "imperfections" of the self, "where habits both good and bad are brought into subjection and thus . . . purged." To the modern reasoning mind, the idea of "purification" does not add up rationally; that is an archaic, medieval term applicable to the mystical experience but of little value to us. We cannot even imagine that a pathway already in place deep within us has awakened because of a life crisis or in response to an inner conflict that has brought us to a crossroads. The very thought is incomprehensible. Yet the presence of that pathway was a given for mystics such as John of the Cross and Teresa of Ávila, as it was for all the great spiritual masters. They all understood that the incongruent and chaotic nature of life would ultimately bring the person into a crisis in which the limitations of the ego would require the resources of the soul. This truth remains as active within each of us as it was within these great mystics who lived 500 years ago or more. That they lived reclusively and experienced these inner phenomena with heightened sensitivities speaks only of their personal spiritual callings, not of the uniqueness of the pathway, which is open to all of us.

John of the Cross directed his fellow Carmelites to navigate the dark night by embracing its purpose, cooperating with the need to purge themselves of "imperfections." The Buddha would have called an imperfection a "distraction," an illusion, a fear that has authority over you. Perhaps you have an ambition that is so all-consuming that you become blinded to the consequences of the thoughts, actions, and deeds you are initiating to achieve your goal. The need always to win, always to be right, is yet another kind of imperfection that causes us to do harm to others as well as to ourselves. We develop these behavioral patterns largely out of the need to exert power and control in the world. Most often, these patterns or habits are rooted in fear, and so they create fear or harm, because fear only generates more fear. The purge during the active dark night, according to John of the Cross, brings us into a confrontation with these habits that represent fear-based behavior. The ego and reason would have us believe that we are in charge of our lives. To face the truth that we are actually being controlled by fear, like puppets on invisible strings, is devastatingly humbling. Prayer, silence, and grace are essential, he added, because as the darkness descends on us, the atmosphere can become thick with feelings of powerlessness.

The Active Night: Applied to Healing

Following a medical diagnosis or a personal crisis that destabilizes one's ordinary life, an individual will automatically be drawn into an interior process of evaluation. No one really has to be told, "You had better think about what just happened." Even if we don't want to think about it, the progression of inner evaluation begins, because it is part of our natural healing mechanism. Just as the body has systems that automatically react to a physical injury, such as the inflammatory response, the psyche and the soul respond to a crisis by reviewing which systems have broken down, allowing the crisis to happen. We want to know what went wrong. When did the systems in our life begin to malfunction? Did we miss the signals or did we simply not want to notice them?

This evaluation will automatically progress from matters of reason to matters of the heart, in which the focus is placed on seeking what needs to be fixed, repaired, and healed. Relationships, values, life choices, regrets, and priorities come up for review during this stage, because there is something about a life crisis that automatically makes us want to reprioritize what has meaning for us. This resembles the standard protocol in our health-care system, in which a patient goes from following a physician's orders to the phase of organizing an emotional support team for healing. We engage in this process of healing in part because, as research seems to indicate, healing requires that we examine the underlying stress patterns influencing an illness. But our healing therapies are also modeled around the deeper archetypal need to undergo a purification process upon learning that we have entered a time of crisis.

In the early part of my career as a medical intuitive, I thought, as so many others in the world around me did, that if people got to the "root" cause of their emotional or psychological stress, then their illness was 90 percent healed. The rest would take good nutrition, a handful of the right vitamins, and daily exercise. I also learned through doing medical intuitive readings that there are as many different stress patterns as there are personalities. But what all people share is the need to purge themselves of their wounds, emotional traumas, and memories of hard times or abusive relationships. Regrets also need resolution, as healing requires that we look at whom we have injured, not just who has injured us. I learned that forgiveness was essential and that the inability to forgive is as painful as the wound itself. Yet, in spite of that, forgiveness remains the greatest hurdle of all for most people.

Given all the healing options available and the flood of research that continually validates the connections between stress patterns and the development of disease, I anticipated that increasing numbers of people would achieve the goal of healing their illnesses. At least they would make great strides in breaking through patterns of depression, chronic pain, debilitating fatigue, and recurring cancer. Certainly healings occurred along the way, helped by medical breakthroughs combined with the rise of integrative healing modalities. But the initial enthusiasm of the holistic health movement had suggested that treating the whole person would open up unprecedented avenues for healing, because we were finally dealing with all the facets involved in the cause of an illness.

When that promised spurt of holistically inspired healing failed to materialize in significant numbers, I wrote a book entitled *Why People Don't Heal and How They Can*. In it, I investigated a pernicious syndrome that I called "woundology," by which I meant the tendency people have to use their wounds as a kind of shadow power that makes healing a less attractive proposition. Carl Jung used the term "shadow" to refer to the part of our psyche that we find unacceptable, and about which we purposefully, yet more or less unconsciously, keep ourselves in the dark. In this sense, most people are largely unaware of how they play on their status as wounded victims—victims of incest, of a dysfunctional family, or perhaps some physical ailment—to profit in various ways. I was shocked to realize that so many people believed that healing represented the loss of a certain kind of power they had grown accustomed to using as "social currency." Manipulating or controlling others through the use of one's illness or suffering, for example, was—and remains—extremely effective for people who find they cannot be direct in their interactions. Who argues with someone who is in pain? And if pain is the only power a person has, health is not an attractive replacement. It was apparent to me that becoming healthy represented more than just getting over an illness. Health represented a complex progression into a state of personal empowerment in which one had to move from a condition of vulnerability to one of invincibility, from victim to victor, from silent bystander to aggressive defender of personal boundaries. Completing this race to the finish line was a yeoman's task if ever there was one. Indeed, in opening the psyche and soul to the healing process, we had expanded the journey of wellness into one of personal transformation.

The field of healing became more complex as I continued to work with people through the years, so many of whom were "halfway there." They had gotten to a place where they had unearthed from their history wounds, memories of abuse, and shadow patterns that continued to haunt them. However, they still could not heal their skin disorders, depression, chronic pain, heart conditions, fibromyalgia, or cancer. One woman I know developed breast cancer and had a mastectomy, followed by chemotherapy and radiation. She immediately set a course for healing that included proper nutrition, spiritual direction, and other practices that she felt would serve her. Her cancer went into remission for 18 months and then another malignant mass showed up. She had to undergo the entire chemo-radiation program again. This time, her faith in her ability to beat the odds was not as great, but still she continued. I asked her about how she viewed this illness. "I'm not really interested in the reason I got cancer," she said. "That doesn't serve me. I'm interested in getting rid of it. I believe that if I am meant to live, I will. If not, I won't. I want to live, but I don't see any purpose to going backward and thinking about the past."

This woman eventually got an all clear on her second round with cancer, only to be diagnosed one year later with skin cancer. So she dealt with that, still with no desire to understand its origins. Although healing is a mystery, to be sure, could it be said that she was not trying hard enough? I couldn't help wondering if there was something she was not doing that she should be doing, and why her cancer, like so many other people's, kept coming back. I had seen situations like hers time and time again, in which people almost healed and then the disease returned. The frustration of having to ask why was indescribable.

Then I encountered the work of Teresa of Ávila, or what I call "my Teresa experience," which drew me into the domain of healing as a mystical experience. The piece I had been missing was the power of grace. Since absorbing "mystical reasoning" into my consciousness, and teaching the work of Teresa and now John of the Cross, I have seen people heal completely and permanently. As I said in Chapter 1, some of the healings were instant and others occurred over months, but none of these people have experienced a return of their diseases. Let me state clearly that their healings have nothing to do with Catholicism. This is not a treatise on healing through Catholic teachings. Further, most of these people were not Catholic and did not suddenly convert. The addition of "mystical reasoning" was a missing piece that I consider to be "cosmic" or "spiritually archetypal" rather than related to any particular religion—a universal truth that has filtered into all the major world traditions in some way, much like the teaching "Thou shalt not kill."

Once mystical reasoning was put on my radar, and in particular the work of Teresa and John of the Cross, I realized that most people conduct their healing process in the "active night" of the dark night. During the active night, we identify our hurts, what was done to us, our regrets, our stress patterns, all the things that are wrong. Perhaps we repair some of our relationships or try to make good on some of our regrets, but rarely do those efforts reach the source of why we really suffer or cause others to suffer. For all the determination we put forth in identifying past wounds, the identification process ends up being only an exercise in crime solving unless we complete the healing with forgiveness. Identifying a wound does not heal the wound. Healing must include getting to the source of why we struggle with forgiveness, why we want to hurt others, or why we hold on to our wounds hoping to make others feel guilty. This is where we encounter our true "inner demons," which John of the Cross referred to as the seven deadly sins in the passive stage of the dark night of the soul.

The Passive Night

Beyond the ego and reason, beyond the active night, comes the source of who we are and why we do what we do. Our word *mystery* comes from an Indo-European root meaning "with closed lips" (as in "mute"). The mysteries of the soul, then, are silent on clear or obvious meanings. Yet, the works of the great spiritual masters resonate with truth that is beyond language and reason. This knowing beyond logic and ordinary intellect informs us that the existence of the soul and its teachings, as in the dark night of the soul, contain truth that is "born" within us, in our spiritual DNA. The ego and reason manage our behavior, but they are not the fuel of our behavior. The impetus comes from another source, a deeper, more complex reservoir of the Self that pulsates with sensations of destiny, impulses of intuitive awareness, instincts that compel us to develop unrealized potential from within the Self, and an inherent desire to transcend the ordinary. These are impulses of power, sparks of positive and negative forces that are expressions of your individual charisma.

For John of the Cross, the soul was the container of the core substance of the human being, the unrefined power that needs conscious refinement. This core of each person is the nuclear force of pure love just waiting for God to ignite it. But the way through to that love requires us to confront the dark passions within that make unselfish, unconditional love impossible. According to John of the Cross, these dark passions—or what he calls the seven deadly sins—inflame our negative actions, words, and deeds: pride, avarice, luxury, wrath, gluttony, envy, and sloth. As a Catholic, John of the Cross viewed sin as a negative act that we consciously choose to initiate, knowing that others might be harmed but weighing such consequences as insignificant given the dark passion fueling our ego. That the deed is consciously enacted and that we or others suffer is a violation of the soul's creative power or nature, and, as such, it is more than just "wrong." John sees such action as a celestial or cosmic violation, the very archetypal meaning of a sin. Conscious negative action that is self-serving, incidentally, is also the kind of violation that accrues karma. Cleanse these dark passions from the soul, instructs John of the Cross, and what remains within a person is not just the capacity to love, but the desire to love others.

THE SEVEN DARK PASSIONS AND HEALING

As a medical intuitive, I realized that our attachments to memories, fears, superstitions rooted in our religious or ethnic heritage, or anything that drains our energy anchor us in "time." That is, such attachments cause us to carry more psychic weight in our energy system, mind, and emotional body, because we must continually supply these old, negative patterns of consciousness with energy as the years continue to pass. Think of this in terms of living on an "energy budget," with which you pay out energy allotments. Like bad debts that keep accruing interest as we fail to pay them off, at some point the buildup of your negative patterns from the past will begin to consume the majority of your daily energy allotment, leaving you less and less power with which to manage the demands of your daily life: your health, your creativity, your relationships, and the subtle movements of the natural laws. You will not have enough energy left to participate in, say, the high-functioning dynamics of creating opportunities for yourself or healing an illness. Simply put, your negative history creates psychic weight, and the more psychic "weight" you carry around with you, the longer you have to "wait" for anything to heal, or for anything to change in your life, for that matter. You will compromise the capacity of your soul to heal as a timeless vessel, because the psychic or time "density" of your ego literally converts into lengthening physical time for any experience in life, including suffering, the length of an illness, or the time it takes to move through a life transition. Holding on to past wounds and negative history is more than just an emotional or psychological problem; it drains us of the energy we need to rebuild the present in a healthy and functioning manner.

People hold on to the past during the healing process for any number of reasons. Some simply refuse to release their suffering consciousness, because without pain they have no other identity, no other way to imagine who they are in this lifetime. Others cannot imagine healing rapidly; that is, their image of the healing process is one that must "take time," and, accordingly, in their imagination they have charted a healing course over a period of years, processing their wounds slowly and methodically. For these individuals, it is inconceivable to "be healed" of their inner pain just like that—even though that is precisely what they insist they are striving for in their inner work.

From a completely different, more mystical, perspective, those who find the healing process intimidating, and therefore cling to the past as a way of slowing down their healing, face the greater challenge of arriving at the inner crossroads of personal transformation. I realized a long time ago that no matter how much we think we understand all we must do to heal—including forgiveness, exercise, and proper nutrition—there is always another layer in us that fights the healing process. Here again we are dealing with a part of us that defies gravity by going "beyond reason," but resides in the shadow of reason. I often refer to the part of us that compromises our healing as the Saboteur archetype, but until I looked through the lens of the dark night, I never fully grasped what fuels the Saboteur. It is the battle between the ego and the soul that occurs when we are in a situation that holds the potential for profound transformation.

Sometimes we find ourselves on that battlefield because of illness or a life crisis, and sometimes deep inner suffering strikes us out of nowhere. Regardless of what brings us here, whether it is a crisis or a choice to explore the spiritual path, this interior point is also the marker between time and timelessness in our psyche. This is the place within the psyche where mystical law and physical law merge, allowing the healer to channel a current of grace powerful enough to initiate a "timeless" healing while still in the realm of physical time.

At this crossroads, we ideally confront our dark passions with the intention of dismantling the destructive authority each particular passion has in our life. These are the underlying dark inner currents that direct our actions and behaviors. They fuel the fears of the psyche and make us unable to face the power of truth. Directly encountering the dark passions allows us to realize our experiences as illusions, stage settings essential for an endless stream of life dramas. Experiencing the core of our inner self in such a visceral way, we are then in a position to understand that we are truly responsible for the creative power that is contained within the soul. At this point, we are forced to release the illusion that others are responsible for the difficulties or the sorrows of our life. Here, the privilege of blaming another or feeling that you deserved better begins to fade. In your interior center of power, you confront the cosmic reality that either you are responsible for the whole of your life or you are not. Which is it? And if you are not, who is? And if you are, then it's time to appraise how well you have been directing this power that is the force of your soul into acts of creation.

Just as there are seven dark passions, there are seven gifts or jewels of the soul. The dark passions make it difficult for us to access or even recognize these jewels, much less use them in their full measure. People so often tell me that they fear being success-ful or fear their own power. I would say instead that they fear the power of their hidden jewels, because these are their true gifts, the ones that genuinely unlock their highest divine potential. People fear how their lives would change if they really let themselves understand the "enemy," shattering the walls of the heart to make room for those we never thought we could feel compassion for, let alone love. And from such deeper feelings we begin to see the deeper truth that we are but one humanity. And from that insight come inner changes about who we are and how we want to be and what we want to do in this world of "one humanity."

We wander through life, searching for that special something, for that "thing" we are meant to do or discover, when all the time what we are really feeling is the impulse arising from the unlocked potential of these treasures. But they remain hidden in the background because of the power of the dark passions. John of the Cross obviously made no mention of the seven chakras when referring to the seven deadly sins, any more than Teresa did in describing the seven mansions of her interior castle. And yet, I cannot help but see a connection between the chakras—the seven potent energy centers that interpenetrate the physical and ethe-ric bodies in the yogic tradition of India—and the seven deadly sins or dark passions, as well as the seven gifts of the spirit. So in my commentary on each of the dark passions, below, I have also included the chakras. In Chapter 5, where I discuss the gifts of the spirit, you'll find a more detailed discussion of the way these energy centers connect to our spiritual life.

THE FIRST PASSION: Pride

Pride in its shadow form is often called hubris. For all the fears that have a controlling influence on human behavior, none is as potent as the fear of being humiliated, which is, of course, a matter of pride. Most often, when people speak to me of a struggle with forgiveness, what they cannot forgive is having been humiliated by someone. Pride can be positively defined as self-respect or dignity, but that hardly sums up what this power encompasses within the psyche. Pride is our most vulnerable nerve ending, because it goes directly to our sense of purpose and identity, of having a place and a role in life. Pride is an energy that can feel as if it attaches you to your life's purpose, and your life's purpose is supposed to be kept uncontaminated. We fear shame and humiliation so profoundly that we will shame or humiliate others just to protect our own pride. We will avoid trying anything daring, even if we would grow enormously through our efforts, for fear of being humiliated. Ironically, this reluctance to reach for something outside our comfort zone can make us feel shame about settling for "second best." For all its innate power, then, we have difficulty learning how to manage pride, and it becomes lethal when wounded.

We learn to take pride in ourselves from our tribe, but we also encounter our first scars of humiliation from the tribe in early childhood. Consequently, pride in both its light and its shadow aspects is closely linked to the first chakra, which I call the "tribal" chakra. Traditionally, the first, or "root," chakra is associated with the base of the spinal column, the part of the body that contacts the ground when seated in meditation. It represents what grounds us, and its corresponding element is earth. But I also see this chakra as connecting us to our family and the ethnic, social, religious, and class groups closest to us. Just as those groups can inculcate positive feelings of loyalty and self-respect, they can also create deep scars by imposing their various taboos and stigmas on us for behavior that isn't acceptable to them. Those can be among our most painful scars and, consequently, the scars that can cause us to harm others. Pride is the cause of tribal warfare, of wounds of hatred passed down from generation to generation. In older cultures in parts of Europe, Asia, and the Middle East, many ethnic vendettas have been carried on for so long that the participants don't always remember the original injury. As individuals, we will destroy our own families out of pride. Few people can get this dark passion under control, and when hubris controls a person, it is like being possessed.

- What are you capable of doing when your pride is injured?

- How easily is your ego or pride offended?

- Have you ever truly asked yourself why your pride is so fragile?

- What does it take to get back in your "good graces" once your pride has been offended or you have been humiliated?

- What pain have you caused others as a result of injured pride?

- What have you learned about yourself through this dark passion?

THE SECOND PASSION: Avarice

Coveting another's goods is one way of describing the essence of greed. Greed is a ruthless dark passion that can take hold of you with the force of a tsunami. It is a dark passion that every person has to confront, and it has many forms, like the clever shapeshifter it is. Some people are greedy for money, but then there is power, fame, authority, attention—the list is endless. Greed is a form of insanity. There is never "enough" for the greedy, because greed is not logical. Greed is the perfect example of the shadow side of reason: think of asking a megamillionaire, "How much is enough?"

The second chakra lines up most closely with greed, because it is the power center within the human energy system that governs money. Lower back aches, sciatic pain, and cancers that develop in the region of the second chakra (lower back and genitals) are often related directly or indirectly to financial concerns.

- What triggers your passion for greed?

- In what area of your life is "nothing ever enough"? Love? Money? Gratitude? Attention? Respect? Greed has many, many faces.

- How much of your time and attention is given over to asking, "How will I get my share of this?" and "What do I fear I will not have enough of in life?"

- How has your health suffered because of greed? Possibilities include backaches, sciatica, acid reflux, stomach and digestive problems, stress-related disorders such as anxiety and sleep problems, stress that contaminates relationships, and anger issues.

- What have you learned about yourself through this dark passion?

THE THIRD PASSION: Luxury *(Self-Entitlement and Sexuality)*

John of the Cross interpreted the sin of luxury as one of sensuality, with sexual overtones, and of entitlement. Recognizing that he was writing for monks 500 years ago, I've reinterpreted the dark passion of luxury to reflect challenges of the ego. Self-entitlement positions you to believe that life revolves around you. That belief has hundreds of offshoots, such as believing that all things should work out in your favor, that you are always right, that justice has your name written on it, that bad things should happen only to other people, and that other people were born just to take care of you. Self-entitlement sets you up to have unrealistic expectations of others and to be endlessly disappointed, not to mention bitter.

In an exaggerated form, self-entitlement becomes the right to use others or anything you want to achieve your own ends, be they pleasure or power.

Most people never become genuinely comfortable with their own sexuality. Sex and sexuality become a shadow part of their lives, perhaps the cause of despair in their relationships. Luxury is the dark passion of the third chakra, which is the center of self-esteem and personal power and corresponds to the solar plexus. Numerous physical and emotional dysfunctions arise from stress related to the lack of self-esteem, such as eating disorders, gastric and colon problems, diabetes, and pancreatic conditions. Self-esteem is the cornerstone of personal power, without which we walk shoeless on the rough paths of this earth all the days of our life.

- What do you believe you are entitled to in this life? (We all think we are entitled to something, even if it's as mundane as not waiting in long lines.)

- How much of your frustration and anger is due to things not working out as you thought you were entitled to, such as the "perfect" marriage or a successful career?

- What sexual issues do you struggle with?

- What makes you uncomfortable about sexuality?

- What have you learned about yourself through this dark passion?

THE FOURTH PASSION: Wrath

Wrath is extreme anger, a passion that is destructive, cruel, and merciless. Wrath is a dark passion capable of destroying lives, or of destroying you: you can be as possessed by wrath as by greed. Both are passions that can take control of the "reasoning" mind and convert it into a weapon of massive destruction. We all have anger running through our veins; wrath goes deeper than anger, however, because it is anger with permission to destroy. Anger can flare up in a moment, vent itself verbally, and then be gone. In a loving relationship, partners say they just can't stay angry at each other. But wrath begins to speak in a self-righteous voice, building a case within your mind—your reason—that you are "right" and therefore action is justified. Your reason refuses to relent, stoking the fire of anger constantly, because it takes a great deal of fuel to keep the fires of self-righteousness burning. Wrath eventually consumes you on your own pyre.

The fourth chakra is the heart center, and an angry heart is a tragic, dangerous heart, one that becomes unforgiving. An angry heart turns love into torment, punishing those who we think do not love us enough or in the right way. But there is no right way to love an angry heart, so love is always futile when mixed with anger. Ultimately anger pushes love away, again and again.

How many times have you done or said something that was a spontaneous act of anger, in which you couldn't stop yourself because the anger was stronger than your ability to control yourself?

- Do you use anger to control others?
- How often and in what ways have you harmed others with your anger?
- Have you repaired the damage you've done to others with your anger?
- Do you excuse your own behavior based on your childhood or do you hold yourself accountable as an adult?
- What have you learned about yourself through this dark passion?

THE FIFTH PASSION: Gluttony

John of the Cross identified spiritual gluttony for his monks as going to spiritual extremes—for example, extreme fasting or extreme piety. For our purposes, the dark passion of gluttony deals in mindless consumption, whether of food, drugs, alcohol, negative ideas, the influence of other people's thoughts, material goods, or anything outside yourself that takes possession of your will. To consume without consciousness, just for the pleasure of consuming, makes you unconscious of your own actions or your own power of choice. There is a common saying that a person is a "glutton for punishment." This is directed toward someone who is oblivious to either extreme self-abuse or abuse coming from another. The abuse is apparent to everyone else, as is the person's inability to speak up to stop it.

The fifth chakra, which is the power of will and corresponds to the throat, aligns with the dark passion of gluttony. To take command of your will and maintain it against the controlling influence of other people, of outside fears, of all the illusions that prey on us, is the meaning of "becoming conscious." To command your will means that you have taken conscious control of the choices you make; that you are conscious enough not to compromise the power of your mind, your integrity, your body, and your soul out of fear for your safety in this world. The dark passion of gluttony represents an absence of control over your will, the opposite of what it means to be conscious. The body, the mind, the emotions, and your entire life suffer when you abdicate your willpower to drugs, food, the influence of others, the need for approval, or any outside source. Taking command of your own willpower, your own choices, embodies the challenge of becoming conscious.

- It would be difficult for you to refrain from your patterns of gluttony because _____.

- Gluttony represents self-abuse, as opposed to the other dark passions, which tend to give us permission to abuse others. Is abuse of yourself something you approve of?

- What are your best excuses for allowing yourself to make poor personal or health choices?

- What does this dark passion teach you about yourself?

THE SIXTH PASSION: Envy

The dark passion of envy has not changed over the centuries since John of the Cross wrote about it, nor even before he put pen to paper. Envy can destroy the mind, possessing it like a fever. Envy makes people think that they have been cheated out of opportunities or that they should have what someone else has. People can be driven to near-madness when envy takes hold of their reason. Suddenly all they can see or think about is the person or situation at the center of their obsession, which becomes a twisted, toxic visualization that they play and replay constantly. You can't reason with envy, because it is an illness, rooted in the illusion that you were cheated or that someone got something that should have been yours. This dark passion causes us to diminish all the good in our lives. The inherent command that each of us has to love and cherish our own life is violated by the toxin of envy, as it makes us see only dead-end streets.

The sixth chakra is the mind, comprising intellect and intuition, a power center that the dark passion of envy contaminates. Envy blocks your ability to see opportunities; it makes it impossible for you to appreciate anything wonderful about who you are.

- Are you by nature envious?

- Everyone has had at least one encounter with envying another person. What created that experience for you? What did you learn about yourself?

- Do you envy others even for their spiritual attainments?

THE SEVENTH PASSION: Sloth

Sloth refers to laziness with a tendency toward procrastination. That the word is also the name of a tropical mammal that hangs upside down from branches and feeds lazily on fruits and vegetation gives us a potent visual image of slothfulness. That it should be so easy to be lazy just doesn't seem right or fair, but somehow that's part of the game of life. So many people suffer from living in their minds, from imagining all that their lives could or should be, but find that they can't make their bodies cooperate with the actions required to make their ambitions come to fruition. Getting off the couch, getting to the gym, returning calls and messages, and developing disciplined work habits are all that stand between us and making those dreams a reality. I've listened to so many people tell me that they "know" they are meant for something great, but just what that is—um—they can't figure out. I can. They are waiting for someone else to make their dreams come true, someone who isn't afraid to work hard and take on the responsibilities that go along with making decisions. Some people prefer life "in the mind," where it's easy and safe and nothing really happens. That's the shadow of the passion of sloth. Life goes by and nothing really happens.

- As one of the deadly sins, sloth implies inactivity in the practice of virtue. That it should be the dark passion of the seventh chakra strikes me as extraordinarily perfect. The seventh chakra corresponds to the crown of the head, the "thousand-petaled lotus" that is said to explode like a fountain of light at the moment of enlightenment. But the lazy spiritual mind is one that maintains awareness of God through books and thought rather than through spiritual action; the slothful mind does not push beyond reason into the deeper waters of the soul, but gives up at the first indication of discomfort. It might know what the right thing is, but does not proceed to actually doing it.

- In what area of your life is laziness most destructive?

- Where do you give up spiritually? Do you prefer to meet your spiritual life in books or does your spiritual life include soul devotion?

- In what ways does slothfulness affect your health?

- Do you ever feel that your life is just slipping away and nothing at all is happening? Review the choices that you make each day that contribute to a lack of movement in your life as opposed to choices that create change.

- What have you learned about yourself through this dark passion?

FROM THE DARKNESS INTO THE LIGHT

The dark night of the soul is a journey into light, a journey from your darkness into the strength and hidden resources of your soul. Navigating the dark night requires interior dialogue, contemplation, prayer, quiet time, and sharing with those who understand the profound nature of inner transformation. When you are in this interior place, you stand at the crossroads of your power, between your ego and your soul, between time and timelessness. This is a journey of learning how to view the world as a mystic does, through a timeless lens that perceives beyond reason. Yet, as the mystical sojourner learns, only through encountering the power of your dark passions can you defeat them. As a result, from the darkness come the seven "gifts of the spirit," illuminated graces that naturally heal that which is diseased or in pain. Though these graces are not the result as in reward of the dark passions, they are the balancing forces that govern the power of choice in all acts of creation, from the grandest act you initiate to the most subtle thought you alone hear—and yet there are creative consequences in some immeasurable way to even those unspoken words. These graces are present within every person, and yet, although they reveal themselves in subtle ways throughout our lives, it is the dark passions that tend to dominate our everyday choices. You may want to call someone you love and apologize for saying a cruel word, but pride and anger cause you to decide, "No, I won't call." In the end, years of heartache accumulate, all because the dark passion of pride eclipses the abundance of love that is also present but that we unwittingly suppress.

Complete healing requires that we not even look at the actions of others, but only at the controlling influence of our own pride and anger, because that power is the real source of our suffering. When we release the fear of loving, all that remains is the desire to love. By releasing the false pride that prevents us from reaching out to another person, we unleash the ability to act on our fundamental instincts to help others. In confronting the fear that leads you to believe that you must come first, that there won't be enough wealth or attention or love to go around if others get more than you, you discover the abundant generosity within your own heart.

There is nothing simple about this journey, and yet, as all the great mystics have tried with such enthusiasm to communicate, acting from your many gifts of grace is far more natural to who you really are than acting from your shadow. How much more natural and in keeping with your deeper instincts it is to act out of love than to act out of fear or greed or anger. Indeed, it is unnatural to act from our wounds and, so, to wound others merely because we are hurting—unnatural because we are yielding to the power of our shadow instead of the power of our light.

One of the most common expressions of hope is "There is a light at the end of the tunnel." At the end of the dark night, that light is a vibrant awakening to an empowered psyche and soul that recognize the gifts of the spirit as the essence of our highest potential. And as you'll learn in the next chapter, these graces have as much force to heal and to transform as the shadow passions have to destroy—if not more.

Chapter Five

—————— THE FOURTH TRUTH ——————

Rely on the Power of Your Graces

O ne school of thought that dominates the Western approach to healing assumes that once people confront their history of trauma or painful secrets, or recognize areas of emotional under-development, the state of health just naturally shows up to fill the void left by their vacated wounds. This assumption is so prevalent that many of us have come to believe that simply to "speak our wounds" is the same as healing them. The notion behind this practice is that health is maintained by vocalizing your wounds as well as your present needs, which have arisen as a consequence of your wounds. As a result of this approach, healing practices often dwell on the negative, hesitating to encourage people to actively pursue the richer qualities of their inner nature, such as creativity and the capacity to initiate dynamic changes in life. It's not that these practices deny more positive qualities; it's just that positive qualities cannot compete with the power of vulnerability and the resulting emotional support granted to the wounded individual, as mentioned in Chapter 2.

The emphasis on the negative comes from a set of beliefs, among which is the idea that each painful situation conceals a lesson. Once we discover this lesson and then complete its require-ments, the pain and the illness—or the crisis—will vanish. And so we pursue the pain as the culprit, rarely extending our view to consider the more mature truth that life includes painful transitions. Not all pain is an indication that something is wrong, either in your physical body or in your life. Frequently we are alerted to a cycle of transition by sensations of enormous discomfort, as if our bones have grown too large for our skin to contain. Such discomfort is natural. We really ought to feel, for example, as if we can't breathe unless we leave home and get on with our own life.

And then there is the kind of interior fire-pain that comes from yearning to bring forth something original. This passion is its own agony and ecstasy, a merger of sublime delight and wretched anguish as the writer or artist or mystic strives to see or listen or find the right form to capture inspirations that present themselves before the inner eyes of the soul as sacred messengers. The anguish that a person feels when she realizes that she has failed to find a perfect medium that allows the mystical mist to slip into comprehensible thought is indescribable, yet it is not a pain she would ever anesthetize.

Negativity and pain, therefore, are misunderstood in terms of the purpose they serve within the greater scheme of our life. We fool ourselves by assuming that all discomfort must be immediately converted to comfort and that order must rapidly be introduced into all chaotic situations, as if that were even possible. Such thinking comes from fear of personal harm and loss and the need to reestablish control. So, retreating to the familiar world as soon as possible seems the reasonable thing to do. Yet when we make such choices, we undo the entire reason that a crisis or illness happened in the first place. A woman named Jean told me that she had a long history of excruciating migraines. In time, she realized that her migraines developed within hours of confrontations with her husband. During these arguments she would express her discontent with something and he would end the conversation by saying, "Let's not discuss this any further. You've had your say. Now let's just go back to the way things were."

Jean understood that she would continue to have migraines until she did something other than follow orders to "go back to the way things were." She realized that although she could continue with her migraine drugs and acupuncture treatments, all those healing strategies were useless once she had recognized that her pain came from repressed rage at betraying her dignity. Her husband recognized through their conversations that she was in need of a far more respectful dynamic in their relationship, one he was not able to provide without feeling disempowered himself. He wanted to reestablish control by returning to old, familiar patterns, which only intensified the crisis, although he saw it as his way through the crisis.

In truth, Jean and her husband each required their own healing path, which went well beyond the diagnosis of migraine headaches. As so many people discover, the actual physical illness represents but a part of the challenge of healing. Beyond the breakdown of the body and interior wounds lie much more complex psychological, emotional, and spiritual dynamics that require extensive excavation, among them the dark passions. We have even more to discover about an interior self that is shaped not by a history in need of repair, but by a potentially profound mystical empowerment yet to be realized. We rarely uncover the route to that realization, however, because our tendency is to believe that the healing journey ends once we release the last wound.

Consider that as the wounded self dissolves through the healing process, we experience a loss not only of our "wounded identity," but also of the feeling of power that has accompanied that identity. Sal spent many years in psychoanalysis to work through his difficult childhood, which had left him unable to form healthy relationships with women. Sal built a life around the theme of self-protection, a pattern he desperately wanted to change. At the same time, he developed a lifestyle that was comfortable enough, yet left him lonely. A significant part of his therapy was built around the idea of having a goal and meeting that goal. In his case, the goal was to forgive his parents for raising him in such isolation. Through therapy, he came to realize that his parents did not isolate him out of cruelty; it was unfortunate that they were unable to give him more attention because they worked long hours and that he lacked for friends. But he finally understood that none of that was due to his parents' wanting him to be lonely.

Sal felt great relief in this realization, which signaled for both him and his therapist that he had reached his goal. The absence of this wound and the declaration that he was healed also held the promise that his social life would immediately change. For Sal, reaching a goal successfully always meant that you got the promised reward. He genuinely believed that he would leave his therapist's office that day and somehow walk directly into the girl of his dreams on his way home. But he arrived home only to discover nothing had changed. The apartment was still empty. He was still lonely. And he still had no place to go in the evenings. His only companions remained the television set and the computer. An even greater shock to Sal was that he now lacked even the company of his wounded childhood memories, having matured into realizations that would not permit him to blame his parents for his shyness. At the same time, he lacked any self-image as a healthy, social male, any sense of himself beyond the son needing to forgive his parents. Ultimately the weight of the void proved too much and he was drawn back into his darkness, a place with which he was intimately familiar.

Everyone can relate to Sal's story in some way, because we are all goal-oriented, especially when it comes to rigorous undertakings like rebuilding our physical, emotional, or mental health. Yet most people can also relate to his remarkable experience of entering the void, of feeling that after all the inner work the quality of his emotional life remained unchanged. We can relate to this sensation of the void, because we all know what it is like to identify the loss of power and to go on psychological expeditions to retrieve our sense of feeling directionless. More often than not, we return from those expeditions feeling a bit let down, not quite as transformed as we had anticipated.

But these expeditions to discover where, when, how, and by whom you were wounded are not really about self-empowerment. These expeditions are about discovering why you feel disempowered. The empowerment journey that is critical to your healing—and to your life—comes from progressing through the deep waters of your dark passions and continuing onward to discover not what has been taken from you, but what you have yet to give and who you have yet to become. To be left in the void as the end point of your healing is to be left in darkness, without a sense of any new life growing within you. The substance of that new life is built on seven graces, all of which need to be explored with the same vigor you would pour into examining a buried wound, for these graces are powers that have been just as repressed as hidden wounds, though for different reasons. For one thing, most of us view grace as an imaginary force or perhaps as a vague divine substance. In our five-sensory, reason-bound world that so values control, if we can't see it or control it, bottle it or market it, then what good is it? It certainly isn't "real," as far as the mainstream definition of real goes. So how practical is it to say that the hidden you, the truly empowered you, the fully healthy you, requires your graces to complete the transformation?

For an accurate answer to that, I would refer you to your own inner guidance. Those who know what it is to battle with becoming an honest, integrated person know that the battle is fought on the interior landscape, somewhere between the ego and the soul. They also know that to be incongruent, to say one thing but do another, is a surefire way of sabotaging the quality of their life, because deceit is a dark passion—and a powerful one. Battling deceit or greed, envy or lust, is not something the mind can do by itself. You can't "will" yourself to not be greedy. You can't "will" yourself to tell the truth if you are, by nature, prone to telling people what they want to hear because you want to be accepted. The decision to battle those inner forces requires something far more than willpower: it requires grace.

So, is grace real? In a word, yes. What would you be like if you recognized the power of your inner graces, and knew how to utilize them in your everyday life? Grace is not just an emergency substance, a kind of divine Rescue Remedy. Grace highlights qualities in you, enhances your strengths, heightens your inner senses, and sometimes gives you a craving for silence so that you can listen deeply.

To know yourself through your graces is to come to know yourself all over again. Perhaps for the first time you will truly come to love who you are. You cannot be a fully healed, or even slightly healthy, person without your graces flowing. This begs the question of whether you have to know about your graces in order for them to flow through your being. I don't believe you do, but I believe that knowing them can help you realize new levels of awareness. Imagine how different your life would be if you had an intellect full of ordinary knowledge blended with a soul alive with the mystical awareness of its inherent qualities.

WHAT, THEN, IS GRACE?

Grace is not just a vague divine substance or some poetic ideal that mad mystics came up with while in an altered state. Grace is a subtle force that is, once again, beyond the grasp of reason. It is not logical or rational or an intellectual power that can be contained within one clear definition. It needs to be experienced, recognized by the individual from within, in the same way that authentic inner guidance is deeply understood by the recipient to be genuine. It is a divine power, a force that the laws of nature are often subject to rather than the other way around, as in the matter of miracles.

Grace is associated with many spiritual traditions, but in particular with Christianity, and specifically with Catholicism, because of its long tradition of mysticism and theology. But reference to grace is also found in Hinduism, especially Vedanta, in which grace is ever present to all who avail themselves of it. W. W. Meissner, a Catholic priest, maintains that a "psychology of grace" will help the modern individual realize the relationship of the spiritual life to the process of personal development and maturation. Abraham Maslow concluded that the fully developed person is capable of seeing the sacred, the eternal, and the symbolic in the world. The 20th-century Indian mystic Sri Aurobindo described the spiritual journey as similar to the mystical meaning of the Trinity: First, we must realize that we each have a soul. Then, we must become aware of an inner guide that is the carrier of a truth that we absorb through experience, reflection, and meditation. Finally, we have to become humble and sturdy enough to ascend into a relationship with the Divine. Such a journey relies on a continual infusion of the graces.

Everyone's life has been touched by grace, no doubt more times and in more ways than can be counted. Thoughts and ideas that strike you "out of the blue," that change the course of your schedule or compel you to do something unusual, and that in general serve a positive end you could not have planned may be said to be the work of grace. Anyone who has ever been in a heated argument knows the quiet voice of caution that warns, "Are you sure you want to say that?" Listening to that grace-filled whisper saves relationships, but refusing to listen out of pride causes pain so wretched that the resultant wound breaks open again and again.

Grace has many expressions, and Teresa of Ávila offers superb wisdom on the ways in which it works. She often used water as a metaphor for grace; in one example she writes that you can dig your own well in search of water and, indeed, find it. That water will certainly be pure and will quench your thirst, but because you've created the well, you will have to replenish the water supply by continually finding new sources. As an example of this, let's look at how you might use the grace of Understanding. I give a more extensive definition later in this chapter, but for the purposes of this example let me just say that, like all the illuminated graces of your soul, this grace of Understanding has a far richer meaning than the conventional definition of "to comprehend or listen with attention." For example, the grace of Understanding opens your field of vision not only to comprehend what another communicates, but also to deepen your capacity to appreciate what is being told to you. This is a grace that creates a unified field of understanding, enhancing the ability to share difficult and often life-transforming information.

Let's say, for example, that you recognize that a different level of understanding needs to be introduced into a conversation for a resolution to be reached. Perhaps you're not a naturally good listener and you know it. You can feel that to be true in every bone in your body. You also know that you are capable of listening more carefully and respectfully to what the other person is saying. And yet you hesitate. Perhaps you don't feel the other person deserves that extra care, or maybe you are looking for a response in kind. From a different perspective, you might hesitate to offer an understanding shoulder to lean on, because you fear personal rejection. Or maybe in offering to help, you really want to be admired for being so thoughtful, and you're worried that your motives will be obvious. The ego often has a conflict over how to handle the power of grace, because the ego is motivated by personal agendas.

All of these situations represent examples of conflicts with inner guidance in which you are drawn to reach out to another and yet are uncertain about offering help. Such conflicts do not reflect poorly on you. Instead, they indicate that you have potential goodness that has yet to be expressed. Your ego often views what it is asked to give as "unreasonable," because the ego measures what it gives so carefully. Teresa describes this kind of giving as "digging your own well of grace," because grace is not yet flowing "naturally" from you to another. This hesitation to be spontaneously a giving person exists because consciously or unconsciously, giving is recognized as a form of empowering another person. Withholding the gift of empowering another person, most especially when you know that you are able to give that gift, creates an automatic inner conflict about your sense of hesitation, as the ego is naturally drawn to the opportunity to act on your highest capacities and qualities, which are indeed your graces. But the ego fears empowering another person and therein lies the root of the human conflict: do I empower you when I intuitively sense that I can or do I withhold this gift because I fear you may become more than me? And yet, you see that the use of these qualities anytime, anywhere, and with anyone always improves, settles, heals, or calms a situation. And even if the situation doesn't require a resolution, still your qualities that are rooted in the seven graces are those which people love most about you, the ones you rely on to illuminate any room you walk into. One of the signatures of grace is that you are always spontaneously drawn to act on it and the grace you are called upon to use inevitably heals the other.

The ego relies on the physical senses to maneuver in the world, whereas the soul relies on its graces and spiritual senses. To say this differently, you rely on your senses to control your external world, whereas the power of your graces works to transform your world. To act from grace should be second nature, as that is the calling of your true, liberated, intuitive self. If you were to shed the fears that burden your ego, what would remain would be a clear intuitive soul that would effortlessly respond to others, because your spiritual senses draw you toward others and not away from them. Teresa often said that as we develop a rich interior spiritual life, we no longer have to dig for our own graces, because a divine well of grace is endlessly supplied. We simply live in a field of grace, generated by our own soul. Grace has become second nature to us. Think of life's journey as an endless series of experiences that lead us more deeply into that second nature.

Such a description can sound unattainable, like a state of perfection just shy of enlightenment. But that is an "all or nothing" approach. A more realistic approach is to recognize that we are simply making a more conscious effort to act from inner resources that are in harmony with the very essence of spiritual, mental, and emotional health and well-being. Perfection should never be the goal; practice is the goal. Live in awareness and nurture your practice.

Grace, then, has many expressions and qualities. A woman named Sally told me that she was overcome by guidance instructing her to "be silent" in the midst of a horrible argument with her husband. She said that typically she was very argumentative and their battles usually escalated to the point of screaming at each other. But this particular time, just as their argument was getting ready to explode into all-out war, she heard an inner instruction telling her to be silent, to which she responded immediately. Her husband continued screaming and raging, but she remained not merely silent but still, more awestruck by the intensity of her guidance than by the dramatics of her husband. Finally, he stopped and asked, "What's the matter with you?"

"I'm not fighting any more," Sally said. "I just know this isn't working." What she meant was that screaming and yelling wasn't working as a means of problem solving, but her husband understood her to mean that the marriage wasn't working. He immediately calmed down and said, "Look, I don't want a divorce. I just want to work things out." From that day on, they agreed never to speak to each other in anger again, and in the six years since that day, they have yet to break their promise. For Sally, the intervention giving her that instruction to "be silent" was pure grace, as it was guiding her to act out of character by making herself vulnerable in a verbally violent interaction. She told me that, given her nature and personality, she would never have thought to act in such a way. Sally could, of course, have ignored that grace, as people so often ignore their inner instructions. Yet those who have followed such guidance know exactly what it is to have a direct encounter with the power of grace.

ENTERING YOUR LIGHT: COMING TO KNOW YOUR GRACES

Just as you must be led into your darkness, you need to be led into your light. As much as grace is second nature, animating your graces requires more than being able to define the meaning of each grace's name. The mind cannot comprehend the essence of grace as if it were a mathematical equation. Words used to define grace cannot fully express the power of grace. Grace-filled moments are present in all of our lives. They come and go unnoticed for what they are in terms of "grace," though we recognize them as special for the end product of that grace. For example, a reconciliation between you and someone you hold dear that you thought could never happen is truly an act of grace. Running into someone you haven't seen in a long time who is especially dear to you is far more than a sweet coincidence; it is also an act of grace. Remembering that today is someone's birthday and realizing how hurt that person would be had you forgotten is also an act of grace. These are just small samples of the power of grace as it silently maneuvers through your everyday thoughts, inspiring you to take action that always—always—has the healing or betterment of someone else's life, or your own, as its intention. That you do not credit grace as the source of these inspirations is irrelevant.

Then there is the moment at which you pray for grace, directly, quietly, to come into your life. Usually this prayer is said during a time of need, and it is then you might wonder, "What is grace? How will I know when this grace that I am asking for has arrived?" This is the point at which understanding the nature of grace becomes a matter of spiritual significance. Grace is a mystical substance, not a mental concept. As a mystical substance, it must be experienced to be known. You cannot read your way into an understanding of grace, or discuss your way into it, or find a definition that finally opens that passageway into an experience of inner illumination. Grace makes itself known to you through prayer, by filling you with a sensation of tranquility that you cannot come to by telling yourself to "relax." To know grace fully and directly, you must turn inward.

Consider, for example, the nature of joy. Telling someone who is sad to "imagine feeling joyful" is like telling someone who speaks only English to suddenly begin speaking Hindi. What exactly should that person imagine as she tries to "picture" joy? Poetry? Sunsets over Malibu? Being deluged with birthday presents? Is that the meaning of joy? If you lack a genuine experience of joy, then trying to imagine joy on the count of three or as a therapeutic exercise is preposterous. It cannot be done. Joy is a grace that you need to experience within the context of your life.

You have always lived within the field of your graces, of course, most likely unaware that you are drawing on their resources as often as you do. Graces such as kindness, compassion, patience, and wisdom routinely arise in our interactions with others, but rarely in their fullest radiance. These graces filter into our lives as our finest personality characteristics. But despite the fact that people find these traits our most appealing traits, they are actually a dilution of the pure essence of grace. This is not unlike the way in which pure perfume is diluted in order to make cologne: the fragrance of the cologne is of the same essential substance, but it has much less intensity. Giving an expensive perfume to a girl still too young to understand the value of the pure rose oil contained in the small bottle, for example, is an error in judgment, because she has not yet learned to appreciate all that is involved in acquiring and preparing that oil. It's not that you do not want her to have such a treasure, but the wise elder withholds the treasure until the child comes of age. Then with great delight she is given an ounce of pure perfume as a gift she can appreciate and use appropriately. One thousand baskets of rose petals must be crushed to acquire one ounce of perfume, so precious is the purest version of this oil. Each tiny bottle of pure rose oil represents centuries of masterful knowledge of how to cultivate rose bushes, how to know exactly when to select the right roses, how to pull the petals off the roses so that their minuscule amount of oil does not dry up before it becomes a part of the one thousand baskets being gathered for the ritual of deriving the precious oil from this most exquisite flower.

You cannot acquire or command such refined grace through rituals of reason or knowledge. Like the bottle of pure rose oil saved for just the right moment, "perfume-quality grace" is a gift, a blessing of profound mystical significance that awakens within you. You can't "go after grace"; it pursues you. Grace emerges out of your own inner work and the healing of dark passions. It comes through prayer and through discovering that you thrive more on truth than on fear. Grace comes to you as you learn to rely on it, drawing on it as a primary resource within your thoughts and actions.

I've frequently asked people in my workshops, "When you are not distracted by ordinary thoughts, what do you naturally tend to think about?" Most people respond that their thoughts automatically drift into some negative harbor in their minds or hearts, such as financial stress, relationship problems, unresolved emotional crises, health problems, or job issues. Most people's thoughts drift backward. And if they do send their attention into the future, it tends to be for the sake of worrying over something that has yet to happen. I can't recall a single person who told me that his or her thoughts naturally drifted to gratitude or to an inner reservoir of tranquility. Our society is weighted in favor of what's wrong, what's in pain, and what's missing in our lives, as opposed to what's right and what is enough. No commercial has ever been made that has told the public, "You probably already have more than enough. What else do you need?" The decision to consciously drift into a field of grace goes against a raging psychic current in the collective unconscious that continually reinforces the negative in our lives. Because that psychic current is so strong, the choice to dwell in grace has to be reinforced again and again until it becomes second nature to you. And then your second nature will gradually take over and that grace will take hold.

THE SEVEN GRACES

I have partnered the seven graces with the seven chakras, using the same structure I created for the seven dark passions. By understanding the currents that flow through each chakra, you can better connect grace to areas of your life and your physical body that are in need of healing. In Chapter 4 I emphasized that although the seven dark passions are also called the seven deadly sins, the shadow characteristics represented by these "sins" provide an accurate list of the root causes of human suffering and injustice. The seven graces also have their origin in Scripture: Paul in 1 Corinthians 12:8–10 offers a list of the "gifts of the Spirit," as does Isaiah 11:2–3. As I've mentioned before, Jesus is the Western master teacher most closely associated with grace, not only because he is known for healing, but also because he initiated the cosmic archetype of the Holy Spirit. He let his Apostles know that the "powers" that he had were within them and that his presence would be known to them through a cosmic spirit that embodied the sacred. The substance of that spirit would filter to them in the form of the many graces.

Although grace flows abundantly to all, there is such an experience as "being gifted with a grace," in which you feel a heightened awareness of a particular grace or graces. By this I mean that you become empowered with a particular grace, as opposed to just having an intellectual understanding or appreciation of it. People genuinely empowered or "gifted" with a grace are not difficult to spot, even in a crowded room—everyone wants to speak with them, because there is something rare and unusual about them. Often we say that a certain person "radiates" an energy that is uncommonly calming or loving, and I believe that emanation comes from grace.

THE FIRST GRACE: Reverence

In the scriptures, this grace is called "fear of the Lord," but that isn't the most effective language for impressing modern intellects. "Reverence" offers a better sense of all that this grace represents. In order to appreciate this grace more fully, let's begin by examining the first chakra. As we saw in Chapter 4, the first chakra relates to what I call tribal consciousness, which covers an enormous spectrum of information. Located at the base of your spine, where it makes contact with the earth when you are seated in the classic meditation posture, it is also called the root chakra. This is the energy field through which your circuits of energy are "rooted" or grounded in the physical world. Through this one chakra, your circuits of energy are connected to all matters related to your personal tribe as well as the greater social and planetary tribes. Here, "tribe" refers to any group of people who, for reasons of their own, whether through religion, politics, ethnic origin, or sexual preference, constitute a tightly bonded clan. The archetypal role of the tribe is to pass on social law and tribal wisdom in the form of religious and social traditions and family experiences. Tribes teach loyalty and unity, the idea that "blood is thicker than water." Within a tribe, respect is the law, and respect is also the ego's expression of the grace of Reverence. A tribe will go to war over the loss of respect, for example, particularly if such a loss occurred in humiliating circumstances. The grace of Reverence, on the other hand, grants a perception of unity in which the suffering of one tribe is understood to be interwoven with the suffering of all tribes. The mystical principle associated with the first chakra can be stated this way: what is in One is in the Whole.

Penetrating Reverence: Reverence is the grace that enables us to see that all of life is an interconnected field of cosmic activity that has its origins and endings in divine consciousness. Reverence is the grace through which we are able to grasp the significance of that incomprehensible truth and internalize it, meaning that the vastness of the universe becomes internally personal while remaining externally impersonal. Through such a heightened state of consciousness, you become aware of the difference between the nature of an absolute truth—that which is eternal and constant—and the lesser domain of scientific facts that rise and fall in their significance like yeasted dough. Life, from a mystical perspective, is more than a scientific system of impersonal laws that can somehow be reduced to comprehensible order to satisfy the curious human intellect.

Reverence also leads one ever more deeply into a sense of awe. The presence of the sacred is perceived as the source of life, and your soul is deeply connected to that source. To be filled with awe is the response of the humble before the Divine, a response that acknowledges that the power governing life is not contained or defined by intellectual parameters. Life is defined by a force much greater than can be measured by the human intellect.

Reverence can also be the root grace of the intuitive system, made up of spiritual senses that have two distinct paths of expression. The lower spiritual senses animate your survival intuition, which includes your gut instincts, the fight-or-flight response, and the tribal laws that influence your conscience, integrity, and mindfulness of justice toward others. These intuitive senses are attuned to the exterior environment for self-protection. The more refined spiritual senses are inner-directed, attuned to the advancement of your spiritual life. Having a sense that you are not on the right path, for example, that you are in a spiritual crisis, or that you are awakening to a compelling desire to discover the deep realms of your own creativity and need to express a unique vision—all these are examples of inner-directed senses that advance your spiritual life. Finally, the instinct to question the meaning and purpose of your life is yet another example of how the grace of Reverence shows up in your life, inspiring you to search for your place in the cosmic scheme.

I have no doubt that many people who question the meaning and purpose of their lives are, in fact, starved for the grace of Reverence. Life has ceased to be sacred or holy for so many people. Yet we need awe in our lives. We have a fundamental need to seek out the sacred and experience contact with a source of divine power. We need the grace of Reverence in order to surround ourselves with a sense that we are living in the landscape of the sacred.

Invoking the Grace of Reverence: You invoke a grace through prayer, whether for healing, strength, stamina, insight, other personal needs, or simply to sit in quiet reflection. Reverence connects you with a sense of unity and wholeness. Asking to be given this grace in times of crisis enables you to perceive the whole of a situation instead of focusing on one or two aspects whose importance then becomes exaggerated. Reverence will ground your intuitive senses, helping you to trust your own instincts when situations become chaotic. This is also the grace that heightens your connection to your conscience, to knowing what choices are right or wrong for you.

Reverence thrives on unity and humility—qualities of the soul that nurture health. An attitude of superiority, for example, which is the shadow of humility, fosters arrogance. Arrogance leads to acts of separation that in turn result in psychic, emotional, and mental tensions. All this ultimately results in physical turmoil.

Prayer for Reverence: I invoke the grace of Reverence so that I might be one with all life and that my life might serve the whole. I ask that this grace alert me to all that I do that keeps me separated from my vital life force, so that I might make wiser choices. I ask that this grace alert me to when I am compromising my intuitive guidance because I don't like what I am hearing. I ask for the courage to hear what I must hear and to act on the guidance given to me.

THE SECOND GRACE: Piety

The classic meaning of piety is devotion to God. But for our purposes, we must take the concept of devotion a step further and ask, "How should piety be reinterpreted for the contemporary individual?" After all, the expressions of grace evolve as humanity changes from century to century. The old-world definition of piety is no longer expansive enough to contain the contemporary psyche and soul. Our examination of this grace begins, then, within the context of the second chakra, which provides a window into the stress patterns of the modern personality.

The second chakra, located in the lower back and genital region of the body, is the energy center that relates most directly to our need to create and to connect. Everyone needs to create and everyone needs to be in relationship. This is the energy center of your body that resonates most intimately with the need for companionship, romantic or otherwise. Because it is the command center for personal relationships, the second chakra also harbors all competitive instincts, some of which can become highly negative, if not ruthless. One-to-one power plays are among the most destructive of all human relationships, just as one-to-one friendships and romantic unions are the most fulfilling. The second chakra is where several illnesses begin to form that are rooted in stress related to finances, sexual conflicts, power struggles, and acts of betrayal. These will prove to be significant for the grace of Piety.

The second chakra harbors the fear of rape as well as the desire to rape. This is one of those desires that reveal the shadow aspects of reason; that is, rape is a desire located beyond reason in the dark area of the psyche. As a dark instinct, the desire to rape needs to be defined more extensively than the violation of the body. From an expanded perspective, rape includes the dark desire to forcibly take another's property, finances, power, status, achievements, fame, or any other targets that we want. This dark urge is balanced by the fight-or-flight instinct that alerts you when you are in a circumstance making you vulnerable to some form of rape, whether of power or of your physical body. The idea of "having your defenses up" refers to putting your second chakra on red alert, which means that you are with a person or in a circumstance that you sense is high-risk.

Piety may seem an odd grace to be associated with the second chakra, given the description of this energy center as a hotbed of activity connected with the outside world. And yet, that is precisely what makes the second chakra the most appropriate place for this special grace. The respect derived from humility is a crucial quality with which to imbue all our relationships.

Penetrating Piety: Whereas the instinctual reaction of the second chakra is to mistrust another person, to look for flaws, or to enter into a power play, the grace of Piety seeks that which is divine in others. To put it in less lofty language, Piety is a grace that brings out our spiritual instincts, such as sensing that someone is in need of kindness or nurturing. It is a grace that draws us to interact with those in need and to give generously to those who in an earlier time would have been viewed as competitors.

Teresa of Ávila uses a special name for a certain type of relationship in which the individuals are able to support each other's life's journeys with great generosity of heart and soul. She says that it is rare to find another person who understands what it means to be devoted to becoming "illuminated"—to seeing the truth about oneself and God clearly. As we progress on this path of illumination, we sometimes find others along the way who Teresa says qualify as "soul companions," individuals who have the depth of knowledge and experience to understand our personal journey. Yet another expression of the grace of Piety is to want to give the best of your inner resources to help "illuminate" another who turns to you for guidance.

Many people find matters of the second chakra to be among the most overwhelming: finances, relationships, sexuality, and all matters that relate to survival. This chakra also corresponds with gut instincts and grounded intuition, but someone who is frightened often finds it difficult to follow inner guidance. This is a grace that can help us easily recognize when we are frightened about our survival and out of touch with any sense of what to do next. Others gravitate toward this grace, as if they instinctually recognize that Piety is a provider of "God in the details" of your life, meaning that the nature of the Divine is a constant creative expression, exactly like the second chakra.

Invoking the Grace of Piety: You call on Piety when you feel yourself slipping into a dark power play with another person, or when you fear that you are becoming contaminated by negative thoughts about others. Remember that these negative energies harm your mind, heart, and spirit—not someone else's. The grace of Piety immediately shifts how you view another, enabling you to see with a softer heart. Or, to put this in more classic terms, it enables you to look beyond people's egos and focus on that which is divine in them. This practice takes the teachings of the great spiritual traditions and brings them into everyday life, where our choices matter.

Prayer for Piety: Piety is the grace of God in constant creativity, continually supplying my life and all life with endless energetic and physical resources. If I do not see those resources, then it is because I am looking through the lens of fear. I ask that the grace of Piety surround me and endlessly flow from my second chakra, replenishing all that needs healing. Let this grace dismantle my fear of others, of not having enough, and of hardship, and may those fears be replaced by this grace that illuminates the way I see others. Let me be available to care for others and to be a vessel of kindness for human beings. This is the grace of Piety in action.

THE THIRD GRACE: Understanding

The ego views "understanding" on the personal level, as the ability to listen clearly to what someone is saying, or, conversely, as the need to be heard clearly by others. It may also refer to a mutual agreement, as in the statement "We've come to an understanding on this matter." The grace of Understanding, in contrast, grants us the capacity to transcend matters transpiring at the personal level. This grace opens our capacity to see beyond the illusion of a circumstance and understand the deeper truth of what is really taking place. Two people who get into a shouting match over a parking space may claim that their argument began over who was there first, but the truth about the conflict goes beyond the parking space. It is about two people with histories of needing to win at all costs. Whether the source of contention is a parking space or a football game, both "contestants" share a ferocious need to be first. Though other parking spaces might be available, the person who didn't get the space would not even consider one of those, because that would mean he was the "loser," and in his mind he was second best and humiliated. A second parking space would never "heal" either driver, because the source of this conflict needs to be understood within the context of how people behave when devoid of healthy self-esteem. The role of power becomes a critical factor as the drama between two people unfolds, and with a trained eye one can see that even the cars and the parking lot have a symbolic role. Nothing is in your life by accident, but you need the grace of Understanding to see this clearly.

The third chakra resonates most strongly with the grace of Understanding, which includes common sense. But in this case, common sense is uncommonly grounded. We are born with instincts that are the equivalent of our species DNA, and they provide us with an archetypal understanding of the natural laws that govern the order of life. This is an expression of organic divinity—God in our bones and blood—and the essence of common sense, a sense that directs us to know what to do in a crisis, to help deliver a baby or to rig a structure in order to survive a storm.

Common sense is the thread that connects the species to its collective advancements, like a vibrational phone line that alerts us as a whole that the 100th monkey has finally learned a skill and so the skill can officially enter the pool of collective knowledge. And all humanity benefits, because that is the nature of common sense. In this regard, common sense can be thought of as a fruit from the tree of the grace of Understanding.

The third chakra, which is located in the solar plexus, is the center of your personal identity and, so, of your sense of self. Self-esteem, self-respect, and personal responsibility are centered directly in the solar plexus. Without a doubt, however, self-esteem is the epicenter of this chakra, like the maypole around which all other matters of the third chakra spin.

The "ingredients" that make up self-esteem are essentially the same ingredients that energetically contribute the most to your health. Self-esteem is an integrated set of qualities that serve as positive-energy supply lines to your major organs. The absence of these qualities renders you emotionally and psychically powerless, regardless of how much education or status, wealth or external power you may have acquired. None of those external props of protection are of any use, because they cannot protect even the most powerful individuals from their greatest fear, which is that someone or something has the ability to humiliate them. As long as we suffer from low self-esteem—and it is a suffering—we will both fear others and crave their approval.

Every inner skill, from the ability to heal oneself to the ability to listen deeply and receive inner guidance, then act on it, requires us to develop self-esteem with the greatest soul stamina, beginning with the graces of this chakra. The absence of self-esteem causes us to compromise our personal power and often to betray ourselves for lack of courage or integrity. And the stress of such actions becomes the negative energy currents that fuel disease. All the healing techniques available can bring us only temporary comfort when we lack the essential ingredient of self-esteem, which is ultimately needed to initiate life-transforming changes. Without that, we slip right back into the patterns of behavior that created the illnesses.

Penetrating Understanding: We are always seeking reasons why things happen as they do, but as you now know, events cannot be reasoned. You can look at the same object or situation in different ways. There's your way and there's my way. And then there is the way you would perceive something if you deeply understood that all events are simultaneously personal and impersonal. An event is personal to the individual in the midst of a situation, yet the event is also a gathering of impersonal forces governed by laws of motion and energy. Some of these laws are influenced slightly by the individual; most have their source in patterns of energy that cannot be identified. The impersonal laws, however, hold the key to the significance and higher purpose of an event. This is different from seeking the reason for personal suffering. Trying to understand the higher purpose and significance that is present within every experience elevates your focus toward wisdom and personal empowerment.

I once received a call from a man who had moved to the Middle East to head the financial office of a growing investment firm. Caught up in the financial windfalls of the oil markets and the real-estate development companies, Lanny and his associates disregarded their ordinary, grounded common sense and overinvested in stocks and hedge funds. One partner, knowing that the investments were going bad, made a quick exit from the company and the country, leaving Lanny to shoulder all the responsibility for such huge multi-million-dollar losses that the company was effectively penniless. At the time he called me, Lanny had yet to inform the senior partners that their company was bankrupt. He asked me, "What should I do?" I told him that all I could offer was to lead him into a deeper perspective on the chaos now threatening his life—and his life was actually on the line. He had to break free of the grip of fear or he would never see his way out.

I consciously prayed for the grace of Understanding and common sense—and all the other graces—that could be given to me as I spoke with Lanny. Even with the little that I gleaned about his situation during our phone call, still I felt that his only way out was the wisdom route. That meant calling a meeting of his superiors and revealing the financial status of the company, explaining his reasoning for the investments and how they had gone bad when the global market crashed. Common sense maintains that someone who walks into even the most hostile environment with dignity and self-esteem will command respect. That is one of the natural laws written into our DNA. Lanny had to rely on these graces now more than ever, as he was about to deliver the worst news a corporate board could hear. I knew that if he could truly understand what I was saying to him—not intellectually, but deeply within his soul—then he would be guided by this grace.

Finally, after a long conversation with Lanny and his wife, I asked him what he intended to do. "I don't know," he said. "I'm not sure. I think the only thing I can do is to call a meeting and inform them directly of the status of the company. I don't see any alternative."

It's hard to appreciate how grace works in our life, but in my experience it often sets up the path for us to take because there is no alternative. The grace of Understanding is a transcendent force that directs our attention to what is necessary and useful. It would not have served Lanny in this particular crisis to look backward to understand what had gone wrong with all of the investments he made. The search for that kind of information is ego-driven; its purpose is to blame someone else for things going wrong. A part of him may have wanted to do that, but grace directs you to what you need to do. He needed to find a way to survive what was ahead of him, not behind him. He needed an impersonal perspective about the unfolding global changes, of which his company was a part. He needed to understand that no organism—or organization—exists outside the dynamic of change taking place, no matter how many safeguards you put in place. The power of the whole is always dominant over the individual parts.

You should call upon the graces of Understanding and common sense to illuminate the depths of your own personal mysteries. The pursuit of self-knowledge, for example, is endless. There will always be more to understand about the nature of your own soul and the many gifts you have yet to discover about yourself.

As long as you are alive, you will encounter other crossroads and opportunities. You owe it to yourself to dig as deeply as you can into why you think as you do and why you believe what you do. You should ask yourself every year on your birthday, "What shall I do this year that will teach me something new about myself?" Never stop searching for the depths of your soul.

Similarly, these graces grant us the ability to help articulate for other people what they may need to understand about themselves. To offer the grace of Understanding to another should rightly be seen as an act of healing, because in being able to assist others, often you release them from profound suffering.

Invoking the Grace of Understanding: Like all graces, Understanding and its fruit, common sense, are not self-serving but elicit your capacity to serve others. They are forces that rebuild your life so that you can help others heal. There is no end to the influence a grace can have on your life, but no grace can be commanded. You invoke its power through prayer, and it is released into your life to penetrate your situation, not to make the situation go away but to heighten your spiritual senses in response.

Understanding and common sense help you grasp how the Universe works and how you can reason like a mystic while cleverly disguised as an ordinary mortal. The universe is governed by laws, yet those laws are governed in turn by the Divine. If you can understand that system, you will grasp the essence of healing. Pursue your own mysteries. Never run away from what you do not understand about yourself; that part of you does not evaporate just because you don't want to look at it. What you do not like or what you fear becomes a psychic free radical in your system. And just as physical free radicals lead to devastating ailments, those shadow fears eventually become a psychic disorder and perhaps a destructive pattern in other areas of your body or life. Use the grace of Understanding to see yourself clearly so that you can serve others with that same grace.

Prayer for Understanding: I seek the grace of Understanding in all matters of my life so that I may clearly see beyond the obvious and the personal. I ask to see the wisdom path and to understand the deeper truths about my own nature. May I always use the graces of Understanding and common sense in the service of others, and may I always be able to act on the guiding instincts that flow, even without my needing to ask, from the grace of common sense.

THE FOURTH GRACE: Fortitude

The grace of Fortitude refers to a quality of courage that goes well beyond the kind associated with standing up for ourselves, or even, as the dictionary defines fortitude, the strength to bear misfortune or pain calmly and patiently. The grace of Fortitude is essential for those who have awakened, for example, to the challenges of their highest spiritual potential. I realize that "highest spiritual potential" is a phrase that needs to be defined, and that is probably the best way to get to the core of Fortitude.

Penetrating Fortitude: The ego associates "highest potential" with the perfect occupation that will not only guarantee our success, but also guarantee that we will be admired with no possibility of humiliation. The ego imagines its highest potential to be the fulfillment of fantasies, some generated by ambition but many arising from the desire to prove our self-worth to those who have ignored or emotionally abused us. Listening for so long to people's descriptions of their ideal highest-potential fantasy, I have come to the conclusion that most of us imagine self-serving, high-end ambitions that essentially represent the end of all earthly problems. Rarely has anyone imagined that his or her highest potential could be a path of service that also includes right livelihood, such as creating an economically feasible way to care for the elderly or new ways of utilizing barren farmland. Some people might discover that their highest potential is invisible, that they offer their greatest service to others by holding them in prayer through difficult times.

I frequently put entire groups on the spot by asking this question: "What if an angel came down and offered you two choices? The first is the highest potential your ego desires, with all the bells and whistles and applause and admiration you are craving—except that it's really not your highest potential. The other choice is far less grandiose in appearance yet far more potent as a means of making a difference in the world: becoming a vessel of grace in service to others, though many of them will never even take notice of you. Which would you choose?" After I employ my customary methods of pressuring audiences for honesty, most people admit that they would choose their fantasy of their highest potential, even when offered the authentic alternative, because they would want the experience of abundance, security, admiration, and fame. On occasion some people even admit that they would want the power to make others feel bad for having humiliated them.

Potential, by definition, is something we grow into. In this context, our highest "spiritual" potential is not something a fragile ego could ever value, because the fragile ego can seek only to serve itself. Not until we set about the task of investigating our fragility can we begin to construct an inner scaffolding solid enough to withstand the battles we continually wage between who we are within our ego and who we long to be within our soul. Even the need to search for our highest potential is a destined battle between our ego and soul that is encoded in our spiritual DNA. We cannot help but wonder if there is "more" for us "out there" somewhere. But our ego often jumps in and confuses the process, corrupting the genuine search for spiritual identity with a quest for the ideal physical situation with a promise of monetary security. Maybe that Holy Grail, says the ego, is to be found in the next romantic relationship, or in the next town, or in the next job. Our experiences take us down this path, weaving us through disappointments and accomplishments, heartaches and heartthrobs. Life moves us ever forward, always on a path of discovering more about our potential.

But what exactly is this potential? The word refers to our capacity to become spiritually illuminated and, so, spiritually empowered. The goal of life is spiritual empowerment—to learn to use the power of our souls in acts of creation guided by divine instruction. This is a mystical perspective, not a religious one. Your soul does not belong to a religion; only your body and mind participate in religious rituals, if you happen to be a part of a religion. Your soul is a cosmic force that creates through every breath you take. The goal is to become conscious of what you are doing with your breath, the quality of your thoughts, your emotions, and what you believe to be true about life. Breath, thoughts, emotions, and ideas are your vessels of power. Your potential grows as you exert conscious dominion over these forces and all that influences you, blocking the negative and embracing truth. You can know this a thousand times, read about blocking negative thoughts and opening up to positive ones a million times, but it is nothing compared to actually experiencing the power of just one of your thoughts in an actual act of creation. To actually experience your own self in slow motion, receiving an inspiration, then forming a thought, then reshaping that thought into a choice, then making a choice, then watching that choice flow out of your field of personal energy and into the greater field of life, influencing all of life—that would truly be a moment of mystical awakening. Then you would really begin to understand what it means to become illuminated—to become filled with truth, which is another word for light. (The Islamic tradition includes the 99 Beautiful Names of Allah, two of which are Haqq and Nur, Arabic for "Truth" and "Light," respectively.) Truth is power, and becoming strong enough as a soul to consciously realize cosmic truth while living as a human being in the land of illusion, as Buddha would say, is the ultimate challenge for each human being. This is the test of this journey of life: how much truth can you absorb on this journey of illusion while still living within the illusion?

The progression of life experiences moves us along a path with only one objective: the empowerment of our spirits. One way to think of this journey is in terms of how we progress through the stages of power that we experience: begin with training for and holding a job; move on to building a career and then to having the mystical experience of being called to a vocation, which represents our highest spiritual potential. This analogy elegantly explains the different expressions of the grace of Fortitude. Each of us has had the experience of getting our first job, usually in our teenage years. The challenges we face in holding down a job are minimal because at that "job" level, we are not responsible for running the company, making payroll, or planning for the future. Our "potential" for developing the power to effect any real change is minimal at best, and in such circumstances, the external world has more potential power.

While holding down a job, your concerns, at least initially, are not likely to be focused on making life better for the other employees. The balance of power is such that you would be more inclined to "mind your own business." It takes enough courage at this level to show up for work and mingle with your co-workers. The sort of courage you need to rely on at this stage is survival courage—knowing whom to trust, when to speak up, how to function within a group, and how to protect your personal responsibilities. Courage of this kind is indeed a grace, but it is Fortitude diluted, so to speak.

Eventually, however, you begin to want to have more influence over your environment. To extend your field of influence, you must progress to the next stage, which is a career. A career requires you to shift the focus of power to your inner resources. The intellect needs to be honed and advanced along with other skills. Strategic thinking and more refined capacities of observation need to be developed. How well you process data, think through problems, and arrive at solutions matters more, because the consequences have a far greater impact at the career level than at the job level. You now have to think of how your choices affect the well-being of others. Ascending to this position, you need a different sort of courage, one that begins to tap into the grace of Fortitude. When you act in the service of others, a grace intensifies, just as the fragrance of perfume is an intensified version of cologne.

In order to appreciate what it means to be called to a vocation, which is the next stage, we need to address another characteristic of Fortitude. Keep in mind what I said earlier about the grace of Understanding, specifically, that it grants you the capacity to perceive beyond ordinary reasoning and see into the laws of nature that are present within any situation. Now look back at events or moments in your life when you needed courage. Situations that require courage most frequently involve the polarity of good and evil. We live in an archetypal universe that functions on countless polarities, such as male and female, day and night, left and right brain, right and wrong, good and evil. The root of all fear is precisely this polarity. Over the years I have encountered many people who wear talismans around their necks for "protection," and although they are loath to say the word "demon," they also wear crystals, rabbits' feet, and other good-luck charms as their way of battling evil.

Don't get me wrong. I believe that evil is real, just as goodness is real. Fortitude is the grace that specifically protects us from encounters with evil in whatever form it takes. And evil has many manifestations, from child abuse to abuse of animals and the environment, from corrupt governments to genocide. The absence of civil rights in society as a whole is an evil. It takes enormous fortitude to stand up to the perpetrators of institutional policies that abuse innocent people, because you are battling evil on behalf of those who cannot do so themselves without a great leader. Heroes who have taken up exactly such causes include Gandhi, Martin Luther King, Jr., and Susan B. Anthony.

When you are working within the field of Fortitude, you may end up in a situation in which you have no choice but to help out. You may start an organization on behalf of a particular cause, even though this is something that you never intended to do. Some form of humiliation is often part of the picture, so you may face obstacles that will humiliate you while you are trying to ground your vision in everyday reality. The reason for the humiliation is mystical in that you are forced to relinquish your personal vision of how something should be accomplished, allowing for the divine plan to be set into motion. Finally, through some unforeseen turn of events that usually marks the beginning of divine intervention, something or someone will help you succeed in ways that you could never have anticipated. The success may not be huge by earthly standards, but following the humiliation, if you continue with Fortitude in the face of adversity, inevitably the most appropriate expression of success will unfold.

One striking example of this grace in action is the environmental work of Al Gore. All the while Gore was involved in politics, he was also involved with environmental causes, although most of America was unaware of that during his vice-presidential years and his run for president in 2000. Although Gore won the popular vote against George W. Bush, Bush and the Republican administration in several key states managed to maneuver a win, and Gore conceded the election and retreated into his work as an environmentalist. This drained Gore's political currency at that time—indeed, he was often criticized for seeming to concede so readily instead of fighting to the bitter end—but his "retreat" should be recognized for what it really was, a return to his highest spiritual potential.

The release of his documentary film An Inconvenient Truth brought the environmental movement into the forefront of the global community in a way no other single event had done. In bringing forth this message, Gore faced further criticism and lack of support from jealous colleagues and threatened lobbyists, even as he inspired millions around the world to change their environmental lifestyles. Winning both the Academy Award for his film and the Nobel Peace Prize for his work, Al Gore has continued his efforts to lead the world into a new era of environmental consciousness, accomplishing far more as what I would call an "environmental mystic" than he ever could in the political forum, where his message would have to be carefully edited, if not repressed completely.

Progressing from job to career, we move on to our "calling," our soul's vocation. But note that a vocation is precisely that—you are called, as the Latin root of vocation implies. A vocation isn't something that you can force or gain access to intellectually. It happens when—and if—you are ready. But a career with Fortitude, so to speak, is a target attainable by everyone. To be of service to others through your inner gifts, your intuition, your courage, your talents, and your creativity is possible for all those who are willing to respond to the needs of others. Toward this end, you must see yourself as healed, as having completed the unfinished business of your past. While you may visit your wounds every now and again, you can no longer emotionally or mentally reside in that contaminated psychic field, continually processing wounds that are decades old. Your focus has to be in the present moment. This is where your power is, and being in the present is what your health requires.

Invoking the Grace of Fortitude: Everyone needs courage. It takes courage even to manage the fearfulness that can fill the privacy of our thoughts and emotions. But beyond mere thoughts and emotions is the intuitive guidance on which we must rely to negotiate the many choices that chart the course of our daily lives. Most people reading this book think of themselves as intuitively awake. Intuitive guidance by its very nature is guidance that "defies gravity"; that is, instruction that comes from the mystical realm and supplants the laws of logic and reason. It takes great courage to follow such guidance, because this guidance is often neither reasonable nor logical and can even appear to be foolhardy. That is when you have to rely most on your spiritual senses and find a level of courage that goes beyond your ordinary reasoning skills and into the inner domain of faith and grace, the instruments of the mystic.

Prayer for Fortitude: I ask for the grace of Fortitude to keep me steady in times of chaos and uncertainty. It is easy to be seduced into fear, and once fear gets hold of my thinking, it is difficult to break free of its influence. It is, as Teresa of Ávila described it, a reptile in my interior castle. I ask that this grace keep me alert and surround me like a castle wall with a field of grace powerful enough to help me stay centered, whether in the privacy of my own thoughts or in my interactions with others. Let fear never take command of my thoughts, my heart, my actions, or my soul.

THE FIFTH GRACE: Counsel

We all know what it means to get advice from a friend or to go to a counselor to work through emotional or psychological concerns that we are unable to resolve on our own. These examples of basic counsel, once again, qualify as eau de toilette or cologne rather than pure perfume. Advice can be well intentioned, for example, yet lack wisdom. A counselor may be well trained academically but unable to overcome personal biases in certain matters. The grace of Counsel is present in all these instances, but not in its perfume strength.

At its highest level, the grace of Counsel grounds mystical truths with human reason. This is what Buddha and Jesus attempted to do through their teachings—reveal truths that the ordinary person could grasp and then begin to work toward. Buddha's teaching that "all is illusion," for example, is a mystical truth, not a literal one. If I dropped a large book on your foot, that would not be an illusion. You would feel the pain of an unabridged dictionary, because it is big and heavy. Telling you that such a weighty tome was an illusion would be ridiculous, at least on the literal level of meaning.

But on the mystical level, we must approach the scenario from a completely different angle. When the Buddha spoke about illusion, he didn't mean physical realities such as the weight of one object relative to another. The specific element I believe he was referring to is power. As always, we return to the fundamental ingredient of the human experience, which is the power of your soul and how you manage that power through what you believe. The pursuit of cosmic truth takes on enormous significance when you realize that the great spiritual masters were teaching that mystical truths are the ultimate means of personal empowerment and inner liberation. A mystical truth is not something you "learn," but something that is revealed to you; and in the process of revelation, you are transformed by the power of that truth. It becomes a part of your own consciousness. You are no longer separated from divine truth, no longer merely searching for divine truth; truth has found you and transformed you. Such truth shatters the limitations of ordinary reason.

You can study the mystical truth "All is One," for example, for years. But one day while you are just sitting at your desk, you might find yourself quite suddenly elevated into an altered state of consciousness, lifted into a vast domain of the cosmos in which the entire universe seems to fit inside of you while you see it all around you simultaneously. You are filled with a consciousness experience of the truth that "All is One," a truth that is literally—divinely—incarnating in your blood and bones, in your psyche and soul. In this microsecond of a mystical experience, you realize that a grand cosmic truth has paid you a visit and transformed your very being for all time. Nothing can or will ever look the same again. In all grains of sand, you see the universe. And in the universe, you can imagine every grain of sand. No human face will ever look ordinary again. Yet your reason cannot convert this experience into words that can convey the force, the power, the majesty of the actual visitation of the Truth itself.

Mystical truth gives you the means to learn how to reason as a mystic, combining the brilliance of cosmic wisdom with the strategic capabilities of the human intellect. Yes, the book hit your foot. But what really matters is whether you lost any emotional or psychological power as a result of my dropping the book on your foot. Could you remain detached from the experience, as Buddha taught his disciples to do? Or did you find the experience so humiliating that you have an issue you now need to "process" in order to forgive, indicating that you did indeed "attach" to it? If that's the case, the experience now owns a part of your spirit, controlling your emotions. If, instead, you had remained detached and in control of your perceptions and your emotions, you might have experienced a physical sense of pain, but you wouldn't take it personally. The real secret to health is not to retrieve your power from all the injuries of the past, but to become so clear and wise as a soul that you do not lose your power over illusions in the first place. See clearly. Recognize illusions. Keep your soul intact at all times. Look for God in the smallest details of your life, not in the grand scheme. You can't comprehend the grand scheme, so don't go there. Stay where you belong—clearly focused on the present and spiritual journey that is your life.

Penetrating Counsel: The grace of Counsel seeks truth, so we must ask what precisely we mean by truth. Again, let me refer to the example of perfume. At the level of eau de toilette, truth is diluted to "that which is true for me but not for you." The critical ingredient that makes something a universal truth is missing. I was born in Chicago; for me, that is true. But because it is not true that all people are born in Chicago, it falls into the category of eau de toilette. Anything, in fact, that is personally true falls into that category, particularly subjective sentiments, because feelings are especially mutable and shift from day to day. They are the least reliable containers of truth.

Scientific and historic facts are almost as unreliable, because we are always discovering new facts that challenge or completely change what we believed previously. What was an undeniable truth in science yesterday quickly becomes false following a new discovery. Wine is bad for your health one day, good for your health the next. Pluto is a planet for some astronomers, but no longer for others. How many scientists in the same field argue constantly about what's factual? Global warming, for example, is still a myth for some of the less enlightened factions of the scientific community. And, so, I put sciences such as biology, chemistry, pharmacology, and even astronomy in the category of "cologne truths," because the truth they produce is only temporary.

Then there are "perfume truths." These truths are constant and universal, never changing, applying equally to everyone. Mathematics is a universal science with fundamentals that are constant and universal. The laws of physics and nature, such as gravity, cause and effect, magnetism, and the rhythm of the tides, are constant. Included in this category are mystical truths that are also constant and universal, such as the energetic principles of yin and yang, as well as these:

- What is in One is in the Whole.

- As above, so below. Within every physical event is hidden a symbolic counterpart that represents the higher or cosmic purpose for the event.

- What goes around comes around, a truth also known as the law of karma.

- Forgiveness is the great healer of the soul.

- The truth will set you free.

- Energy precedes the creation of matter.

- Thought precedes form.

- The archetype of death and rebirth, recognized in the myth of the phoenix rising from the ashes, is a formative force in every person's life.

- All experience is impersonal. How we interpret our experiences, whether we see them as negative or positive, failures or successes, is what personalizes the events of our lives.

- Every life has a purpose that unfolds amid a journey of endless opportunities. The choices we make, and the underlying motivations that determine these choices, influence the quality of the next opportunity.

No one lives outside the governing force of these laws. Further, these mystical truths belong to no religion. They are universal, transcendent of any religious tradition. With or without the man-made politics of religion, these truths still hold sway. They are cosmic principles governing the evolution of the human spirit. They are not "reasonable" truths, in that the human mind is incapable of comprehending the full meaning of these teachings. These are truths that must be personally experienced through an act of mystical revelation. When you are gifted with a personal encounter with the power of one of these truths, it's as if the power of that truth and all it represents melts directly into your soul. Such an experience shatters the limited vista of your five senses, and it may render you incapable of offering a reasonable or intelligent description of what you have realized to be true about life as a result. Imagine, for instance, that you had an out-of-body experience or a near-death experience a century ago, before humanity knew of the existence of the more than 200 million other galaxies that fill this endless universe of ours. Back then, the Milky Way was the only galaxy, the center of the Universe. Now imagine that you returned from this cosmic—indeed mystically galactic—experience with the realization that Earth was but a tiny, tiny part of an enormous cosmic blanket of galaxies, suns, planets, and stars. Your entire sense of proportion—of size, dimensions, life, even how you saw yourself—would be shifted instantly. But how would you communicate that to others? Could you? Would you even try?

Even mystics have this kind of difficulty interpreting how a cosmic truth can take command of your lower senses—and yet it does. After one such experience, Teresa of Ávila said that her brain and her senses wanted to join in the experience in order to comprehend the full measure of the mystical domain, but she found that "they were incapable of joining me." She could say only that such experiences left her filled with ever-deepening sensations of love—not ordinary love but vast cosmic love that, again, was indescribable.

Many mystics from both Western and Eastern traditions have experienced extraordinary encounters with inner divine phenomena, as I've already mentioned. While their experiences may vary according to their traditions, the common ground that they share is that they have accomplished a sojourn into the spiritual realm, a realm most human beings visit only through books or faith. These mystics bear witness to the truth that there is a divine presence that participates in our lives in ways we will never be able to comprehend—that, too, is a mystical truth. One way in which some mystics have described an expression of this divine presence is by saying they came to realize that this universe is governed by both physical and mystical laws. Physical laws govern the order of the physical world, such as the law of gravity, the movement of the tides, the speed of the planets, the cycles of nature—all the constants that manage the systems of life.

Mystical laws, on the other hand, are porous while at the same time ever-present and constant. They are "truths" more than they are "laws" per se, and yet we are governed by these truths. The law of karma is one such truth: we are responsible for the causes and effects of our actions, yet a sincere act of love or generosity can wipe the slate clean of a thousand dark sins, according to many mystics who understand the meaning of the cosmic Buddha of Compassion and the Sacred Heart of Jesus, or the "cosmic heart of the sacred."

To say that truth can set you free, or that the truth heals, can sound vague, and yet those mystical laws are literal truth. At one of my workshops, an angry man said to me, "So long as I can speak my truth, I'm fine." I asked him to share one of his truths with me.

"I need people to understand where I'm coming from," he said, "and what my emotional needs are." This man was burning up with rage, not truth, and it showed in his hands and feet, which were disfigured with arthritis. "Your hands look like they could be quite painful," I said. "Why don't you try forgiving all the people you are so angry with? Why don't you let that truth heal you?"

He was infuriated by what I said. He made it plain that I obviously hadn't heard a word he had said and, furthermore, that I had no idea of all he had been through, so how could I even suggest that he suddenly become forgiving? That ended our conversation, but I couldn't stop thinking about it. What would have happened to his mind, his body, and his spirit had he released his illusions about his wounds and his "truth" and taken hold of the mystical power of forgiveness? That power would have set him free and healed him, ending his fire and rage and healing the burning in his joints and in his heart. The truth does indeed set you free, but you have to be able to hear it, absorb it, and use it.

The grace of Counsel is not an easy grace with which to be gifted, even slightly. The great mystics have often written that theirs is a painful journey. The kind of pain they are speaking about, however cosmic, is not physical, but the deep interior pain that comes with knowing that truth is incomprehensible to the ordinary mind. They come to realize, for example, that "All is One," not just intellectually, but through the eyes of their soul. That "oneness" is a cosmic truth that some of them can actually feel, as Francis of Assisi did. Imagine having sensitivities that allow you, compel you, to feel the fears of animals or the consciousness of trees. Or having such a grasp of human nature that you understand how an event will affect society, not because you're psychic, but because you have a profound knowing of how groups of people behave when they are paralyzed by fear. You would be able to see the inevitable cycles of destruction that have to occur in order to reestablish balance, but if you offered such counsel to society as a whole, it would fall on deaf ears. Destruction and fear could often be avoided if only people would listen to the counsel of those who can read the patterns, but such information strikes the ordinary mind as useless and impractical, or even as nonsense. How many people are ready to believe that animals have feelings and that they, too, are frightened about the environment? In the face of such great truth, many of the mystics write, the pain of having to be silent and keep one's own counsel is enormous.

Now let's reduce the proportions of "counsel" from the grand scale of receiving cosmic revelations to the local level of being a container for a friend's secret. Just think of the times in your life when you have been asked to keep someone's counsel. You look your friend in the eye and say, "Oh, no, I wouldn't tell a soul." But if you're like most people, you tell someone else immediately, making that person swear not to mention anything about the information you've just shared. Few people in that instance then pause and admit, "I've just betrayed my good friend, because I gave my word not to tell anyone and I just broke my word." Holding someone's counsel takes grace, because the ego wants to gossip—especially if the news is tragic or involves the breakup of a romance. Gossip makes people feel as if they are a part of a secret society, that they know something no one else knows, and that someone else's life is in worse shape than theirs. That's what sells millions of supermarket tabloids every week.

Truth, on the other hand, is a force of transformation, which is why people fear the truth. Truth always causes change. There is no such thing as absorbing the power of a truth and having your life remain the same. In some way, at some level, every truth changes your life. This mystical phenomenon is also why truth has the power to heal and clean out the soul. This is why you have to build up the stamina to manage the power of truth. The temptation to counsel others for personal gain is precisely what requires us to continually revisit our dark passions and work with the graces. You cannot reflect on the influences of your dark passions once and think that you're done with them, and now on to the graces. Once you are aware of these shadowy forces, you must remain in intimate contact with them, just as you remain in an ever-deepening relationship to your graces. No one lives just in the light, any more than he lives only in the dark. The day contains the night and the night always moves into the day, like the black dot within the white swirl in the yin-yang symbol. The same is true of our natures.

We must learn how to absorb the power of truth, beginning with an examination of what is true about our dark passions. The discovery of your inner graces is contained within this process, as you simultaneously begin to detach from negative beliefs or attitudes that you realize are simply not true. This isn't easy to do. We start with our personal beliefs and continue with beliefs that are more impersonal and so have a greater capacity to shift the field of our reality. I often ask my students, "What do you need to believe about your version of God? Do you need your God to be born on December 25? Do you need your God to take on the image of a man and be a father figure? Or do you prefer the image of a Goddess as mother and life-giver? Or are you more into pantheism? If so, what would happen if you had a mystical experience and suddenly found yourself hovering outside your physical body, away from this planet somewhere in the vastness of universal space, dead center in the realization that the many gods of planet Earth do not exist anywhere else? What if you became saturated in the truth that out in the vastness of eternal space, the only force that exists is a sense of divine, nameless Light—no costumes, no churches, no synagogues, no ashrams, no mosques, nothing. Just Light."

For some people at my workshops—indeed, quite a few—such a revelation was just too much to take in. They still needed the costumes provided by their respective religions, which is fine. But divine light has no religion—and that's the cosmic truth.

Invoking the Grace of Counsel: Introduce the practices of reflection and self-examination into your daily life, focusing on your ability to identify and articulate ever-increasing insights into what the truth is about who you are and how you view the field of your life. Begin by asking:

- Did you compromise speaking the truth in any way today, and if so, how and why? Note how many times you will excuse not speaking the truth because you don't want to make someone else uncomfortable. In doing this exercise, you'll begin to appreciate that people fear the slightest use of truth, because it's so powerful. Even answering a question directly intimidates most people, including something as simple as, "Is it okay with you if we eat at the Italian restaurant this evening?"

- Examine your personal beliefs on a regular basis, such as what you accept as true about yourself or life or God. "I'm always unlucky in love," "I'm always unlucky with my investments"—these are illusions, not truths. Counsel yourself through the practice of inner reflection, examining your beliefs and noting those that are illusions. Replace those illusions with a cosmic truth, such as "All things are possible with God" or "Fear is the absence of faith in my own life purpose. So long as I have life, I have purpose."

- Do you fear truth? Is it difficult for people to share their insights about you?

- What do you believe that you know is not true but hold on to anyway? And why do those illusions have such power over you?

- What truths would you like to make a part of your inner life? Take one at a time and reflect on what it means for a month. Look for that truth in action in your life. Live by it. Live in it. Live with it.

- Look for the presence of truth in counseling others. Look beyond illusion. Be mindful of your truth, the other person's truth, and the governing presence of mystical truth.

Prayer for Counsel: I ask to be shown the truth within myself that I might never harm others with my illusions. I ask for the stamina of spirit to contain the transforming power of cosmic truths as I come to understand them. Let truth be the guiding force in my life. Let the grace of truth continue to sustain me and to heal me when I slip into illusion.

THE SIXTH GRACE: Knowledge

The grace of Knowledge in its purest form manifests through us as a revelation about the nature of the Divine. In rare instances, one can have a revelation of knowledge directly from God, as occurred in the transmissions of Rumi, who was said to speak his mystical poetry while in a state of ecstasy. Teresa of Ávila began the writing of her masterpiece, *The Interior Castle*, with the vision of a crystal holding the soul's seven mansions. Sometimes the transmission may come through an intermediary, as when the prophet Muhammad received the word of God, which was to become the Quran, through the angel Gabriel. Scientists who are able to combine the best of their genius with their receptive intuitive skills to bring forth breakthroughs in medicine are also working with revealed knowledge in an effort to help humanity. Revealed knowledge does not just come through saints and mystics, though I refer to them continually because their work is so well known. Revealed knowledge is given to those who are vessels of service to humanity in ways great and small.

This grace is the door to that most secret garden of knowledge that is beyond the grasp of human reason. This knowledge may be expressed through a deepening comprehension of the human experience in relationship to the Divine, or an enrichment of the mysteries inherent in our quest to understand the essence of God in which a person sees a revelation of a cosmic law in action within a scientific field. That was the experience, for example, of Isaac Newton when he understood the law of gravity. Or this knowledge may take the form of a medical discovery—a much-needed vaccine, perhaps—that has baffled the ordinary range of understanding because of a missing piece of data. When experiment upon experiment fails to provide that data, it sometimes is revealed through a moment of inner revelation.

Sacred scriptures were no doubt inspired with the grace of Knowledge, which synthesizes our intellectual skills with our spiritual senses so that we may perceive a single interior message with absolute clarity. This is a grace that draws us inward toward the pursuit of the knowledge of God as it expresses itself through our inner yearnings and personal mysteries that cannot be solved or satisfied by the riches of the world. Knowledge gives us a ferocious craving for divine intimacy, an experience that is so completely beyond reason that it has led many mystics to use only one word to describe it: ecstasy.

Penetrating Knowledge: The grace of Knowledge shares the location of the sixth chakra, which is the energy center of the intellect, the mind, the brain, and intuition. This chakra is headquarters for the perceptions, myths, beliefs, and attitudes that you carefully or carelessly weave together into the reality-tapestry of your life. While the spiritual senses are vastly important to all the chakras and all the graces, the sixth chakra stands as a mystical turning point. To appreciate the inner evolution of your spiritual or intuitive senses under the umbrella of this grace, we must separate what is considered "knowledge" into our now-familiar categories of eau de toilette, cologne, and perfume.

The three categories of knowledge are information, active knowledge, and gnosis, or knowledge revealed through grace. Your spiritual senses develop through these three levels, moving from organic survival gut instincts to an awareness of inner guidance motivated by personal need and, at last, to a devotion to mystical illumination. One way to appreciate the elegant manner in which this evolution takes place is through an analogy of three men, each coming from one of those levels of consciousness, interacting within the same garden.

Someone focused only on information would certainly know what each plant needed from the environment, when the vegetation was ripe, and whether a plant was edible. If the plant produced edible fruits or vegetables, they would indeed nourish him and he would know how to prepare them. He would know what fertilizers and pest-controlling plants to use to get the most out of the land, because the instinct to survive ranks practicality and productivity high on the value scale. It is important to see, feel, touch, taste, and smell the ripeness of one's efforts to know that all is well in the garden of life.

The next person looks over the same garden knowing all the same environmental information, but in addition he knows the interior nature of the plants. This man has active knowledge that some of the plants are not just edible, but also medicinal. He knows which herbs and plants are useful for healing chest colds, indigestion, and fevers or reducing inflammation. He has learned how to prepare medicinal teas that relieve aches in the body or help one relax. For this man, a garden is not only a means of nourishment. It is also a living pharmacy.

The third man knows how to tend to the earthly needs of all the plants, and he is aware that his garden is a living pharmacy. But beyond that, he is humble and aware that, because these are living creatures, they are part of nature's collective soul. They, too, have a consciousness that is sacred. He prays in his garden and speaks to his companions. As he observes the eucalyptus plant, knowing that it contains properties of menthol that are healing for a cold, he is also connected to the power of gnosis, or sacred knowledge. He knows that the spirit of the plant is more powerful than the substance. The spirit of the plant animates the substance in an act of divine alchemy, converting the substance into a vessel through which a subtle energy merges with it, producing a refined healing force akin to homeopathy. He knows that if he were to tell the first man about this, he would think this knowledge was magic and superstition. The second man would be open to this knowledge, but, lacking in humility, he would be "loud and arrogant" with this sacred truth and so it would sound foolish coming from him. He has yet to learn the value of silence. And learning to listen in the bliss of undistracted silence and the comfort of inner humility is required for the gift of revelation.

The garden feeds each man abundantly. None is starved for lack of the other realms of knowledge or punished for actions that might poison the garden. The motivation to fertilize comes from instincts to survive, and these instincts are also an expression of the grace of Knowledge, but felt at the organic level—that is, God manifest in our blood and bones. One day the land will be poisoned and the garden will cease to produce life and the grace of Knowledge will draw us to realize instantly, "You are poisoning your own land." Grace never punishes; it always directs us to awaken. We make choices, and choices have consequences. We are not saved from the consequences of our choices, which is why we have an inherent fear of making choices. Lawyers thrive in their practices because we want to force others to be responsible for our choices, so we put others under contract in order to hold them accountable for the consequences of our own fears. We ultimately know that we are responsible for our actions and our choices. We were born knowing this truth, just as we are born knowing that killing another human being is a moral wrong. We are born already aligned to a natural law that governs our fundamental instincts as a species, and this natural law is also an expression of this inner knowledge that is deeply embedded in our spiritual DNA.

A Deeper Knowledge of Ourselves: Our spiritual senses are far more powerful than the rational mind, and within their natural interior impulses continually direct us to come into a conscious alignment with our souls; that is, to recognize that we are living but one path and that path is only a spiritual one. We have a sense, however dim, that there is an ultimate power somewhere—but where? We cannot stop searching for it, although that quest may take many forms, such as fame, goods, money, thrills, and drugs, to name a few. The immortal myths, legends, and even some fairy tales remind readers that the path they are seeking has been within them all along. Our lives are this spiritual quest—nothing more, nothing less. And our spiritual senses pull us along our interior route, transmitting impulses to us that mature as we do, shifting from survival instincts to a self-centered desire to know secret knowledge about ourselves, and finally—we hope—discovering a craving to experience the knowledge of God.

Grace is not a mystery to me. People are far more of a mystery, because we don't see ourselves as we really are. We think of ourselves as a rational species, when in fact we are fundamentally an intuitive species utilizing our rational skills to repress the high-functioning abilities of our spiritual senses. Rather than allowing our spiritual senses to develop naturally alongside our other skills, we repress our spiritual senses in early childhood, turning our full attention toward our rational intellect as our power base. And yet the impulses stemming from this grace have a way of expressing themselves. But having repressed these intuitive instincts for so long, we are more likely to express them in a negative form that thrives from our baser power-seeking instincts.

The craving for secret knowledge runs in our spiritual DNA because in its purest form, this desire is a craving for knowledge of God. Without developed spiritual senses, however, people will fill the void at the shadow ego level (or eau de toilette) with a myriad of social, political, or sexual secrets, gossip, cults, and secret organizations, because secrets represent contact with knowledge that has the power to transform our lives. In many schools of knowledge, from the mystery religions of Egypt and the Mediterranean to the early teachings of Kabbalah, there were legitimate reasons for secrecy. Perhaps the most urgent was to protect members from the potentially lethal opposition of outsiders. But there were also serious concerns about protecting the uninitiated from the possibility of inflicting harm on themselves and others through the misuse, purposeful or inadvertent, of advanced spiritual practices and techniques.

When the secret you are holding on to is something dark and ruthless, however, or when a group maintains secrecy to hide ego-based activities that benefit its members at the expense of others, there is great danger. Secrets—especially dark ones—can give you a shadow taste of the power of knowledge to transform the life of another person. Dark secrets represent the archetype of Dark Truth, so the need to "come clean" or to "confess" is more mystically liberating and psychically essential than you may have considered. No one can ever hold your life in the palm of his hand when your history has no secrets.

While grace is never really absent from your field, you can be intuitively numb. But the inability to perceive or sense the influence of grace does not eclipse the need for it. In the absence of the grace of knowledge, for example, you might experience a lack of discernment, a vulnerability that leads to negotiating your integrity and common sense. In other words we are willing to compromise the integrity of our soul in exchange for entry into a dark circle of power that gives the appearance of a social safety net, such as a secret society or even a "get rich quick" scheme. Many groups present themselves one way but in fact operate from behind the scenes by dark principles—which is to say no principles.

The grace of Knowledge certainly manifests positively at the ego level, as do all graces. For example, this grace expresses itself through countless ways in which people seek information for the betterment of humanity. The desire to improve the lives of others is an expression of this grace that finds its way into research laboratories, cancer treatment centers, environmental projects, and all other areas in which people pioneer uncharted territories of data in order to benefit life. It is irrelevant whether we are aware of being motivated by grace or goodness or humanitarian urges. All of these activities are expressions of the grace of Knowledge in that we are driven by an inner impulse to discover unknown elements in this universe. The drive to know the unknown—on whatever level it is pursued—is a metaphor for knowing the Divine.

At the cologne level, the pursuit becomes a more conscious effort to acquire knowledge of a transformational nature. This knowledge may be associated with secret codes that require the student to find a master instructor who is capable of passing on the secrets of the code. The Zohar used in Kabbalah is the most renowned of these coded scriptures. Scholars of these texts believe that because ancient Hebrew letters also represented numbers, a numeric code is hidden within the letters of the words. The numeric code translates to the cosmic meaning of the text, adding room for multiple dimensions of interpretation.

Astrology, numerology, tarot, and the enneagram are other forms of occult (meaning secret) arts that offer the student a means of cracking cosmic codes. The goal of the student, of course, is to find an advanced or mystical system of logic and order in the universe, which is yet another way of gaining access to the Divine Mind. The goal of a student devoted to the study of mystical wisdom contained in these fields of spiritual alchemy is to make personal choices in harmony with cycles of change as well as to understand the greater cosmic patterns of transition that guide human evolution and to continually examine the interaction between the personal and impersonal dimensions of the personal and cosmic domains.

As a rule, however, we turn to the occult arts to find a way to outwit earthly chaos. Rarely does one turn to a Tarot reader to find a way to advance on the spiritual path. The questions most people ask have to do with finances, relationships, and occupation. My personal experience as a medical intuitive for 25 years validates that point. Prior to writing *Entering the Castle*, I was rarely asked questions that directly related to spirituality. Many people exploring consciousness through this door are seeking to understand the practical relationship between the power of heaven and how it can be directed to influence events—mainly personal ones—here on Earth.

But from a different perspective, the desire to pursue the eso-teric arts is deeply indicative of the fact that we are seeking a way to encounter the Divine through the safety net of logic and rea-son. From the perspective of an astrologer, this is completely ratio-nal. After all, planetary cycles exist within the consistent laws of mathematics, thereby hinting at the possibility, indeed probabil-ity, that the creator of this vast universe must have a logical, con-sistent nature that can somehow be decoded. The secret must lie in understanding the relationships between the planetary forces and their individual characteristics, which operate in and out of synchronistic orbital patterns, as do our lives. We want to crack this code because deep in our spiritual DNA we know that our lives are influenced by the cycles of these planets. How exactly that happens, however, is not logical. We have a mystical connec-tion to the planetary forces through the mystical law that main-tains, "What is in One is in the Whole." The mechanics of that law are beyond human reason, even if the function of the law gov-erns our lives. And, so, we seek this knowledge and other esoteric knowledge, because we know it is the logical route to that which is not logical—namely, the nature of God.

Works of esoteric literature also reflect the grace of Knowledge in an unconventional way. One example is *A Course in Miracles*, which was channeled by Helen Schucman, and the works of Alice Bailey, an Englishwoman who channeled a library full of spiri-tual literature over the course of thirty years. The phenomenon of channeling is yet another form of interior spiritual dialogue that not only defies the gravity of reason, but also challenges how we envision the external or internal distance between the physi-cal and the divine dimensions. Without a doubt, a great percent-age of channeled work is the product of the imagination of the authors, as I learned from my own years in publishing. As an edi-tor, I received stacks of manuscripts from people who claimed to be channeling one spirit or another, including extraterrestrials and the spirits of former Egyptian pharaohs. Comparing those manuscripts to *A Course in Miracles* or the work of Alice Bailey, it seems clear to me that Schucman and Bailey were working in unison with a quality of grace that was not self-serving. Instead, their work came through them to the benefit of others.

And there are many other extraordinary expressions of the inner desire for a secret path to God. The South American Guaraní people, for example, believed in a Land Without Evil where the world still existed as it had been from the early days of creation. People were at ease with the gods in this place. The Guaraní believed that this land was their missing homeland, the place of their origin, and they set off on a quest to find it during the 16th century, just as South America was being wracked by the invasion of the Spanish conquistadores. Though unsure of exactly how to find the Land Without Evil, the Guaraní were certain that obtaining this knowledge would require sacred rituals—dancing night and day into states of trance and constant prayer, hoping that someone would be graced with a revelation of the map to a mythic homeland.

Invoking the Grace of Knowledge: A "reasonable" person might wonder how any group of people could believe in such a thing as the Guaraní people's mythic land, but the truth is that we all do. No matter how reasonable we think ourselves, our spiritual DNA is stronger than our rational minds, and it keeps us on a quest for the sacred, even if we do not call it by name. Indeed, that quest calls us. We are the incarnation of the sacred quest itself. We cannot stop ourselves from seeking the Divine. Perhaps the only choice we have is how conscious we want to be about this journey of becoming conscious. And when we reach the point of asking ourselves that question, perhaps we will be open to dropping the neutral language of "consciousness" and shifting to the vocabulary of the soul. The human experience is not just about becoming conscious; it's about becoming illuminated, becoming a person who has come into the knowledge of his graces and has awakened to an intimate relationship with the Divine.

Prayer for Knowledge: I ask that the grace of Knowledge guide my thoughts and illuminate my awareness of all that transpires within the vast resources of my mind. Grant me the inner light to enter into a deeper knowledge of who I am and help me to listen to that still, small voice that is unlike any other, that I might recognize truth when it is being revealed to me.

THE SEVENTH GRACE: The Grace of Wisdom

With the grace of Wisdom, we return to that commonly used phrase, "God must have a reason for why this happened to me." That reason cannot be found in logic or human rationality, but it can by seeking the grace of Wisdom. This grace, in its purest form, reveals guidance about who you are, how you are living, and how you are using the power of your creative soul, which is a much different perspective from that of human reason. Reason seeks personal justice, as if we have been wronged in some way. Wisdom assumes that no action is intended by the Divine to harm us; yet all actions must include the active ingredients of human consciousness in the constant balancing of yin and yang, the positive and the negative.

Penetrating Wisdom: The grace of Wisdom coincides with the seventh chakra, the most etheric of the chakras. The seventh chakra, linked to the pituitary or pineal glands in various yogic systems and corresponding to the crown of the head, is described as the energy center most receptive to the spiritual realm and to our spiritual life. Wisdom is truth acquired through experience; it is the capacity to consider the consequences of our actions seven generations into the future. Wisdom gives us the strength to recognize that life cannot be lived without pain, but that we can minimize our suffering by learning to make wise choices. If we don't learn from our experiences, we are fools and, as the wise adage warns, destined to repeat our mistakes. Experiences are meant to be teachers, events from which we extract lessons about the choices we make.

I grew up in a close-knit family that was held together by ethnic traditions, religion, and the rule of wise elders. All my grandparents came from Europe as teenagers, immigrating through Ellis Island in the early 1900s. They did what all immigrants did back then—they moved into their ethnic enclaves, immediately went to work, and, shortly after that, married. Hard work and family formed the backbone of their lives, along with saving money. Buying something on credit was unheard of for these wise elders, except, of course, for a home. Their philosophy was, "If you can't pay for it up front, you don't need it." Such wisdom was drilled into all of us grandchildren from the time we could walk.

"But I want them now," I once said to my grandmother on our annual shopping day in downtown Chicago. I was standing in Marshall Fields, the hallmark department store in Chicago when I was growing up. My grandmother had a tradition of taking each of her granddaughters on a special day downtown with her, including lunch, a movie, and shopping for one special treat. And this was my day. I had spotted a pair of shoes with heels that were too high, too "mature" for me, a 13-year-old. These inch-and-a-half-heel shoes were the loveliest shoes I had ever seen and I had to have them—I had to or I would just die. I knew I would, right there in the store. I would force myself. I would hold my breath until I turned blue.

My grandmother held her ground. "No," she said. "There'll come a time when you can get those shoes or any kind you want, but not now. You're too young. Get another pair."

"No, I want those," I said. "I'm not too young. I'm a teenager now. I'm a grown-up almost." But my eyes filled with tears because I knew she had won that argument. Then she asked me, "Why do you want to grow up so fast? Do you think it's easy being an adult? You will be an adult faster than you can imagine and you will stay an adult for the rest of your life, but you can never be young again. It's wonderful being your age and having a grandmother take you out for a day. Don't take that away from me, Carol. Stay young for a bit longer. I promise you, you won't regret it."

After that we left the shoe department and went to see the movie *Flipper*, which had just come out, about a boy and his pet dolphin. By the time we got to the movie theater, I had completely forgotten about the shoes and was already on to my next treat, which was hot buttered popcorn. Stay young a while longer and don't rush your life. My grandmother was right. Those years passed more rapidly than I thought possible, but I cherish her wisdom. The young part, well, that has now taken on new meaning, as we all tend to redefine the meaning of young with each passing decade. I adored my grandmother and I always will. (Incidentally, I was officially old enough to wear "high heels" at age 16, and guess who bought them for me? My grandmother—of course.)

Grandma was not the only wise elder in my family. All of my grandparents had that wise common sense that came from realizing they needed each other to survive, as immigrants but also as family. They bonded through love, humor, music, and weekend banquets. They had a way of judging whether a dispute was worthy of anger; observing their methodology was watching wisdom in action. Unless a deed was deceitful or dishonest, cruel or abusive, ah well, everyone was entitled to a bad day. "It's not worth it," was a favorite expression of my elders, as they weighed the consequences of having critical natures against the wisdom of learning to overlook meaningless squabbles.

Almost everyone is familiar with the wisdom of the great elders of the Native American traditions, such as Chief Joseph and Chief Seattle, who warned, as he noted the inevitable future of the red man, that the time of the decline of the white man's tribe would come as well. The words of this wise elder prophet foretold the end of his people, a people who related to the earth as kin, and their replacement by those who had no awareness that life was a sacred tapestry. He could see that the white man would pay a price for this arrogance, though it would take generations for that butcher's bill to come due.

Although multiple versions exist of his now-famous 1854 Treaty Oration, it is widely accepted that these are the words of Chief Seattle: "But why should I mourn at the untimely fate of my people? Tribe follows tribe, and nation follows nation, like the waves of the sea. It is the order of nature, and regret is useless. Your time of decay may be distant, but it will surely come, for even the white man, whose God walked and talked with him as friend to friend, cannot be exempt from the common destiny. We may be brothers after all. We will see."

Here is wisdom that extends far beyond the practical earth guidance of elders to children, transcending the personal and drawing upon cosmic wisdom. Chief Seattle is speaking not for himself but for his people. He is speaking as one who has accepted a decision that he may even see as originating not with "our good father in Washington," as he referred to the American president, but with divine forces that manage the destiny of all humanity. The red man and the white man are players in a larger cosmic drama, and on this day, Chief Seattle is saying, it is his tribe's turn to begin the journey of decline. But no one can escape that journey of decline, he notes, and that truth is not in the hands of any mortal. It is a common destiny, and he was able to see that the archetypal force of common destiny had descended on his people. This visionary insight is the grace of Wisdom in a true act of revelation, evidenced even further by the fact that the full content of his speech has continued to inspire countless numbers of people beyond his intended audience. It may well be, in fact, that his profound words are about to come into their full power as "the white man" now enters this same cycle of decline, sharing in the common destiny of all tribes to which Chief Seattle referred, this time brought about by environmental and ecological destruction.

Many people might balk at the idea that a divine force would include in its organic evolutionary plan of life the ruthless demise of the peoples of the earth. Yet here was a man—a chief and a visionary —who was given the grace to perceive that, in some way that is beyond the grasp of ordinary reason, no people, whether individual or nation, exist outside the governing cycles of death and rebirth.

Could any words of Chief Seattle's wisdom have shifted the environmental crises of our contemporary world? In an ideal universe, we might imagine leaders referring to words of wisdom in the same breath with the practical matters of the day, but this is far from an ideal world. It's a practical world that is fueled far more by fear than by faith and goodness. As a rule, goodness picks up the pieces after fear-based decisions have done the damage. Ask yourself how often you have paused in your own actions to position the wise choice against the fearful or foolish one. And then ask yourself: which of them won? Mind you, the wise choice does not mean the safe choice, because wisdom often dictates that you walk the path that offers you the most risk, precisely because you need to rid yourself of your fears rather than be controlled by them.

No one exists outside the cycle of death and rebirth. When it is necessary for a cycle of new life to begin, the old way must die. That is not cruel; it is essential. Suffering and pain are part of the cycle of change because, as Buddha so wisely taught, we cling to what we do not want to release and we fear the unknown. Wisdom is the grace to see what has to happen because there is no other way for the whole of life to renew itself. Wisdom is the grace to glimpse the cosmic compassion that is the nature of the Divine. We think in the immediate, in terms of how the events of today are affecting the stuff we own and the immediate plans we have for our lives; but celestial forces move the whole of life. If a forest gets destroyed, it is not a tragedy, because nature can replenish a forest or a lake or create a new one, even if it takes centuries. If nature gets disrupted in its capacity to renew itself, however, all of life will diminish. The whole perceives differently than does a particle. A particle must learn to think as if it were that whole being, because it is governed by the whole by virtue of being contained within the whole.

The grace of Wisdom also expresses itself through the experience of personal revelation. Teresa of Ávila was particularly known for her numerous experiences of direct revelation. She felt that she could reveal the contents of some of these inner dialogues with God, but that others were just for her. She noted, however, that dialogues with the Divine did not occur within the context of a conversation as such. Instead, they were multisensory, experiential events for which the human senses had no reference. But though these mystical experiences were indescribable with the limitations of ordinary vocabulary, they left their mark. Teresa experienced quantum leaps in the depth of her perceptions about human nature. Her understanding of the archetype of the mystical Soul's Journey became cosmic as opposed to Catholic, meaning that she became fluent in the nature of the mystical domain, transcendent of any religious tradition. And her capacity to love deepened in an effortless way, even as she increasingly became the target of resentment and jealousy from members of her own religious community as well as authorities in the town of Ávila, Spain, where she headquartered her main convent.

The Dalai Lama is a current example of someone who draws from the grace of Wisdom, as evidenced by his teachings and writings. But perhaps this grace is most evident in the wisdom that pours through the replies he offers to provocative questions about the Chinese invasion of his home nation of Tibet. Many times he has been asked how he feels about the Chinese after knowing how many of his monks and countrymen have been beaten or killed as a result of their occupation. His response has consistently been, "Compassion. I have compassion for them and for my people."

Compassion is a baffling response to those who live by the law of reason, because reason tells us that the Tibetans have suffered decades of brutality and abuse that has been ignored by the world authorities, who must have decided that there is little practical value in defending Tibet against a military power like China. This great spiritual master, who is the reincarnation of the Buddha of Compassion, is perhaps the living embodiment of this grace, if not all the graces. He is one for whom the effects of compassion need not be seen in order to be known. In his wisdom, compassion is a response of the perfected soul, an example of turning the other cheek in the face of violence and absorbing the pain of the aggressor. Who knows the depth of the Dalai Lama's personal grief? Grace does not erase personal pain by any means. But it does grant the gift of a higher perspective than any you could attain with the limited skills of reason. In these experiences of insight that are beyond the boundaries of the mortal landscape, it is grace that helps you to defy the gravity of earth so that you may take an enlightened view of the whole.

Using examples of saints such as Teresa of Ávila and the Dalai Lama may seem to put this grace beyond the reach of ordinary people, but that is not the case. My point is that this grace is very much a part of all of our lives. I use saints as models because their lives contain extreme examples of this grace, and because saints have the one ingredient so many of us lack when it comes to gaining access to grace—they are humble enough to pray for it. The grace of Wisdom comes to everyone, not only to highly evolved souls with big followings. If any two people could have indulged in intellectual arrogance, Teresa and His Holiness might have gotten away with it. But fame made Teresa all the more reticent and it has made the Dalai Lama all the more humble and loving. Wisdom dictates that the more you are seen, the less noise you should make. The grace of Wisdom is obvious in the writings of both Teresa and the Dalai Lama, because their teachings lead their students to become oblivious to the destructive influences of this world and to remain silent about the inner powers that unfold as they pursue the path of inner truth.

Invoking the Grace of Wisdom: Perhaps you are not accustomed to thinking, "What is the wise thing to do?" You may be familiar with basing your decisions on the best thing to do, or the right thing, or the most practical thing, but "wise" may not be a value that has seen a lot of action in your decision-making equations. Now consider what the grace of Wisdom represents: the presence of God unfolding guidance within the events of your life while you seek to respond with wisdom in the midst of the changes. Wisdom dictates that you recognize that you cannot ask to see what can never be shown to you; that is, you cannot ask, "Why did this happen to me?" That's a child's question. It is asked by people who think that the world revolves around them. In situations of loss or pain, such a question also assumes an injustice has been done that requires an explanation.

Wisdom recognizes that when a process of change has begun, ultimately no one person is responsible for any enormous enterprise of transition. All changes have multiple sources and points of origin, even though you might be able to identify one or two people who appear to be the initiators. Wisdom dictates that all crises have more than one level of origin—the level you can see and the many other levels of influence that rise as high as the cosmic plan of evolution and the common destiny of humanity. The question you must ask yourself then is "How wisely do I want to perceive this? Do I want to see this situation through wisdom or through woe?" Woe is the result of taking events personally, as if all pain and suffering were intended just for you.

Wisdom is the choice that recognizes pain and suffering as part of the human experience. It is inevitable that we will cause each other to suffer in some way. At times these actions will be deliberate and at times they will be unintended. It is wise to recognize yourself in everyone else. Wisdom allows you to melt into others, and the more you melt, the more compassion is awakened.

Seek the wise response in all events in your life. Ask:

- What wisdom is hidden in this?

- What is the wise way for me to respond?

- What changes are happening that are necessary?

- What changes am I fighting that are bringing me pain?

- If I am in pain, am I taking something personally that has nothing to do with me?

- Am I blaming someone for something that would have happened anyway?

Prayer for Wisdom: *I ask that the grace of Wisdom guide me on my path. Let me respond with wisdom to the problems and challenges of my life, rather than with fear and hostility. Let me build a soul with the stamina to absorb the grace of Wisdom so that I may serve the whole of* *humanity with the actions of my life, acknowledging as I now do that all I do, think, say, and feel influences the well-being of all life.*

LIVING THE GRACES

Life is not just active energy. Life is sacred, and that sacredness has a source that is divine. As you recognize the power of the graces within you, that divinity becomes apparent in sublime and subtle ways. The way you perceive the ordinary world shifts, for example, because nothing can look ordinary again when you are aware of the presence—or absence—of grace. Neither can you ever again look upon your problems as insurmountable. Rather, for someone who knows what it is to rely upon grace, the only realistic choice becomes the most unrealistic one: the choice to defy gravity by turning to your inner resources in combination with your external abilities. This is the true description of the whole human being.

Chapter Six

THE FIFTH TRUTH

Defy Gravity and Learn to Reason Like a Mystic

Both the Buddha and Bodhidharma, the Indian patriarch associated with establishing Zen Buddhism in China, are said to have remarked: "I am but a finger pointing to the moon. Don't look at me; look at the moon." The implication of this often-repeated saying is that the wise master was aware that his followers would look upon him as the ultimate manifestation of truth, and he cautioned them to bypass him for the more authentic target of their own inner enlightenment. Jesus told his followers, who were captivated by his miracles, "I tell you the truth, anyone who has faith in me will do what I have been doing. He will do even greater things than these" (John 14:12). Jesus knew that his healings appeared to be miracles to the unenlightened observer, but in fact they were a natural by-product of his many graces and the way he understood the intimate workings of the Divine, as expressed within the mystical laws of the universe that naturally empowered a fully awakened soul.

As human beings, Buddha and Jesus each underwent a complete transformation, a transfiguration in which the power of their souls became dominant over the temporal power of the body. Buddha attained enlightenment under the Bodhi Tree. Jesus came into his authority through his baptism by John the Baptist and later through his transfiguration on Mount Tabor before three disciples. Although full enlightenment or divine realization can be difficult to define, one way to imagine this level of consciousness is to consider that it embodies the precise harmony of the laws of the universe: energy precedes the creation of matter and cause precedes effect. Attaining this perfected harmony of soul and matter, truth free from illusion and love without limits, transformed the souls of Buddha and Jesus into fully awakened cosmic forces that could *defy gravity*. They resided in physical form and were certainly subject to the vulnerabilities of the physical world, yet their enlightened souls also knew how to draw on the higher governing laws that commanded their interior reality. And so, when Jesus declared, "Be healed," a physical disease yielded to his command and the individual was immediately cured. Time was not a factor, nor was the critical condition of the patient. Jesus was able to heal lepers and cripples, release demons from the possessed, and even raise Lazarus from the dead, because illness and fear and death were no match for the force of his consciousness, which was not anchored in the acquisition of earthly power. Yes, such reports appeared to be miracles then, as they still are now, but not to someone who has had the slightest experience of the inner power that Jesus and Buddha fully embodied. Their life mission, ironically, was not to perform miracles but to disprove the need for them by demonstrating that you could become a source for miracles in this world, if you understood the true nature of your soul and how to open fully to that power.

Obviously, Jesus and Buddha are the ultimate templates for the cosmic healer and the enlightened soul. But they did not incarnate to razzle-dazzle people with their capacity to walk on water and meditate for months without sustenance. Their task was to introduce new archetypal paradigms of consciousness, like unraveling the next wave of human potential, and to defy gravity—that is, to align physical life with spiritual nature. The magnificence of Jesus and Buddha is seen again and again in their capacity to illustrate that the soul is naturally in harmony with a domain of truth that transcends the limitations of the physical world. As challenging as it is to comprehend this mystical truth, it is true nonetheless. Through practicing a truth, you eventually embody or become that truth. As you become a truth, its power animates or transforms your soul into a vessel of that truth. This is how Jesus could command the forces of nature to do his bidding, though he could not command the will of another person. Jesus and Buddha became the truths they were teaching; they became fully congruent cosmic forces embodied as fully human beings. Jesus didn't merely teach love; he was love. Buddha didn't just teach about enlightenment; he embodied it.

As models for unconditional love, Jesus and Buddha set the bar rigorously high for the ordinary mortal. I suspect, however, that their message was not so much "Look what I can do," but "Look what you can do if you absorb the truth I represent." Few people will ever achieve full enlightenment or become saints capable of manifesting unconditional love. Yet for most of us it may be enough of an interior awakening to be able to defy gravity even in small ways, perhaps during a healing crisis or a period of deep personal transformation. Ironically, most of us have little awareness that every time we pray, we are attempting to defy gravity by asking for some form of divine intervention, or that any time we rely on our intuition for guidance, we are defying gravity by reaching for information from the energetic domain—said another way, information that is "weightless" in that it has a predictive or directive quality as opposed to a historic one.

Learning to defy gravity requires more than just the occasional intuitive hit, however. You must ascend to a refined realm of spiritual consciousness in which you learn to work in harmony with the laws that govern the subtle, silent nature of your soul. Mystical laws do not exist as independent rules that order the structure of our external life. Instead, these are the laws that influence our interior or spiritual life, like a parallel universe that contains all the same information, except that it lacks the influence of time, weight, space, and gravity. The next part of this journey introduces you to laws that, like the physical laws of nature, form an integrated system of truths. Whereas the physical laws govern that which has come into physical creation, these laws govern the dynamics of creation itself. The two sets of laws operate in tandem with each other, as energy flows into matter and matter, in turn, influences the flow of energy.

When a system of life lacks knowledge of one of these realms of law, that system automatically falls into patterns of dysfunction. The failure to realize that your attitudes influence your behavior, for instance, has a direct effect on the quality of your relationships, which in turn affects the quality of your life. To repair damaged relationships, you have to begin at the root cause, which takes you to the energetic influences of your own patterns of fear or woundedness. Consciously living these truths is no easy task, but neither is healing or rebuilding a life after a devastating crisis. Renewal of who you are is not something that occurs within the mind. Healing is far too great an enterprise for the mind alone to handle. Renewal of your life, your health, or your very being is a mystical undertaking, and you have to be willing to work with truths of cosmic proportion to accomplish such a profound transformation.

THE REALM OF MYSTICAL LAW

An examination of the lives of Buddha and Jesus illustrates that three sets of laws govern human existence: physical laws, social and religious laws, and mystical laws. Our physical lives are governed by the laws of gravity, time and space, cause and effect, and magnetic attraction, among others. We see these laws in action and can test their authenticity. And, so, what we consider to be "real" derives from the consistency that the physical laws of the universe provide. It is incomprehensible that one day they would function and the next day they would not. They are as they are—period.

Societal and religious laws, such as the Ten Commandments or the Sharia of Islam, structure social order. These laws represent another type of order entirely from the domain of the physical laws that govern all humanity without our having any choice in the matter. While these laws are presented as religious absolutes given to human beings by God, in practice they turn out to be laws that we either choose to observe, as in not stealing or murdering, or risk punishment by breaking. As we know all too well, many people do break certain social or religious laws without getting caught and pay no material price.

But existing in a parallel universe are mystical laws that operate within the same essential harmony, yet outside the equation of time, space, and matter, and outside social and religious convention. We are born with a resonance to this realm of truth. Our innermost self does not learn these truths but awakens to them, meaning that we come into an awareness of that which we have always known. The truest meaning of the spiritual path is to come home to these truths, to awaken again to what is already within you: the knowledge of the mystical realm.

To embody one mystical law is to embody them all. Each truth enhances the others without conflict. You may choose to break the laws, but if you do, some part of you immediately knows you have violated something deep and profound within yourself. You may not be able to give a name to that violation, but you can feel it through an immediate sense of disempowerment and self-betrayal. Most people can remember the first time they told a lie. We all remember that first lie because it represents a dark cosmic ritual of sorts, crossing over a line we knew we should not cross. If your conscience was functioning, all systems would have alerted you to the violation of a deep code of honor within yourself. You betrayed your relationship with your own conscience, a voice you could hear loud and clear. And in telling that first lie, you were also given the awareness that if you continued to lie, your capacity to hear that clear voice of your conscience would diminish. A ferocious sense of guilt washes over you during that dark ritual of the first lie, as the soul fights to keep the voice of the conscience louder than the instincts of fear and the other dark passions. You remember that moment precisely because it was a moment of cosmic transition—the first time you tampered with that precious, delicate connection between your conscience, your consciousness, and the voice of your soul. And you remember whether or not you set things right after that first lie. Either you compromised your integrity through that first momentous lie or honesty became a personal creed.

That mystical laws already govern the nature of your soul is a given; what you must develop is your capacity to consciously draw on their power, and this is the definition of learning how to reason, think, perceive, and act with awareness within the physical world. This is the definition of your highest potential in the most spiritually evolved sense of that concept. The soul seeks to be in harmony with the mystical laws because creating in harmony with mystical consciousness results in a life that is governed by love and not fear, one in which your life's work reflects your strengths and talents rather than your limitations. If you are in harmony with truth, there is nothing about yourself that you need to hide.

You need not be deeply involved in a spiritual tradition in order to have a strong mystical connection with your soul. Most historical mystics who belonged to specific spiritual traditions, such as Rumi or Hafiz, Swami Yogananda or Bede Griffiths, placed God and the soul at the center of their quest by choice. Yet such a choice is not necessary to attain a sense of awareness, and today, in fact, most mystics emerge from the ranks of ordinary life. Among those who have been mystics outside monastic settings are Emily Dickinson, Abraham Lincoln, Albert Einstein, and Helen Keller. Mystical consciousness means finding your route to seeing truth clearly in your world, transcending the limitations and burdens of conventional fears, superstitions, and social beliefs. The great American poet Emily Dickinson found nature to be the expression of God, and she celebrated it in hundreds of short poems that can be read with both secular and spiritual overtones. Einstein found his transcendent consciousness at the end of the universe that he discovered had no end. His quest for truth took him to higher and greater questions, as it does every pilgrim who continues to pursue the nature of truth. First, you are compelled to ask what is true about your own life, and that inevitably leads you to ask, "What is true about life?" Eventually all mystics, regardless of what motivated their search for truth, meet on the same cosmic ground.

You do not learn the mystical laws for only one specific purpose, such as the need to heal, because that assumes that once your goal is met, all the discipline and learning poured into your healing can be discarded. That is the same mentality shared by people who go on a diet to lose weight, only to regain it all because they reward themselves at the end of their achievement by releasing their discipline and knowledge of good nutrition, returning to their old eating habits. You learn these laws because they represent a higher level of consciousness that redefines your core relationship to power, and in particular to your power of choice. At some point, the goal of healing, for example, is replaced by the search for truth. You'll know you have made a profound shift in consciousness when a crisis is no longer required to motivate change, but instead an attraction to truth is enough to draw you toward the next stage of life.

For example, a woman I know named Janis approached her 60th birthday with an admitted sense of trepidation. Those "0" birthdays are significant crossroads in our lives, and the 60th is one that signals the beginning of the last third of your life. Janis could sense a potential psychological crisis on the horizon as she approached this turning point, and so rather than allow the despair of aging to overwhelm her, she chose the creative option. She happened at the same time to be reevaluating her career, and she was not afraid to reinvent herself or take her work in a new direction, even if such a decision introduced financial risk into her life. So prior to her 60th birthday, Janis did what is not typical for most people, but very typical for her—she thought about what she should do as opposed to what she would like to do. She decided that she should face the truth that she was frightened about aging and about what turning 60 represented. In response to that, she enrolled in a class on clowning as her birthday present to herself, because clowning would help her confront her fears of self-expression and dissolve her masks.

Janis gave herself the gift of a truth, and from that gift, different and more dynamic doors of self-realization opened up in her life. In fact, Janis drenched herself in the graces of Revelation, Counsel, and Knowledge as a part of her gift to herself for having journeyed 60 years on this Earth. Truth always brings some form of liberation into your life. Sometimes discovering a personal truth may liberate you from a dismal relationship or occupation, although that realization may shatter your familiar world in the process. Yet few will say that their lives are anything but more enriched for having gone through the shattering of personal illusions so that they might come to know who they truly are. We fear truth not just because it shatters our illusions, but also because from the shattering comes change. Truth and change go hand in hand.

One benefit of choosing to become more conscious is the power of forward thinking. We are far more accustomed to using the tool of conscious thought for repairs, analyzing what went wrong in our lives in the past. With that knowledge we attempt to create a field of gravity around us in the present that includes commitments not to repeat the same mistakes and to heal the old wounds. While that kind of rearview assessment is natural to our way of thinking, introducing a forward-looking view that evaluates what we need to do to meet the exigencies of the road ahead represents the essence of intuitive wisdom. Mothers who anticipate the empty-nest syndrome are intuitively responding to emotional signals that they are in for a tumble unless they find something to fill the gap once all their children are gone. You should think of the subtle voice of your intuition that alerts you to prepare for the coming life changes as a sort of mystical experience: your soul is directing your conscious mind to what will soon manifest in your physical world.

FROM ENERGY TO MYSTICAL CONSCIOUSNESS

Energy is the first way we identify power in the mystical realm. Thoughts and intentions are expressions of energy that move at the speed of light. Physicists crossed over into this dimension of energy consciousness once they penetrated the field of quantum physics, gradually revealing the relationship between thought and its influence on particles of light. But from a mystical perspective, this light or energy that is the counterpart of matter is not just "conscious energy," but also an expression of the sacred itself. It is the manifestation of a divine life force that enlivens all of creation.

The transcendent state is often described as lacking the physical limitations of time and space. Some mystics have spoken of experiencing a sense of timelessness during a mystical experience, perhaps in a moment of spiritual quietude in which they receive the grace of comfort at a time of great difficulty. So many people tell of "being taken over by a sense of knowing" that immediately leaves them calm and filled with inner strength. This is not a rare mystical experience but a common one. What is rare is recognizing it as a genuine mystical occurrence. Although it might last but a moment, your consciousness fully enters a timeless realm in which all the ingredients of your life suddenly, almost magically, look better.

You are no stranger to mystical experiences. The mystical incident visits everyone in various ways. Simply defined, it is an event that takes you beyond the limitations of your five senses, heightening the intensity with which you are able to relate to the profound beauty or significance of something. Often, in this moment of heightened sensitivity, you feel a oneness with whichever "other" you are in relationship with at the moment. Such a union could take place between you and nature, or between one person and another—such as a mother and her newborn—or between an individual and God. Sometimes an original idea can lift you into the mystical realms, as the power of a fresh perception has the voltage to reorder your entire reality in an instant. It flushes out all that you thought was dark and unsolvable and leaves you with a profound sense of optimism and hope. To be lifted beyond the limitations of ordinary thought, beyond the boundaries of logic and reason, and into the cosmic fresh air, where you feel suspended in the weightlessness created by a temporary absence of fear—these are the signatures of a mystical experience. These are also mystical experiences that blend easily into everyday life. Everyone has had at least one of these precious occurrences, whose potency never fades.

Mystics such as Teresa of Ávila and saints from the Eastern spiritual traditions deliberately chose a path of spiritual illumination. Their experiences were of a highly refined spiritual nature; Teresa in particular was known for her many and extraordinary mystical encounters with Jesus. She shared many of her experiences in *The Interior Castle*, often noting that the particulars of mystical experience cannot be described precisely, because the level on which the soul travels is beyond the comprehension of human reason. For this reason, William James wrote that genuine mystical experiences are both "ineffable"—more like states of feeling than of intellect, shaded with nuances that are difficult to convey in language—and "noetic," that is, partaking of knowledge, insight, and illumination beyond the grasp of the rational mind. So precise was Teresa in her intimate knowledge of the fine lines between the psyche and the imagination, or between the imagination and the soul, that she noted that while the imagination is capable of constructing a vision so far as a mental image is concerned, the imagination cannot force or produce a true mystical state. The mystical experience is one that "comes upon you spontaneously," to use her phrase, and is recognized by the soul rather than through the mind. In a profoundly mystical state, the mind is left completely baffled by an encounter with transcendent consciousness.

THE FIVE MYSTICAL LAWS

Teresa was certainly not the only mystic known to levitate. I had read about a meditation master who not only could levitate but could also dry sheets dipped in ice-cold water or melt snow from the force of his meditations. I had the opportunity to ask a Tibetan Rinpoche about this particular master and he giggled all through our conversation at the innocence—or foolishness—of my questions. "Of course he can do those things," he said, "but do you know why they happen?" I said that I did not and he giggled some more, never answering. What stayed with me, however, was that he asked me if I knew why the master experienced levitation and not how. Why did he levitate and melt snow? Why implied that it was the natural consequence of something, whereas how implied that it was the result of something he himself was initiating. Mystical actions follow their own logic, a logic dictated by forces that we are unable to comprehend and that seems irrational to us—beyond the bounds of our ordinary consciousness. And yet what is extraordinary about such events is not that the mystics to whom they happen are living in another, more ethereal world, but that they are so firmly rooted in the realities of this world, of the here and now, undistracted by anything that doesn't absolutely matter.

THE FIRST MYSTICAL LAW: There Is Only Now

The heart of so many mystical disciplines is "Stay fully present." Learn to keep your spirit fully in focus, so that you know where all of you is at all times. Such a profound truth is one that the mind simply cannot grasp, because the intellect cannot get to this place called "now." Only the soul can travel there. I never forgot my conversation with the Tibetan lama, and as I pursued healing in the mystical realm, the why began to reveal itself to me. My own experiences doing countless medical intuitive readings gave me a better understanding of the human energy system. In doing a reading, I could determine energetically where and why a person had lost so much energy to a past crisis, or why he or she was currently losing energy to a specific situation—losses of energy that, in turn, influenced the health of the physical body. The simple formula, obviously, was to identify and detach from whatever historic pattern was causing the energetic hemorrhage and move forward with positive choices. Simple enough on paper, as they say, but brutally difficult for most people to do in real life. As I've already pointed out, the need for an explanation or someone to blame, far from bringing release, locks most people into their histories. And when you are feeling weak and broken in spirit, it's difficult to get on with the emotional and psychic demands that healing requires. So while it may sound easy to say, "Just detach and get on with your life," there is nothing easy about it. Yet, like it or not, we are left with only two choices at the end of any crisis: We can either get better or become bitter. No one stays in neutral. We all choose one of those two paths when we are faced with difficult changes.

Quite a few years ago, I realized that the need to settle our unfinished business with the past was far more than just a psychological or emotional healing ritual; it was also a deep need of the soul that affected our ability to heal. Simply put, holding on to the bitter parts of your past—recent or distant—is like carrying credit-card debt that incurs an ever-increasing interest rate. Eventually all the energetic currency you need to run your present-day life gets redirected toward maintaining the interest on your mounting emotional debt. Finally, when you can't afford to pay your present-day "energy bills," you fall into "emotional bankruptcy"; that is, you become ill, because too much history is colliding with the energy of the present moment. As I've noted previously, the result is that you can move neither forward nor backward with life decisions, because you lack the energy to think clearly, much less make a decision and follow through on it. Because you are in debt, your energy is fragmented across the psychic decades of your life, focused neither in the present nor in any one place where you can find it. You can't heal, because you are still more in the past than in the present; in effect, the past is more emotionally and psychically real to you than the now

Contemporary spiritual masters such as Ram Dass and Pema Chödrön, who have become rich sources of wisdom, love, and healing, frequently speak of the power of living in the present moment, suggesting that such an achievement represents winning a great battle against the illusion of what you think of as "the power of your past." Yet it takes great stamina of soul to master living fully in the present moment, and the reasons are worth understanding. It is not a state of consciousness that can be attained by simply repeating "I am fully present" a dozen times a day. Instead, holding your consciousness in present time is the equivalent of entering a different but parallel dimension of reality. The present moment continually renews the creative possibilities of your life.

It is not that you forget your past. You can hardly forget your past. But being in the present more fully than in your past represents where you position your creative power and your primary identity. The wounded are anchored in their past—that is their primary identity. A time that has come and gone continues to overshadow the present moment. Another choice is to accept the initiatory awakening of wounds, release your resentment toward those who played their roles in wounding you, and nurture the wisdom and compassion that wounding represents. That is, from the broken heart comes a heart that can recognize and identify with the pain of others. A wound such as that must not be wasted or buried in self pity, but brought into the light and examined, reflected upon, and used as a lens through which the lives of others are better understood. Such a choice liberates you from the gravity field of a wounded past, which can hold you hostage to unresolved memories and traumas for decades. The consciousness of present time allows you to keep your memories, but they can no longer hold you hostage, and so they can no longer drain you of your energy, which inevitably drains you of your health.

I've lectured about the power of living in the present moment, and, not surprisingly, nearly everyone asks me, "But how? How do I let go of the past?" It's simple, really, but not easy, and though I've already commented on this point, it is worth yet another go-around with a different approach, because the subject of "letting go" is so difficult. You have to give up the need to punish the people who hurt you. The desire to get even with the people who have humiliated or hurt you is a dark truth; though we rarely admit to it, underneath all the other reasons why we find forgiveness difficult is only this one: the desire for vengeance. This one dark need can keep you tied to your past more tightly than any other trauma you have had, because there is something in human nature that needs to even the score. You may not like to admit it, but admit it you must. And more than admit it, you must get past it and ascend to a higher truth that allows you to focus on what you are meant to learn about yourself through each crisis.

Beyond overcoming the need to get even, you have to be willing to give up being hurt or traumatized as a primary power identity. The "suffering self" can be a powerful social mask that comes with a peculiar type of privilege in our therapeutic culture; being able to say "I'm done with suffering" is not as easy as you may think. Yet it is essential if you are to release the control mechanisms that you've attached to your healing via the suffering motif. The desire to hurt another because you are hurting, for example, is a very difficult power play to give up. The need to let others know you feel entitled to attention because of your pain and suffering is very seductive and releasing the entitlement of the suffering self is more a battle with the shadow of your own pride than it is with anyone else. Yet I repeat with great compassion: None of this is easy, but neither is living in the past, which is the equivalent of living in a psychic cemetery where you confer with problematic corpses on a regular basis.

Although none of this is easy, sometimes a transformation can happen in an instant. I've observed a miraculous healing as a result of an instantaneous shift from living in the past to living in present time. Sharon was battling cancer in her back, which caused her constant, relentless pain. By Sunday morning of one of my healing workshops, she realized that her pain level had been reduced by half, which was extraordinary for her. She e-mailed me three weeks later to tell me that by the following Tuesday she had been pain-free, which made her want to see her physician. He ran several tests, including an MRI on her back, and found that all signs of her cancer were gone. "I said the prayer, 'Now, God. I release the whole of my life to you,'" Sharon explained to me. "I felt as if I went into free fall, as if I owned nothing. I felt as if I had no past and nothing to lose. I had only life to gain. I fell asleep after that prayer and when I woke up, half my pain was gone and my healing had begun."

Sharon believed that the catalyst for her healing was that she had completely abandoned any attachment to what healing would require of her or how she would have to change her life. With that one prayer, she relinquished any attachment to the familiar. Previously she had paced her healing so as not be overwhelmed. Now she could see that she was overwhelmed already and more of the same wouldn't matter, because what could be more overwhelming than dying? Sharon's prayer opened her to the healing power of grace, which before she had experienced only in small doses because of her need to heal in a way that kept her familiar world intact. Sharon's prayer of "Now, God" worked like a cosmic release valve, opening her to an intensity of grace that heals outside the boundaries of time and space, renewing her life force.

Falling into Harmony with the "Here and Now": How do you accomplish being fully present in the "now" of your life? Do you have to wait for a desperate life-or-death situation before you can shatter the blockade of reason that holds you back from ascending to that interior place of surrender? No, not at all. Here's one simple method to help you stay in the present: Change your vocabulary. Specifically, give up the use of the following terms and all that they imply: blame, deserve, guilt, fair, fault. If you cut those five words from your vocabulary, both in your private thoughts and in your communication with others, you will notice almost immediately that it is far more difficult to fall into negative emotional patterns. You will also discover how habitual those patterns had become.

In addition to that simple suggestion, the teachings of the great spiritual masters contain all the wisdom and guidance you need—teachings so simple that they should be easy to follow. But in keeping with the paradoxical nature of the Divine, in their simplicity is hidden the arduous nature of the journey. Mystical laws interact with each other like a flowing, energetic mandala of truth. One law or truth supports another. Living in the present moment is accomplished through creating a spiritual practice as well as a life based on mystical truths and wisdom. You learn, for example, that to live in the present, the practice of forgiveness is essential. Without forgiveness, you remain anchored in your past, forever in emotional debt.

THE SECOND MYSTICAL LAW:
The Necessity of Forgiveness

I have already discussed the role of forgiveness as a factor in consciousness and as a required stage for healing. But forgiveness is also a mystical law. Unlike the other mystical laws, it has made its way into the meat and potatoes of human life, thanks to Jesus, from whom we received the mystical command to forgive, and also because forgiveness is now recognized within the holistic health field as having a practical application in terms of healing. Though other mystical laws have not so far had a measurable influence on decreasing stress or supporting one's healing, scientists, physicians, and psychologists who have researched the relationship between stress and illness have concluded that the ability or inability to forgive affects the outcome of serious illness. People who have a forgiving nature increase their chances of recovery.

Above all I want to emphasize that forgiveness is a mystical, not a logical, command. It makes no sense to the reasoning mind, because the reasoning mind is incapable of forgiveness. Genuine forgiveness is a self-initiated mystical act that requires the assistance of grace to release you from the compulsive and often self-righteous chatter of the ego, which continually enforces a position of entitled anger or hurt. In terms of the financial metaphor I've been using, a genuine act of forgiveness clears your credit-card debt completely, releasing your soul from debtor's prison.

Forgiveness is not the act of releasing the aggressor, though it is usually interpreted this way. Nor is it a way of telling others that what they have done is "okay" with you and "all is forgiven now." Neither of those interpretations even comes close to the mystical essence of forgiveness, which is fundamentally between you and God. A genuine act of forgiveness takes place in the inner landscape where your disappointed, hurt, abused, or angry ego confronts your soul, which holds to a cosmic template of justice.

The ego wants to hold another person responsible for why certain events in your life turned out as they did or for why you were hurt or treated unfairly. We always want justice to serve us and not the "other," which, of course, means we always want to be right. Another way to translate this is that we want our version of God always to support our side, as noted by the creeds of all world religions: God is on our side. All these issues come down to the belief that if you don't get what you want, fate has not treated you as you deserve. Ultimately, forgiveness is a battle between the righteousness of your ego and your capacity to transcend whatever situation you've experienced that has shattered these myths that maintain suffering is deserving of recognition, reward, or righteous vengeance:

- God is on your side and only your side.

- Justice should be logical and reasonable and always serve your side of the story.

- God follows the code of human law—if you do only good things, bad things will never happen to you, and, of course, you never do bad things.

- You are entitled to have all things work out in your favor, after all.

We can't forgive others when these myths fail us, and they do fail us through the relationships and events that make up the tapestry of our lives. Understanding the essence of forgiveness is one of the most deeply healing and liberating gifts you can give to yourself. Among the many ways you can approach it is as a showdown between you and the forces governing your own destiny. For example, often you cannot forgive another person because you believe that he or she has ruined your life. I frequently hear people speak about their parents in this way, noting that if they had had more supportive parents, they would have gone to college and fulfilled their dreams of becoming entrepreneurs or artists or scholars. Much of the pain in people's lives is rooted in the truth that they are unable to make even one personal and empowering choice lest it cost them their marriage or job. They project their resentment at being silenced onto the people who had or have influence over them—their "captors," so to speak—when in fact it's their own fears that cause them again and again to betray themselves. Who, then, is responsible for the choice of remaining in captivity, and who should really be the object of forgiveness in these situations? Whether you think of those forces as Fate or God or just the luck of the draw in the game of life, your arguments that certain things in your life should have happened differently are matters of cosmic proportion. Nothing is as simple or obvious as it appears. You can lock your sights on another person and believe with all your might that this one person destroyed your life, but from a cosmic perspective your life is far more complex than you can measure by the influence of one or two relationships.

I had my own arguments with my destiny that ultimately opened me to the mystical power contained within a genuine act of forgiveness. The arguments stretched across quite a few years, however, so they require a bit of background. Although I was raised Roman Catholic, by the age of 12 my struggles with the doctrines of the Catholic Church had begun. By the time I reached high school, I was in a genuine spiritual crisis with the core teachings of Catholicism, in particular the notion that Jesus died for our sins because of something Adam and Eve did in some garden. The idea that an off-planet God required the sacrifice of a son-God to make things right for the human race struck me as all wrong. Knowing the history of Roman, Greek, and Mithraic religions, I was aware that the way Christian beliefs developed after the death of the historical Jesus involved a blending of myths. These myths involved blood sacrifices on altars, along with the symbolism of death and rebirth as derived from ancient agricultural rituals that predated even Greco-Roman culture. At the same time, I was drawn to the teachings of Jesus as embodied in the Gospels, including the Gnostic Gospels. I never lost faith in the mystical truth of his message of love, forgiveness, and service to others that he so elegantly put forth in the Sermon on the Mount.

And yet I remained truly baffled by the mystery of why he had to "suffer and die for our sins" and by the whole notion of salvation through faith. This mystery grew all the more intellectually confounding, frustrating, and enraging as the years passed and I watched Christian Fundamentalism and Evangelicalism grow around the idea of "salvation." This was no small matter to me. Indeed, trying to understand this core message of Jesus became a personal Holy Grail. It wasn't that I needed to believe in the "son of God" myth, biological or otherwise. What I did need was to have some kind of understanding of the archetype of salvation that was obviously represented by the Crucifixion. I could not grasp what this doctrine of salvation meant to people. The idea of Jesus dying for the sins of humanity was so bizarre, yet it had somehow taken root and possessed the Christian world of close to a billion people. This was such a huge spiritual dilemma for me that I left the Catholic Church, although, as odd as this may sound, I continued to study the writings of Catholic mystics, which I adore. I learned early on to discern the difference between the politics of God and the mystical expression of the Divine; it was the politics of the Catholic Church that I needed to leave far, far behind.

Years after falling away from the church, and after I had been working as a medical intuitive for some time, I was doing a reading on a man with cancer. My method of intuitive reading is that I ask in prayer for all that I can be given to help an individual, and so I asked, "What is the source of this man's cancer?" Instantly I was filled with images of the symbolic meaning of the crucifixion story. I was both stunned and repelled, because the symbolism by then had only negative associations for me. I repeated the prayer, but the same image "downloaded" into my field of vision. With that, I let the information flow into me without a personal response, as if it were any other kind of data. I believed then, as I do now, that what I experienced that day was not about the man for whom I was doing a reading; it was for me personally, although the information also helped him a great deal.

I believe that our planet has been host to many great souls, but that Buddha and Jesus are among the greatest. I consider Buddha to be the cosmic architect and archetype of Compassion, a man more fully human than perhaps any who came before him. Buddha saw the dark side of human consciousness as if it were a freshly cleaned window on a sunny day. He saw how and why people could—and indeed would—so easily find illusions of power more attractive and seductive than their own innermost nature. And I consider Jesus the cosmic architect and archetype of Forgiveness, a man whose divinity is beyond our capacity to comprehend. Jesus incarnated to unveil the inner power of the human spirit—the power to heal, to love beyond the boundaries of one's own tribe, to create peace, and to know God directly and intimately. This power comes at a price, however, and that price is the test that positions the power of the ego against the power of the soul. In order to illustrate the test, the teacher Jesus had to incarnate the entire archetypal journey that culminated with the story of his arrest, trial, crucifixion, and resurrection.

The core of this drama was Jesus's message to us to embody a level of consciousness that transcended human reason: There is a higher law that rules the spirit, a mystical law that holds no allegiance to the laws of religion. If you are able to embody this law, you can heal the sick, feed the hungry, cast out demons (or madness of the mind), and even raise the dead. But the way to this sacred consciousness requires that you release your belief that a self-serving system of justice can be attained on earth. Believing in any system of human justice is the same as believing in righteous vengeance, because the tribe that loses will always feel abused and want to seek revenge. From the ego's perspective, nothing about life on this earth is entirely just or fair, because the ego is fundamentally self-serving. Anything that doesn't materially benefit us is perceived by the ego as grossly unjust. It's not only that good people suffer and bad people seem to have it all, but that I suffer and I don't have it all.

Yet Jesus insisted that the presence of Abba, as he called the father-God in his native Aramaic, is a force of love so powerful it allows you to trust that beyond whatever you may endure lie greater cosmic reasons for your experiences. Reach deep into your soul to surrender to that which your ego cannot comprehend, he said, in terms that even today are difficult for the mind to comprehend, let alone the ego: "I say to you, do not resist an evil person; but whoever slaps you on your right cheek, turn the other to him also" (Matthew 5:39). The greatest challenge is to forgive those whom you could so easily justify retaliating against, for when is your mind so clear of illusions that you truly grasp why events happen as they do?

Having given this lesson, Jesus lives it to the fullest. He prays to God while in the Garden of Gethsemane not to have to suffer the fate that he foresees for himself, to have "this cup taken from me." But there is no response from God. Jesus receives no guidance whatsoever as to why he has to endure the nightmare that is about to unfold; he must surrender in blind faith. Indeed, he is abandoned and betrayed by his friends; he is put on trial for bogus crimes, he is tortured and humiliated. Finally, as he hangs on the cross, Jesus asks, "Father, why have you abandoned me?" But in the next breath, he says, "Forgive them, for they know not what they do," as if his entire crucifixion would have been for naught had that one detail been omitted.

In going through each of those tests of abandonment, betrayal, accusation, humiliation, and torture, Jesus endured every act that a person can "righteously" claim as justification for vengeance. His death embodied the ultimate shattering of the power of the ego against the illusions of the physical world. In responding with forgiveness, he was birthing a new template of consciousness that would show us all how to release ourselves from the hell of the illusion that some cosmic injustice has befallen us. The mystical truth is that forgiveness has nothing whatsoever to do with the person you are forgiving; it is a self-initiated act of transformation in which you release yourself from a level of consciousness that binds you to the illusion that you are safe and protected in a world of chaos and that your God is the only God of justice and fairness for all humanity. For if any one people were truly to have such a relationship with the Divine, imagine how relentless they/we would be? The fairness of the Divine is in the equality of chaos and in our capacity to do evil to each other, as well as in our capacity to release each other from hell. Forgiveness is an act so powerful that a resurrection of the inner self does indeed occur, because you are retrieving your spirit from the dead zone of past traumas and unfinished business.

Falling into Harmony with Forgiveness: No amount of logical chatter can ever motivate us to forgive. I'm not sure how useful talk therapy is in this process, except that it serves to help us release the frustration of not being able to forgive. Ultimately, you have to turn to the power of grace to break through the boundaries of your reason, which can be ruthless in producing justification and hurt pride. Pray for the grace to forgive, and be ready to act on that grace. Let it melt through traumatic memories and do your best not to fight the meltdown, because it will happen. And in keeping with the nature of mystical laws, refer to the power and wisdom of other laws for support, particularly the one that follows.

THE THIRD MYSTICAL LAW: All Is Illusion

I often think of Jesus as the soul who opened the cosmic heart for humanity and of Buddha as the soul who opened the cosmic mind, introducing the mystical path of the Four Noble Truths. If followed with devotion, these truths can lead to spiritual enlightenment. Centered on the rich mystical truth "All is illusion," the Four Noble Truths are these:

- The First Truth: Suffering—Buddha says that birth is suffering, aging and illness are suffering, and death is suffering. Facing a person you hate is suffering, as surely as being separated from someone you love. Not getting what you want is suffering.

- The Second Truth: The Cause of Suffering— Buddha says that the cause of human suffering is

undoubtedly found in the thirsts of the physical
and mental body and in its perceived illusions.
Traced to their source, these thirsts and illusions
are rooted in intense craving. And craving, which is
motivated by a will to live, seeks only what is sensed
as being desirable.

- The Third Truth: The Ending of Suffering—If
  instinctual craving or desire could be removed,
  then passion would die out and all human suffering
  would end.

- The Fourth Truth: The Noble Path to the Ending
  of Suffering—The way leading to a cessation of
  desire and suffering is the Noble Eightfold Path:
  Right Ideas, Right Resolution, Right Speech, Right
  Behavior, Right Livelihood, Right Effort, Right
  Mindfulness, Right Concentration. Buddha says
  that enlightenment can be gained only by the discipline of the Noble Path, and that living without
  the understanding of the Noble Path sets our life on
  an endless labyrinth of illusions, motivated by fears
  and physical desires. All is illusion in life except the
  Noble Path. Only truth is real.

All is illusion. This is one of the more baffling mystical truths,
because every one of your five senses will tell you otherwise.
Imagine this scenario: I step on your shoe. It's not an illusion that
your foot is now hurting or that your shoe is now slightly marked.
But we enter illusion when we start asking why. Why did I step
on your shoe? Was it because I didn't like your shoe? Or was it
because I was trying to stop you from leaving the room? Or maybe
it was because I just don't like you. Maybe I wanted that pair of
shoes and you got to them first. Or maybe, just maybe, I didn't
see you standing there and it was simply an accident. What we do
know is that, left to your own imagination, you will more than
likely reach into the vast resources of your memory archives and

fill in the void of why I stepped on your shoe with some nega-tive association from your past or a negative projection about me in the present. It's not personal, as the Godfather might say, just business. It's what we do. We tend to fill voids with something negative, a fear or insecurity.

It would never occur to you that my accidentally stepping on your shoe was part of an even bigger plan to delay your departure from the building, which in turn made you a few minutes later in reaching a certain intersection on your way home. And maybe that two-minute difference saved your life, because a driver was going to run a red light at that intersection and would have hit you. Is it impossible to believe such a micro-drama could be enacted just to save your life? These micro-dramas occur continually through traffic jams, dishes that slip out of hands in the morning, and last-minute phone calls that keep us from running out the door at a certain time. How do you know why things happen as they do? You don't. You have no idea and you never will. Much less are you capable of knowing what must take place today in order that cer-tain events unfold one or two years or a decade from now. Perhaps a car accident is necessary, or you have to get fired so that you can end up in another position, because that is where you will meet someone you will end up cherishing the rest of your life.

Why events happen as they do in your life, from the grandest or most devastating to the most seemingly insignificant, is beyond your ability to know. You can no more distinguish what is sig-nificant from what is insignificant, if such a thing as insignifi-cant exists at all. Whether something brings you pain or pleasure, happiness or sadness, is not the best arbiter of what really mat-ters, which most of us should have learned by now. Those feel-ings are just temporary responses to your experiences, and even your responses are illusions. You are happy one day, sad the next, melancholy on the third day, bored on the fourth, ecstatic on the fifth, exhausted on the sixth, and on the seventh day you're con-fused about the whole of your life.

The deeper truth is that there is not one reason why a par-ticular thing happens as it does. Every event is the result of the compilation of hundreds, if not thousands or millions, of events that have been in motion for an unknowable length of time. You are alive because of your parents, and your parents' parents, and so on back into the mists of history. So where did your gene pool begin, exactly? You have no idea and you never will. It's an illusion that you know where you came from or the origin of the psychic DNA that you are carrying within you and around you. And if this is the case, there really is no reason why any of us should expend our energy searching for reasons why certain experiences or events happened as they did. That is a cosmic quest, not an earthly one.

But as Buddha noted more than 2,500 years ago, if you want to suffer, then follow an illusion, such as the path of your humiliated ego and its passion to get even with the people who have hurt or abandoned you. You will discover that such a path leads only to more illusions. I've heard my share of stories about people who went into therapy as adults, for example, to heal the memories of an abusive childhood. Part of the therapy included reconciliation with the abusing parents. I know of three cases in which, after all the therapeutic prep work and anticipation of finally confronting the surviving parent, the response was almost as devastating as the original wounds, because the parents denied ever abusing these people as children. In their own ways, the parents were telling their adult children that their memories were illusions, when in all likelihood the memories of these abusive parents were illusory, based on the lies they had to tell themselves. Only one thing was certain: the memories of the parents had nothing whatsoever in common with those of the returning adults who were so intent on finally extricating themselves from their emotional dungeons.

Falling into Harmony with Illusion: The power of all mystical truths finds its way into our lives in some fashion, even disguised in the form of common social wisdom, such as "One never knows what goes on behind closed doors." The deeper implication of that well-known adage is, of course, that what you see and hear in the world around you is nothing but an illusion. You know that to be the case in your own life as well, which is where the practice of the Third Mystical Law begins. The practice of the Third Mystical Law (not to be confused with the Buddha's Third Noble Truth, the Ending of Suffering) is greatly enhanced by the teachings of Buddhism. One way of discerning the power of illusion is through self-examination of your actions and agendas regarding the people with whom you feel you are on an unequal footing. These are the individuals with whom you negotiate your power and who make you vulnerable to behaviors that draw from your dark passions. In seeking their approval, you will adjust your behavior to please them more than you realize. You will morph yourself, your opinions, or your creativity, and you might even negotiate your honor or integrity, just to remain on good terms with these people. No matter what rationale you give yourself for your actions, negotiating your power for the sake of personal acceptance is a form of self-betrayal that results in a loss of self-respect.

Such actions always result in toxic resentment (is there any other kind?), because in negotiating your power you automatically expect some type of reward or recognition, even though you may not acknowledge it consciously. When none is forthcoming, resentment increases and you feel disempowered. Emotional, mental, and psychic disempowerment over prolonged periods of time inevitably turns into cycles of depression, despair, and ultimately chronic illness with elements of fatigue and physical pain. At the root of all this is a desire for empowerment through the recognition of others, which is a path of illusion. The truth is that no one can empower another person.

Instead, you need to turn to the higher truths, reminding yourself: "No one has done anything to hurt or reject me. That is an illusion. It can look and feel that way, because of my own personal needs, but I am in charge of my needs. So, I forgive all these people who I believed had deliberately hurt or rejected me. That, too, was an illusion. They never plotted to reject or hurt me. I projected expectations onto them based on my own desires and they failed to live up to my imagined plans for them."

Mystical truths help you to see clearly, because they provide order when you may be tempted to fear there is only chaos in your life. Although you may experience great pain from losing a job, from health crises, or from going through a divorce, you can also find extraordinary comfort in the mystical truth "Change is constant." To believe that anything can remain perfect, successful, or healthy forever is always just a wishful illusion. We may not be able to know the truth about any one situation, but we can know truth itself, which is often found wrapped in paradox.

THE FOURTH MYSTICAL LAW:
Trust in Divine Paradox, Irony, and Synchronicity

A paradox is an apparent contradiction that nonetheless contains the truth. The power of a paradox, by its very nature, cannot be captured in a single definition. Paradoxical dynamics are currents that animate the wild cards of our lives, sometimes with such dramatic force that they give us pause to consider, "Who could possibly have masterminded such an event?" These are the experiences that open our imaginations to take seriously a truth that mystics have long known: Paradox is one of the languages of the Divine. Unlike many of us, who long for a Supreme Being who communicates in logical celestial codes, mystics see in paradoxical events and situations a "divine irony" that tends to be more in keeping with the nature of divine expression. Paradoxical dynamics are somehow perfectly suited to the eternal tug-of-war between the ego and the soul, and we can learn a great deal by training ourselves to recognize the truth within divine paradox.

Consider the birth of Jesus in a manger, symbolic of an ever-present theme in spiritual life—that divine power always enters your life through the humblest door. In contrast, Siddhartha Gautama, as Buddha was known before his enlightenment, was born into opulence and protected by his father, a king of sorts, from the unpleasant sights of life, such as aging, sickness, and death. But young Siddhartha managed to sneak out of his perfect world, only to collide with imperfection—by seeing an old man and a funeral procession—and that collision shattered his consciousness wide open. The paradox: Buddha needed absolute wealth to understand that no amount of material security could preserve him from the human fate of suffering. From that collision of opposites, he began his search for truth.

The energetic threads that manipulate ironic events, too, reveal the handiwork of the Divine in our lives. I heard about a woman, for instance, whose husband died on the day that their lottery ticket won the jackpot. He had always bought a ticket for her, and she checked out that last lottery ticket purely for sentimental reasons. It turned out to be the winning ticket. In an interview, she said, with tears in her eyes, "He always said he'd provide for me." Ironic events along with paradoxical ones stand out in our lives, calling us to notice them. They come together with rare, once-in-a-lifetime ingredients that may never coalesce again. These facts alone beckon us to take notice that unusual forces have consciously gathered around us to make that one event happen. How we interpret it, of course, depends on the sophistication of our interior skills. I am one, for example, who does not make a big cosmic deal out of finding a parking spot on a crowded shopping afternoon. I'm just relieved. On the other hand, I do make note of receiving a letter from someone I hadn't thought of in years, only to realize I had come across a photo of him the day before and left it on my desk all afternoon, just for the pleasure of remembering times gone by.

While experiences such as these can appear to be random, the element of paradox invites us to consider the possibility that they are not random at all, but reveal yet another mechanism of cause and effect that is governed by the sacred. Whereas the mechanism of paradox is similar in function to Jung's concept of synchronicity—that is, an impersonal function of the collective consciousness—divine paradox is conscious and personal. How often has something happened to us that in the moment we think is devastating, only to discover six months or a year later that it was the proverbial "blessing in disguise"? There is nothing at all impersonal about such events, and those of you who have had the experience of a blessing in disguise know that's true. Sometimes the blessing is simply that these events draw us out of our ordinary "sleeping" state; that is, they cause us to wonder about the greater cosmic map, and that's purpose enough.

But the element of divine paradox is present in how change occurs in our lives, what it looks like, and what it is meant to stimulate in us. The ego is always frightened and cannot discern a blessing from a tragedy, because its only compass is its own survival. As a result, it bases every decision on either what it already knows and is familiar with or what it views as safe, all of which Buddha identified as pure illusion. Times of change are about exactly that—a need to change. But changes of circumstance are the illusion, not the intent. You are always the object of change, never your situation. When life presents you with a crossroads and you are not sure what to do, the ego will always fall back on what it has already done. The ego pulls out its résumé, which is, paradoxically, exactly the wrong thing to do. Change arrives because you need to move forward, not retreat to the past.

So often people say, "But I don't know what to do" or "I don't know where to begin." More and more that is the case as our familiar world is in meltdown and we must now rely on our creative instincts to build a new global community. People who look to their past will not do well, because the past is no longer relevant. We can only go forward and toward the fact—and it is a fact—that learning to rely on divine paradox and wisdom will become a great survival grace.

Falling into Harmony with Divine Paradox:

- What is big is really small; what is small is really big.
- What is frightening is really the safe path; what looks safe is your fear talking.
- What looks like chaos is actually a future blessing in disguise.
- Your greatest power is humility; your greatest weakness is humiliation.

- The mustard seed (one clear soul) has more power than the mountain (a group of people in chaos).

- The power of prayer and grace—knowing how to work in harmony with the cosmos—influences the whole of life, whereas trying to dominate one person destroys you.

- Your ego—and not someone else's—is your most ruthless adversary.

Live these truths. Take them into your life and act on them. Look for paradoxical forces in your life and note that these energies are not accidental but represent dynamics that are cause for a conscious response. And always return to your graces as a way of reminding yourself that your highest potential is worth all this effort.

THE FIFTH MYSTICAL LAW:
Maintain Spiritual Congruency

Whether you strike out on the path of consciousness in order to heal yourself or to engage more profoundly in matters of the spirit, one way of describing your goal is to say that you want to become a congruent human being. Congruency can take many forms, but in essence you are congruent when your beliefs match up with your everyday actions and your spiritual practice. Say what you believe and believe what you say; act on your beliefs and follow through on guidance that comes from inner reflection. In this way, body, mind, and soul finally come into an alignment that allows for the harmony of the graces to flow through you as naturally as your breath. You maintain congruence by honoring the spiritual truths that you have consciously made a part of your interior life. Only you know what you believe to be true about the Divine. Only you know what you believe to be true about your purpose in life and what qualifies as real or illusion for you. Once you make those choices, compromising them is an act of self-betrayal, because you are violating your personal truth. And truth is its own monitoring device; that is, you can never lie to yourself about compromising a truth. Further, your biology itself will show signs of the stress when you become incongruent with a truth.

Truth is such a powerful force that many people dance around making commitments to what they believe to be true, as if they are shopping for political philosophies. In workshops I ask people, "What do you believe?" The majority of them respond, "I'm not sure," or "I don't know," fearing, superstitiously, that God will hold them accountable for their answers. And there's an element of truth in that, because part of us realizes that an acknowledgment of a belief—whether private or public—stands as an official commitment to it, if only before our own conscience. So we often avoid making such acknowledgments, as the acknowledgment may demand a response of congruent action that could be life-transforming. It is safer to remain in a fog about what finally qualifies as a truth worthy of commitment; yet a consciousness left in a fog is incapable of creating any clear path in life, much less of healing anything.

Falling into Harmony with Congruence: There is nothing easy about living a conscious life, but it's even more treacherous to live an unconscious one. I'd like to say "a fully conscious life," but that might seem idealistic to the point of impossibility. Simply being as conscious as you can be at each moment is a full-time job, because becoming a conscious person is all about realizing the full potential of the power of choice. And of all the choices that you can make, none is as empowering as the decision to live in a spiritually congruent way. Each of the mystical laws I've described is in its own way supportive of all the other laws. But perhaps the most helpful practice for maintaining a congruent life is referring to Buddhism's Four Noble Truths outlined earlier in this chapter. The wisdom of those teachings will help you to identify illusions in your life that are draining you of your energy and stamina. It's always important to return to inner balance before you engage in any action. In addition to the Four Noble Truths, you can enhance the practice of spiritual congruence by following this advice:

- Say only what you believe and believe what you say.

- Power originates behind your eyes, not in front of your eyes. Once power becomes visible, it evaporates. True power is invisible.

- Thought precedes the creation of matter. Therefore, your thoughts are instruments of creation as much as your words, deeds, and finances. Become conscious about the quality of your thoughts, because each one sets patterns of cause and effect into motion. Every thought is a tool. Every thought is a prayer.

- Judgment anchors you to the person or thing you judge, making you its servant. Judge others too harshly and you become their prisoner.

LIFE WITHOUT GRAVITY

Every day we will slip in our efforts to live a congruent, conscious life. So what? Get up, try again, slip some more. Imagine life without being controlled by the illusions of fear—fear of not having enough, fear of rejection, and fear of failure. Imagine your fears as having less influence over you. A completely fearless life may be unrealistic, but a life in which you keep your fears at a distance is an achievable goal.

Mystics did not set about learning the nature of God or the higher mystical laws so that they could literally defy gravity—that is, so that they could levitate while they meditated, heal others spontaneously and at a distance, bilocate, or develop telepathic abilities. The great mystics of India warned that such remarkable powers—or siddhis, as they are known in their tradition—could be a great distraction on one's spiritual path. Those capabilities they viewed instead as fruits that fell from the single tree in their garden, which was their passionate love for all things divine. The mystical approach to life is not to see life from without, but to perceive it from within, to sense your energetic field before you allow your body to move into action. Sense the many currents of information that are electrically charged in the atmosphere and interpret that information. Respond to that information, run it through your spiritual senses, and then let that data enter your ordinary mind. Learn to utilize all of your spiritual senses as naturally as you breathe, and always within the consciousness that you are living in a field of grace.

WORTHY OF REFLECTION

- Ask yourself, "What psychic, emotional, or mental weight am I carrying that is unnecessary to my journey? Why am I carrying this?" Be tough with yourself. Don't carry extra emotional baggage. It doesn't serve you or anyone else.

- Seek the truth in all aspects of your life. Ask the constant question "What is the truth in this situation?" Search for wisdom, for understanding, for insight at every opportunity.

- Learn to endure. Remember that no plan unfolds in an afternoon. Have no expectations of anything. Let everything be a surprise.

- Give up the need to know why things happen as they do. How do you know what success or failure is? You've never had a scale that can measure either one of those two ends of the spectrum. Everything is just experience. Reflect on whether experience empowers or disempowers you—that is all. Does each experience make you more aware, more honest, more grateful, kinder, more generous, more compassionate? That's where you should focus your attention.

- Act on your guidance without constantly saying that you're frightened and require proof that you will be safe. You will never get that proof. Every choice in life is an act of faith. Stop letting fear be the one constant voice you listen to with unremitting faith. Be outrageously bold in your belief that you will be guided but do not have expectations of how that guidance will unfold. Keep your attention in present time—always in present time.

- Develop a truly devoted prayer life. Go inward. Find a way into your soul that serves who you are at this stage in your life, but wean yourself of just speaking your surface thoughts to the Divine in a conversational way and discover your interior graces.

These are times of change, and among the most crucial changes is the need for people who would not ordinarily seek mystical teachings to turn to them now with a soul-felt passion. We are past the point when just reading about healing and human consciousness is of any value. All sojourners must awaken and cease the search for who they are in this world. What answer do you need other than "I am a soul in search of truth"?

Your soul knows it can defy gravity. And you know that you can learn the mystical laws. The question is whether you can transcend the boundaries of ordinary reason: that is the great challenge in this human life that binds us all.

Chapter Seven

BEYOND ILLNESS

Living in a Field of Grace

Some years ago I wrote the book Anatomy of the Spirit, in which I discussed the harmonious integration of the seven chakras, derived from Indian yoga and philosophy, with the Jewish Tree of Life and the seven Christian sacraments. The merger of these three sacred traditions with our physical biology revealed what I now think of as the mystical intelligence of our "bio-soul," a unique interplay of active wisdom that exists between our biology and our spiritual senses. My work as a medical intuitive had long since taught me that our biography indeed becomes our biology, but now I realize that our definition of "biography" must also include the biography of our soul, and not in the religious sense. To this model of the three sacred wisdom traditions I now add the dynamic ingredients of the soul—our seven graces and our seven dark passions—as essential to the bank of knowledge for healing as well as for becoming a whole person. These are our core elements, as essential to each of us as breath is to the physical body. Our graces and our dark passions are our link to creation itself. These forces have no religion of origin, nor can they be commanded by beliefs of superiority based on myths that say this god is better than that god. These light and shadow graces and passions come from but a single source—the one God that created all of life.

My decision to add the graces and the dark passions to the bio-soul does not arise only from my belief that, because healing is a mystical experience, knowledge about the mystical realm and mystical intelligence becomes essential to our health—although that much is true. Instead, my belief in the need to learn about mystical reasoning and the bio-soul is in large part the result of an evolutionary process in which we are all involved.

We must now realize that we have already crossed the energy Rubicon, having entered the Age of Energy Consciousness 50 or more years ago. Even someone who has no interest in matters related to the body-mind-spirit approach to healing must respond to questions that are now routinely asked during a medical exam for a cardiovascular condition, such as, "Is there stress in your life?" Stress is an energetic indicator that physical conditions in your life are out of balance because psychological or emotional conditions are too. You need not be a believer in any god, or in the body-mind-spirit template of healing, to engage in a conversation on stress; however, such conversations occur regularly on the "energy" side of the Rubicon. In effect, we are an energy species now, and energy medicine, among the many energy-based technologies that have already reshaped global society, is here to stay. We really should be long past the stage of having to prove that a link exists between the energy patterns of emotion and attitude and the health of the physical body. Indeed, at this stage, such research should almost be considered primitive. To use the parlance of our technological culture, think of your bio-soul as your spiritual Internet: it receives and transmits energy data, transferring it to your spiritual senses and chakras, which, in turn, convert that light-speed data into grounded information recognized by your five senses. This is a portrait of living within an energy hologram, and it presents the reality of who we have become.

It's time to move on to the significant questions that are more far-reaching than mere matters of health and that determine the quality of your entire life. Until now, life traumas and crises of health have certainly been the main impetus for people to seek out alternative ways of thinking about personal empowerment, spirituality, and energy medicine. But given that we must now recognize that we are multisensory beings whose energy anatomy has a complementary authority within the physical body, we must move beyond illness and trauma as our motivating forces and ascend to the level of living according to the rules of energy consciousness. You now need to reflect on the questions that matter most, questions that hold the power to transform the quality of your life and not just your health, such as:

- How capable am I of handling energy consciousness?

- Am I able to become more genuinely intuitive, or do I still need to perceive the world around me at the more reasonable speed of my five senses?

- Can I handle mystical consciousness and maintain my own conscience and actions in harmony with that level of truth?

- Can I live in harmony with the deeper sacred truth that energy is really grace? This truth transforms the world around and within me, calling me to see all life and every person as sacred. Am I ready and able to do that?

Making that one shift in consciousness—from perceiving life as energy to seeing life surrounded by grace—would not physically alter one thing in your world. Yet that one shift in perception would open up your inner vista to the realm of mystical intelligence and reasoning, because the space surrounding every living creature would pulsate with the creative potential of grace.

Imagining the space around every living creature as alive with the creative potential of grace is a highly refined mystical truth that carries with it a call to live according to that truth. This is not a truth you can just "know" and then ignore. This truth demands that you rise to its authority, that you live according to its inherent law of cause and effect. If grace surrounds all living beings, then by virtue of having earned the knowledge of that truth, you are required—required—to engage with others according to that truth. You may rightly ask, "Required by whom?" The answer is that you are required by the mystical laws of evolution, or, if you prefer, by the law of karma, or by the rules known to your soul. If you know it is wrong to steal, are you not required by the laws of our society to abstain from stealing? Of course you are. The only difference is that mystical truths are far more demanding and require much more inner diligence. And yet such diligence is exactly what has always been required of every person who has walked the path of inner illumination.

Actually all people are walking that path, willy-nilly. But it isn't a cakewalk. Someone to whom I put this prospect replied honestly, "I'm not ready to live at that level of consciousness. It's just too hard. It's too difficult to always remind myself that people I don't like are also surrounded with grace. I mean, that's easy with people I love, but not with people I have personal issues with at work. I know that's when acting on this truth matters the most, but I also end up feeling it's unfair to force myself to see them through grace when I know they dislike me. It's just not fair and I end up resenting them, because I feel like I'm doing them a favor while they still get to dislike me."

Nothing is easy about life on the other side of the Rubicon, but once you've crossed that river there is no turning back. You can't decide to become unaware that your attitudes influence your physical health, for instance, or decide that chakras don't exist or that you don't have a soul. You can influence only the speed at which you want to engage with your own transformation, and even there your influence is limited. For example, you can decide to minimize the involvement of the sacred, cutting out the mystical path and retreating into the safety of your intellect. That's fine. Your chakras will still keep working, so to speak. But all choices have consequences, and deciding to envision yourself as merely a physical body with an energy system may result in your turning to conventional reason for support during times of crisis. That's not logical, but it is the nature of fear. Crises scare us and we tend to retreat into the most familiar forms of power and comfort that we know.

In the absence of a developed sense of mystical reasoning, you will more likely turn to your intellectual reasoning skills for a way through your crisis, because logic and reason—including an image of a reasonable God—is what you trust beyond all else. You will automatically look toward your history for clues about how to pursue your future, only you won't find many. What you will find are endings indicating where new beginnings need to take root: the end of a relationship, the end of a job, or the end of a certain degree of health. You might turn to energy medicine to analyze the stress patterns in your life, but you're likely to be afraid to change most of them, because such transformations will introduce corresponding changes in your relationships. You may, of course, take some healing comfort from energy medicine in thinking that at least you're getting a handle on what your stresses are, so that surely has to help.

Indeed, it does help, but only a little and only for a short period of time, because getting a handle on a problem does not heal it. It merely identifies the problem. You might change your eating patterns and maybe force yourself to exercise, but even that won't bring about systemic transformation, because most often the enthusiasm for maintaining these changes wanes rapidly. As you learn how deeply ensconced your fear of change really is, not to mention how crucial change is to your healing, then your goal shifts to seeking out others to help you become someone who "wants to want to change" in order to heal. Energy healers abound, along with organic food, supplements, and self-help literature, all of which are greatly supportive, but gathering a support system is not the goal of healing. *Healing* is the goal. You know that healing is the goal. Yet, as inconceivable as this is to the reasoning mind, the deeper question that inevitably emerges in some way for almost everyone in a health or life crisis is, "How fast can I emotionally and psychologically afford to heal?" In other words, how fast can I handle my life changing? That is the one question that people in crisis cannot believe they ask themselves, but they do. And the reason this question emerges as if out of the blue is that healing is not about the illness or crisis that has befallen you. Healing is about your capacity to engage in your own transformation from fear to courage, from holding on to the past to letting go, from living in illusion to embracing truth. Healing is an invitation to enter your own mystical awakening.

Understood through mystical consciousness, illness or crisis is a catalyst for releasing a set of attitudes and beliefs that no longer serve who you need to become in the future. But as you release these old patterns, the world they held together evaporates as well, and that is the frightening part. Energy precedes matter; cut the energetic strings and the matter attached to that energy is released. Rapidly cutting strings releases matter and changes your world quickly as well. As soon as you ask for guidance, you are always told what strings to cut. Often, you may receive those instructions before you ask. Acting on guidance at the speed of light heals at the speed of light. But few people can handle guidance at light speed—without, that is, the support of the sacred. Light speed is mystical consciousness.

Yet we must recognize that we have reached this critical turning point in our evolution as a species. That we are creatures of energy consciousness we can no longer deny. Now we need to go beyond illness and crisis as the motivators for personal growth and transformation and get on with the business of exploring our spiritual natures, because that is who and what we are—spiritual beings. We should not have to discover such a profound truth as a result of learning that we have cancer or because our marriage has fallen apart. Instead, we should come to rely on the guiding forces of our graces to keep us healthy and to maintain our loving relationships. We are still living backward, as if we were not intuitive.

But we are intuitive, and more than that, we are born to create and to use our spiritual resources to transform ourselves and the lives of others. Inherently, we are beings of light and service, masterful at perceiving who needs to be healed, who needs the grace of joy, who needs to be comforted, who needs the grace of spiritual companionship, who needs to be listened to, and who needs someone to share in their good news. This is who we genuinely are and who, free of the burdens of our fears and wounds, we long to be. With such gifts waiting to be shared in our souls, each of us can become a formidable force for transformation on this earth.

I leave you with the following simple but powerful guidance. These suggestions are meant to help you build a healthy life through becoming ever more aware of your mystical nature and your spiritual senses.

1. Develop a Practice of Inner Reflection

Spend time each day in teachings that are transcendent of ordinary thought and that bring light to your soul. Apply these teachings to the choices you make each day. For example, as I related in Chapter 2, a simple line written by Thomas Merton had a transformational impact on my life. Merton was a great writer and devoted to journaling. On a hot summer afternoon, as he gazed upon the hillside from his hermitage window at the monastery, he noted how the warm breezes bent the flowers, and how the sunset made the color of the hills look bluish-purple. He wrote that it was so hot that day that a bull was lying down under a tree, just waiting for the sun to set. But as he jotted down the small and precious details, he ended by writing, "This day will never come again." That one line went straight through my heart and into my soul as I realized that same truth, looking around my office. That night, as I looked across the dinner table at my friends, I melted them into my memory, thinking, "I will never again be here with you in just this way. This evening of our lives will never come again." My love for them exploded in that instant as I realized it could well be the last time I would ever see them, for who knows when we shall be called to leave this life? I look at strangers and think, "I will never see that face again," and wonder why I am seeing that face at all. And suddenly the face of that stranger is beautiful to me.

Such reflection takes you deeper and deeper into the values that matter and away from dwelling on the insignificant and the useless. Go in search of these rich writings. Discover the wealth that the mystics of all the great traditions have left us; choose but one line and jump into it with all your might, like Alice falling down the rabbit hole. Here's one more that I adore, which comes from my favorite, Teresa of Ávila: "Let nothing disturb you. With

God, all things are possible." Dwell on that and see if it doesn't make your soul just a bit lighter.

2. Decide Whether You Will Learn by Wisdom or Woe

Use these two options as guideposts for your decisions. Are your choices wise or will they result in woe for you or others? Wise choices come in many forms. Draw on your experiences in which you have already learned this, and blend them with the constant flow of intuitive guidance that filters into your thoughts. Study the wisdom of the great masters, the wise teachers such as Buddha and Jesus, who knew the obstacles of the human journey. These obstacles have not changed. Respond to the intuitive signals coming through your biology. Stress in your solar plexus is a signal that you are losing your power to something. Identify that something and take action before it consumes you. This is wise action.

Woe is the choice to wait until your fears consume you, to deny your intuitive warning signals in hopes that the winds of change will pass you by. But they won't. Wisdom rises to meet the challenges of life. Woe is the result of thinking others will take care of your problems or that they will magically disappear. Your problems have your name on them because they are for you to resolve. And each time you resolve them through wise action, you allow more light and grace into your life. Ask yourself before making a choice or taking action: Is this a wise choice or am I courting woe?

3. Don't Have Expectations of Others or of Outcomes

Expectations come from your dark passions and from feelings of entitlement. When you sense an expectation arising in your ego, review your dark passions to see which of these forces is energizing that particular situation. Then choose a corresponding grace and pray for that grace to clear out the perception created by your dark passion. Expectations inevitably lead to disappointments. Make no judgments. Have no expectations. And give up the need to know why things happen as they do.

4. Actively Cultivate Your Graces

Come to know the power and authority of your graces with the same precision with which you have come to know your brokenness and pain. Remember that without conscious effort, you will easily succumb to the gravity field of your pain. You have to work at staying in your field of grace, because it is not natural to your ego, which knows its base of power more in the shadow than in the light.

5. Be of Service to Others

All the great mystics have acknowledged that genuine enlightenment manifests as a desire to be of service to others. If you want to imitate the masters, there is no better way. Healing the self can lead to making the resolution of your own problems all that you see. Without service, your life becomes an experience of self-service, a journey of taking without giving back. Finding a way to be of service to others is the highest path of your soul.

6. Learn to Pray

Pray beyond petitioning for the stuff you want for yourself. Learn to be present to the grace of the sacred. Open yourself to the mystic that you are by nature. Your intuition is not a skill to be honed so that you can figure out how to stay safe and avoid losing money. If you think that, you will never develop more than your gut instincts. You need to challenge your fear of your life becoming unreasonable—because it is already unreasonable. In truth, your life has never been reasonable, it's just that you keep hoping tomorrow will be different and that you will find a way to bring more control into your world.

Prayer and trust and your capacity to reason as a mystic give you the wisdom to recognize that life will always be full of challenges and crises. The wise way is not to attempt to find the one path that promises you will never have to endure the pain of loss and illness, but instead to learn how to endure and transcend when unreasonable events come your way. Learning to defy gravity in your world—to think, perceive, and act at the mystical level of consciousness—is the greatest gift you can give yourself, because it is the gift of truth. And as we are bound to learn again and again in this life, the truth does indeed set us free.

7. Defy Gravity

Live as if you were liberated from ordinary thought, beyond the boundaries of logic and reason. Be bold in your decisions and creative and imaginative in your thoughts. Think and live with the soul of a mystic, seeing the world as a field of grace in which you walk as a channel of light. Live these truths. Become these truths. This is your true highest potential.

And remind yourself each day of your life, "This day will never come again." You will never see the same sunrise or sunset. You will never sit at the same table twice with the same people in exactly the same way. You will never look upon the faces of the people you love in exactly the same way tomorrow, for you might not even be here tomorrow. You will never walk down the same street in precisely the same way. Such tiny realizations are also the most profound soul awakenings. You have resources yet to be unleashed. Make bold, outrageous choices. Live as though you have the power to change the world—because you do.

Acknowledgments

It is my pleasure to extend my heartfelt thanks to several people for their assistance with this book. To my business partner, forever friend, and literary agent, David Smith, my gratitude, appreciation, and love for your boundless faith in our work in the world. My editor and dear friend, Peter Occhiogrosso, provided his keen eye and brilliant insight throughout the writing of this book, and I am deeply grateful for his talent and his diligent nature. My thanks and appreciation also goes to my Hay House editor, Patty Gift, for her assistance in bringing this book to its final stages of birth and for her continual positive feedback along the way. I also wish to thank Anne Barthel for her superb copyediting—what a master you are in the world of micro-details. And to the entire supportive staff of Hay House, most especially Louise Hay, Reid Tracy, and Nancy Levin, I extend my sincere thanks for this opportunity to work together.

Friends and family provided so much love during the writing of this book. I am especially blessed because of the love and support of my mom, my brother, Ed, along with the rest of my family: Amy, Rachel, Sarah, Eddie, Jr., Angela, Allison, and Joe. And of course my cousin team, Andy and Pam, Marilyn and Mitch, Chris and Ritch, and wonderful Colleen Daley and Phil Kruzel, who continually sent messages of love and encouragement, which were more appreciated than words of gratitude can convey. Equal treasures are my friends who do so much for me when I am in a writing frenzy, and I am delighted to acknowledge their place in my heart. I have a rare group of friends that I treasure with all my heart. Some of these friends are also authors and they, too, know the great difficulty that accompanies writing a book. They merit special mentioning because we shared so much of the birthing pains of our books, all written at the same time in the same neighborhood, practically on the same street. Andrew Harvey, a renowned author and the leading voice in the field of sacred activism, is also a best friend, a confidant, a soul companion, and my neighbor. We spend many an evening together on my porch in the summer chatting about the challenges facing our planet as well as the mystical journey into the human soul. I was deeply grateful when he agreed to write the Foreword to this book while steeped in the demands of his own deadline for his remarkable book on sacred activism entitled *The Hope*, as I knew that he understood the vision of this work, having listened to me articulate it so many times over endless dinners and walks through our neighborhood. To my dear friend, Andrew, my deepest thanks and love. Mona Lisa Schulz, M.D., Ph.D., author of *The Intuitive Advisor*, is a soul sister to me in more ways than can be listed. She is also a part-time neighbor but a full-time member of my family. I am deeply grateful for having a friend like her who understands the complex journey of the intuitive life as deeply as she does combined with having a wild sense of humor and a devotion to helping others. And to Ellen Gunter, also a neighbor and an author with her specialty in the field of spiritual ecology, my love and thanks for wisdom, love, and devoted sisterhood and the blessing of having you, John, and Miles as part of my family. Steve Fanning, Ph.D., Professor of History at the University of Illinois, deserves a special spotlight for all he has done for me. I would not have ventured into healing were it not for him as in addition to being a brilliant historian, he is also a gifted healer and an expert in mysticism, as well as an author on the subject. Because of Steve, I began to do workshops in healing which ultimately became the foundation for this work. Thank you is hardly enough. His devotion to healing others has become a part of his life and he generously shares that calling with my students at CMED. And to my dear and trusted companion of my inner life, Tom Lavin, Ph.D., my endless gratitude. And to Jim Garrison, my confidant and beloved friend for half of this lifetime and more yet to come, thank you, yet again.

And to Julie Flaherty, my fellow antique-book lover who has gifted me with more treasures than I can count, I thank you for your endless love and generosity. It is returned. Meryl Martin embodies all that is fun about life, and when I think I am going to implode from the pressure of my schedule, I get on a plane and go to Meryl's place, where I know all will be well. This book required two trips to Meryl's. Georgia Bailey has the soul of a philosopher and the heart of a divine servant. She is one of God's most grace-filled human beings and I am blessed to know her. She is an inspiration to me, and in turn, that inspiration made its way into the pages of this book. Mary Neville is one of my dearest friends, the oak tree in your backyard, whose very presence is enough to remind you that life is good. Cristina Carlino is the type of support person that thinks you can do no wrong. She only inspires others with her genius and I consider her one of the true gifts in my life. My love and thanks to Cristina for her constant support and her endless gifts of Philosophy goodies. Jim Curtan, a forever best friend and a magnificent faculty member at my CMED Institute, kept sending me cartoons and funny cards, many of which happened to arrive just as I would have to squeeze in writing a chapter in between weekend workshops—and there is nothing funny about a deadline like that. So to my dear Jim, thanks for those laughs, because I sure needed them. To Prentiss Prevette, a most extraordinary man, my love and thanks for your constant generosity of spirit and heart. My love and thanks to Tracy Barratt for the gift of an enchanting friend. And finally, to my dear and loving neighbors, Charles and Sue Wells, Priscilla Haddod, my thanks and love for being a part of my life. And to Leslie Meredith—your guiding wisdom and the experience of our years together were ever-present as I wrote every word. You are a permanent resident in my office—and my heart. To all of these jewels of my heart, you make my life so rich and I am so grateful.

Index

release from, 103
sloth, 90, 100–102
wrath, 90, 97–98

Dark Truth, archetype of, 150

death, predetermined moment of, 10

death and rebirth cycle, 10, 77, 139, 157–158

decision guideposts, 204

defying gravity, 194–195, 206. *See also* mystics and mystical laws

depression
  meaning and purpose with, 55–57
  reason and, 33, 44–45
  spiritual, 17, 66–67, 78–79, 188–189

Dickinson, Emily, 168

divine force, 9–10. *See also* mystics and mystical laws

divine paradox, 189–192

E

economic security, 70–75

ego
  behavior and, 89–90
  breakdown of, 83–85
  Counsel and, 142
  forgiveness and, 178–179
  Fortitude and, 129–131
  Knowledge and, 150–151
  luxury as challenge to, 96–97
  Saboteur archetype and, 92
  Understanding and, 112–113, 124, 127

Einstein, Albert, 168

elder wisdom, 155–158

emotional debt, 174

empowerment journey, 109–110. *See also* graces

energetic pollution and, 15

energy (life force), xxiii, 38, 49, 58, 171, 177

energy consciousness, 14–20, 170–172, 198–202. *See also* healing in age of energy

Enlightenment, 20–21, 24–26

enneagram, 151–152

Entering the Castle (Myss), xxiii–xxiv, 1–5

environmentalism, 134, 157–158

envy, 90

esoteric literature, 152

essential Self, 54, 55–56. *See also* meaning and purpose

evil vs. good, 29–30, 39–40, 46–47, 133

expectations, 204–205

explanations. *See* reason

"eye for an eye," 48

F

fairness, 47–48, 177

Fanning, Steve, 7
  fear and fear patterns. *See also* dark passions; graces
  "fear of the Lord," 118
  financial, 70–75
  on global scale, 39–42
  of imperfection, 84–85
  meaning and, 62–65
  mystical law and, 166–170, 172, 194–195, 196
  nature of, xxv, 200–201
  polarity and, 133
  reason and, 34–35, 38, 39–42, 44–47, 52–53
  woe and, 204

Finley, James, 39–40

forgiveness
  as act of release, 30–31
  archetype of, 182
  living in the present and, 175–176, 177–178

About the Author

Caroline Myss is a five-time *New York Times* best-selling author and internationally renowned speaker in the fields of human consciousness, spirituality and mysticism, health, energy medicine, and the science of medical intuition. Caroline established her own educational institute in 2003, CMED (Caroline Myss Education), which offers a diverse array of programs devoted to personal development and draws students from all over the world. Caroline is best known for her pioneering work in energy anatomy and medical intuition and contemporizing classical mystical teachings, as described in her best-selling book *Anatomy of the Spirit*.

Website: www.myss.com

Hay House Titles of Related Interest

YOU CAN HEAL YOUR LIFE, the movie,
starring Louise Hay & Friends
(available as an online streaming video)
www.hayhouse.com/louise-movie

THE SHIFT, the movie,
starring Dr. Wayne W. Dyer
(available as an online streaming video)
www.hayhouse.com/the-shift-movie

•••

*THE BIOLOGY OF BELIEF: Unleashing the Power
of Consciousness, Matter & Miracles,* by Bruce H. Lipton, Ph.D.

*FINDING LOVE EVERYWHERE:
67 1/2 Wisdom Poems and Meditations,* by Robert Holden

THE HOPE: A Guide to Sacred Activism,
by Andrew Harvey

*THE SPONTANEOUS HEALING OF BELIEF:
Shattering the Paradigm of False Limits,* by Gregg Braden

All of the above are available at your local bookstore,
or may be ordered by contacting Hay House (see next page).

We hope you enjoyed this Hay House book. If you'd like to receive our online catalog featuring additional information on Hay House books and products, or if you'd like to find out more about the Hay Foundation, please contact:

Hay House, Inc., P.O. Box 5100, Carlsbad, CA 92018-5100
(760) 431-7695 or (800) 654-5126
(760) 431-6948 (fax) or (800) 650-5115 (fax)
www.hayhouse.com® • www.hayfoundation.org

———

Published in Australia by: Hay House Australia Pty. Ltd.,
18/36 Ralph St., Alexandria NSW 2015
Phone: 612-9669-4299 • *Fax:* 612-9669-4144
www.hayhouse.com.au

Published in the United Kingdom by: Hay House UK, Ltd.,
The Sixth Floor, Watson House, 54 Baker Street, London W1U 7BU
Phone: +44 (0)20 3927 7290 • *Fax:* +44 (0)20 3927 7291
www.hayhouse.co.uk

Published in India by: Hay House Publishers India,
Muskaan Complex, Plot No. 3, B-2, Vasant Kunj, New Delhi 110 070
Phone: 91-11-4176-1620 • *Fax:* 91-11-4176-1630
www.hayhouse.co.in

———

Access New Knowledge.
Anytime. Anywhere.

Learn and evolve at your own pace
with the world's leading experts.

www.hayhouseU.com

MEDITATE.
VISUALIZE.
LEARN.

Get the **Empower** *You*
Unlimited Audio *Mobile App*

Get unlimited access to the entire Hay House audio library!

You'll get:

- 500+ inspiring and life-changing **audiobooks**
- 200+ ad-free **guided meditations** for sleep, healing, relaxation, spiritual connection, and more
- Hundreds of audios **under 20 minutes** to easily fit into your day
- **Exclusive content** *only* for subscribers
- **New audios** added every week
- No credits, **no limits**

Listen to the audio version of this book for **FREE!**

 ★★★★★ **I ADORE** this app. I use it almost every day. Such a blessing. – Aya Lucy Rose

Scan me with your phone camera!

TRY FOR FREE!
Go to: hayhouse.com/listen-free

HAY HOUSE

Free e-newsletters from Hay House, the Ultimate Resource for Inspiration

Be the first to know about Hay House's free downloads, special offers, giveaways, contests, and more!

 Get exclusive excerpts from our latest releases and videos from *Hay House Present Moments*.

 Our *Digital Products Newsletter* is the perfect way to stay up-to-date on our latest discounted eBooks, featured mobile apps, and Live Online and On Demand events.

 Learn with real benefits! *HayHouseU.com* is your source for the most innovative online courses from the world's leading personal growth experts. Be the first to know about new online courses and to receive exclusive discounts.

 Enjoy uplifting personal stories, how-to articles, and healing advice, along with videos and empowering quotes, within *Heal Your Life*.

Sign Up Now!

Get inspired, educate yourself, get a complimentary gift, and share the wisdom!

Visit www.hayhouse.com/newsletters to sign up today!

 HAY HOUSE

 HAY HOUSE online learning